The
PATTERN of
SOVIET CONDUCT
in the
THIRD WORLD

Edited by
WALTER LAQUEUR

PRAEGER

PRAEGER SPECIAL STUDIES • PRAEGER SCIENTIFIC

Library of Congress Cataloging in Publication of Data
Main entry under title:

The Pattern of Soviet conduct in the Third World.

Includes index.
1. Underdeveloped areas—Foreign relations—Soviet
Union.   2. Soviet Union—Foreign relations—Underdeveloped
areas.   I. Laqueur, Walter, 1921-
D888.S65P37   1983   327.470173'4   83-9491
ISBN 0-03-063944-1

Published in 1983 by Praeger Publishers
CBS Educational and Professional Publishing
a Division of CBS Inc.
521 Fifth Avenue, New York, NY 10175 USA
©1983, by Praeger Publishers

3456789   052   987654321
Printed in the United States of America
on acid-free paper

"This study was supported and reviewed by the Department of Defense. D.O.D. review does not imply endorcement of factual accuracy or opinion."

The study was carried out under the auspices of the Center for Strategic and International Studies, Georgetown University. The editor would like to thank Dr. Barry Rubin for his help and collaboration in the preparation of the study. Thanks should also go to Laura Blum for research and editorial assistance and to Sophia Miskiewicz for general administrative supervision throughout the many stages of the project.

CONTENTS

ONE

Introduction
WALTER LAQUEUR

*When Sékou Touré was young and
Nasser and Nkrumah were alive many
knowledgeable people lost their heads
and cried "wolf." There was no solid
empirical justification for calling these
people or their states Communist.
Therefore today many knowledgeable
people refuse to cry "wolf" when the
wolf stands in plain undoubted view.*

Peter Wiles, 1982

The present study proceeds from the assumption that most of the military
and political conflict in the years to come will take place in the so-called
Third World. It addresses itself to the following questions:

1. How aggressive a policy is the Soviet leadership likely to follow in the
   Third World?
2. How much priority will be given to the Third World in Soviet strategic
   planning?
3. Above all, what are the Soviet instrumentalities to make friends and
   influence people in the Third World?
4. What factors are likely to enhance, and which may obstruct, Soviet
   progress in these countries?

   The term "Third World" is here used, with great hesitation, as a very
imperfect abbreviation. Its indiscriminate use has caused a great deal of

1

confusion, for there is an almost infinite variety of "Third World" countries as far as economic development, social structure, and political orientation are concerned. In short, the "Third World" is as much fiction as fact, and its members have seldom cooperated on major issues. The Soviet Union, with all its efforts to woo Third World countries, has never accepted the concept of a Third World bloc.

The present investigation does not deal with the Far East, the western hemisphere, and South Africa, but concentrates on the "nonaligned" countries (another unfortunate abbreviation) between Bangladesh and Morocco, as well as West and East Africa—that is, the Third World heartland.

Since World War II both Soviet expectations concerning the Third World and Western appraisals of Soviet intentions have been subject to frequent and far-reaching changes, summarized briefly below.

1. In the immediate postwar period, from roughly 1946 to 1954, Western governments generally believed that Soviet interest and activity in Asia, Africa, and the Middle East were strictly limited. Once the Soviet Union had withdrawn from Iran (1946), not followed up its threats against Turkey, and not pursued its claims for colonial acquisitions in the Mediterranean (Tripolitania), the consensus was that Russia had no intention of playing an active role in these areas.[1]

2. Change set in around 1954. Following Stalin's death, Soviet foreign policy became more flexible, less dogmatic, more willing to create opportunities in the Third World and to exploit them. As a leading Soviet writer wrote, "The stormy breakup of the colonial system and the anti-capitalist rhetoric of many leaders of the national liberation movement created the illusion that in a very short period the overwhelming majority of the former colonies would go over, if not to be socialist, then to the non-capitalist road of development." This was the era of Nehru and Sukarno, of Nasser, Ben Bella, Nkrumah, Modibo Keita—a new breed of "progressive" leaders, the heyday of the new nonaligned movement, and the vintage sloganism of Bandung. Third World countries were expected to become gradually more and more hostile to the West, and turn into natural allies of the Soviet Union.

3. Soviet disenchantment set in after a decade of such expectations. The "progressive" leaders disappeared, and those who followed them were, on the whole, less desirable from a Soviet point of view. They were less willing to permit Soviet-licensed infiltration; in many places Communism and the other "progressive forces" were suppressed altogether. Soviet Communists began to admit they had underrated the power of religion and nationalism, that the ideology of even the progressive Third World regimes was "slipshod," their links with the masses frequently nonexistent, that

"vanguard parties of socialist orientation" had not been created, that habits of systematic work had not been inculcated in most Asian andAfrican countries, and that fine speeches would not suffice. In short, it was realized in Moscow (first) that even the most friendly Third World regimes were not altogether reliable and that (second) while the Soviet Union had become heavily involved, it was by no means in full control of the conduct of affairs.

4. Since the mid-1960s, Soviet assessments of prospects in the Third World have been, on the whole, more realistic. It was accepted that for the time being, nationalism (with a strong religious admixture) would be the prevailing force; that while this force was to a larger or smaller degree anti-Western in inspiration, it was suspicious of all outsiders, that even the so-called progressive regimes in the Third World would be headed by military men motivated "less by patriotism—let alone socialism—(to quote a Soviet author) than by a purely career-inspired desire to seize power." But the disenchantment, and the recognition that the optimism of the early 1960s with regard to swift Soviet progress in the Third World had been premature, led by no means to resignation. On the contrary, realization that the Asian and African situations were more *slozhnii* (complicated, a favorite term in the Soviet political dictionary) led to a redoubling of efforts.

5. Western assessments of Soviet intentions since the early 1950s in Asia, Africa, and the Middle East have been uneven. Relatively few observers have expertise in both Soviet foreign policy and Third World affairs. Moreover, there has been a tendency to exaggerate both Soviet isolationism and expansionism, to overrate both Soviet advances and setbacks. Thus, to give but one example, an influential school of Western observers argued during the late 1970s that the Soviet record in the Third World was negative, that it had made progress in some countries but suffered defeat in others ("some you win, some you lose"), and that since Asian and African nationalism was obviously so passionate, the West really had not much to fear of Soviet advance.

Seen in a short-term perspective of five to ten years, it is indeed true that the Soviet Union has not succeeded in all places in which it tried to gain a foothold. The most obvious examples are post-Nasser Egypt, Indonesia after Sukarno, and Somalia. Seen in a perspective of 30 years, it is obvious that the Soviet Union has made considerable progress in the Third World. In 1952, China and North Korea were its only allies. In 1982, Vietnam, Laos, Cambodia, Nicaragua, and Grenada in the western hemisphere, as well as Angola, Benin, the PLO, Mozambique, Ethiopia, South Yemen, and Congo (Brazzaville), have to be included in the list as well as "socialist-oriented" (to use the official Soviet term) Guyana, Algeria, Libya, Syria, Zimbabwe, Madagascar, Burundi, Guinea-Bissau, and some others. While some of these countries may turn away from the Soviet Union, it is likely that elsewhere the Soviet Union will find new clients or allies.

A good yardstick for the growth of Soviet influence is the development of the nonaligned movement, which, at the time of its foundation, was genuinely uncommitted and made nonadherence to blocs the cornerstone of its policies. Since then, this traditional nonalignment has been put into question. Thus, the fact that the Soviet Union did gain influence can be denied only on the basis of a short-term (and short-sighted) perspective. Furthermore, the idea that nationalism and religion form an a priori bulwark against Soviet progress is, at best, a gross overstatement. As Brezhnev stated at the 26th Congress of the Communist Party of the Soviet Union (CPSU) in February 1981, "Islamic slogans are, so to speak, neutral, the decisive point is what kind of long-term political aims are pursued by those voicing them." The same applies to nationalism, which per se is not an obstacle to Soviet designs. Few observers will doubt the national motivation of the Soviet leadership, not to mention the Chinese, the Yugoslav, and others. A confluence of nationalism and Communism (or pro-Sovietism) is the prevailing fashion, and not only in the Third World.

After at least a decade of overrating Soviet lack of success in the Third World, something akin to a revolution of perceptions took place in the West following the invasion of Afghanistan. This was seen by many as a sudden turning point initiating a new wave of expansionism. In actual fact, the occupation of Afghanistan was not a turning point; it only came as a shock to Western analysts who had assumed that the Soviet system had become status quo, increasingly moderate. Nor was it at all certain that the Afghanistan precedent was pointing to further military expansionism in the near future, caused by Soviet revolutionary ideology, imperialist tradition, or the innate imperialist thrust of large organizations to eliminate all outside disturbances.[2]

Direct military expansion is not in principle excluded, but it will be undertaken by the Soviet Union only if its leaders are convinced the balance of power has shifted decisively in its favor. In other words, such military intervention will be initiated only if the Politburo feels certain that no risk of escalation into a general military conflict is involved, and that, furthermore, it will have no lasting negative consequences on the attitude of Third World countries toward the Soviet Union.

COMMUNIST PARTIES

For several decades after the Bolshevik Revolution, most of the hopes of the Soviet Union rested on the assumption that strong proletarian parties would emerge within a few years all over the globe. Failing this, the revolution in the East was expected to come as the result of agrarian uprisings and revolutionary nationalist, anti-imperialist movements. These assumptions were not exactly wrong. Even if there was no working class, there was a strong revolutionary potential in the East as developments in China, and elsewhere, were to show. What Soviet leaders did not anticipate was the unwillingness of many Communist parties, especially those in power, to adopt the Soviet model.

If Soviet leaders could choose today between a non-Communist and a Communist China as a neighbor, there is little doubt which, in the light of many years' experience, they would prefer. In brief, Communism is no longer a synonym for pro-Sovietism, nor, on the other hand, is non-Communism a hindrance to close cooperation between the country in question and the Soviet Union. The existence of Communist parties in the Third World gives the Soviet Union certain advantages, but it also creates major problems. This is true with regard to both Communist parties in power and those that are not.

But the Soviet Union cannot wash its hands of world Communism, which, with all the difficulties that have arisen, is still a source of strength to the Soviet Union in many respects. Dissociating itself from Communist parties would undermine the legitimacy of the Soviet claim to be leader of the Communist bloc.

Not counting the Far East and Latin America, there are today nonruling Communist parties in India, Israel, Syria, Lebanon, Morocco, Sri Lanka, Réunion, Iran, Iraq, and Turkey. To these one should add minor Communist groups in Algeria, Tunisia, Egypt, Nigeria, Jordan, Senegal, Pakistan, Bangladesh, Nepal, and perhaps a few other countries. All these parties are pro-Soviet; they are legal (or semilegal), with the exception of those in Egypt, Turkey, Algeria, Iraq, Jordan, Senegal, Nigeria, and Pakistan. However, even the legal or semilegal parties have to move carefully so as not to arouse suspicion.

The existence of a "Russian" party in so many countries (and the absence of an "American" party) is not, in most cases, an unmixed blessing from the Soviet point of view. It does create opportunities for infiltration and gaining influence. But it also means that since all Third World countries are intensely nationalist, there is bound to be a great deal of suspicion vis-à-vis parties whose loyalty is, at least in part, to an outside power (however friendly and progressive). Some of this suspicion will be transferred to the Soviet Union, even if no internal help is extended by the CPSU to the local Communist party. In other words, the local Communist parties are likely to be a stumbling block in interstate relations. It means that the Soviet Union may frequently have to choose between support (even if only rhetorical) for the Communist Party and friendship with a regime that wants to combine collaboration with the Soviet Union with the repression of Communism at home. This dilemma has faced the Soviet leaders almost from the beginning—Turkey in 1919/20.

To reduce the risk, the Soviet leadership in 1964 even recommended to Third World Communist parties, particularly in the Middle East, that they dissolve voluntarily and join the "progressive" official state parties. Several parties temporarily obeyed; others (such as those in Sudan and Syria) refused to do so.

The existence of Communist parties, given Soviet claims to leadership of the bloc, also means that the Soviet Union may have to take sides in conflicts between Communist parties, which have become increasingly frequent during the 1960s and 1970s. This is usually impossible without offending at least one of the parties. Communist parties or front organizations in Third World countries may still be of interest to the Soviet Union if they are well established and have a chance to come to power in the foreseeable future, or at least to share power. The Iranian Tudeh Party may serve as an example, but there are only a few parties in this category. Elsewhere, the Communist Party may take over a national liberation movement or there may be a merger of the two, which is what happened in Cuba. But this is unlikely to happen in many other places.

The Cuban constellation was in some respects unique. Furthermore, Communist parties are no longer the well-disciplined, conspiratorial, monolithic organization they used to be. Frequently, they are rent by internal divisions. If, however, there should be further Cubas, they are likely to occur in Latin America, partly because of the sympathetic (or at least tolerant) attitude of sections of the Catholic Church, partly because of geopolitical reasons—the relative proximity to the United States and the distance from the Soviet Union; Latin American "progressives" will not feel threatened by Soviet policies. Last, there is the possibility, although distant, that a pro-Soviet regime will come to power in a Third World country democratically, as the result of an electoral victory. Thus, a "progressive" party (the MMM) came to power in Mauritius in 1982, but while it is left-wing and neutralist, it is neither Marxist nor (as yet) a Soviet client.

This leads to the question of how to define and to differentiate, in this age of Communist polycentrism, between Communist, pro-Communist, and progressive parties. According to official Soviet sources Communist parties are working-class (in theory, if not always in practice), Marxist-Leninist, and democratic centralist—that is, subject to unquestioning discipline. Lower on the scale are the revolutionary-democratic parties—anti-Western in outlook but not "class parties," not subscribing to all the basic tenets of Marxism-Leninism (for instance, concerning the class struggle and the role of religion), frequently dominated by petit bourgeois elements.

Some of these revolutionary democratic parties are "vanguard" parties, which is to say that they have moved closer to the Soviet pattern than others. However, in the final analysis, these are academic distinctions of limited consequence. What ultimately matters in Soviet eyes is not whether the party in question subscribes to dialectical materialism or whether its leaders are of proletarian, petit bourgeois, or even bourgeois origin, but whether it supports the Soviet Union. If it does, all other sins are forgiven.

As leader of the Communist bloc, the Soviet Union has to support local Communist parties in order to emphasize the central importance of Marxism-Leninism and of a progressive, avant garde party as a condition sine qua non to achieve socialism. "No other class can replace the working class in that historic function," as Professor Roshslav Ulyanovski put it. This sounds very radical and dogmatic, but it actually leads to "revisionist" conclusions. For since a strong working class does not yet exist, the Soviet authors inevitably reach the conclusion that the revolutionary process in the Third World should not be measured in months and years, but will continue for several decades. And it sometimes appears that the Soviet leaders are by no means in a hurry, provided they can get maximum assistance from their as yet imperfect allies.

Dealing with "revolutionary democratic" or "socialist-oriented" parties, or simply national liberation movements gravitating toward the Soviet Union, has many advantages. The Soviet Union cannot be held responsible for their ideology or their political practices. These groups have no right to expect help from Moscow automatically. At the same time, there is much room for pragmatic cooperation. For this reason, the ideological discussions about the noncapitalist road of development characteristic of a "state of national democracy," and similar debates are not terribly significant.[3]

What are the political prospects of the Third World Communist parties in the years to come? By and large, their chances seem dimmer now than in the mid-1960s and 1970s. The growth of Islamic fundamentalism has limited their influence in the Arab world and other Middle East countries, and they have remained small in Africa. It seems unlikely that a Communist party acting on its own will be able to directly challenge a government as the Sudanese party (unsuccessfully) challenged Numery in 1971, or to take over a national liberation movement from within.

However, it would certainly be premature to write off Third World Communist parties altogether; though most of them are small, the same is true of the political elites in general. The fact that overall conditions are inauspicious does not mean that one party, or even a group of parties, may not succeed. A few dozen determined people may well be able to take over an African country, provided they have well-placed allies in the army and/or police. Second, instability in the Third World will be the rule rather than the exception. It is perfectly possible that the ruling political groups in some major Third World countries will break up in the years to come, because of internal quarrels, or inability to cure social and economic malaise, or unlucky foreign entanglements, or ruinous civil wars. This may happen in India or Pakistan, in Iran or the Arab countries, as well as in Africa. In these circumstances, local Communist parties collaborating with other opposition elements will constitute the political alternative, and in some cases they may even outmaneuver their allies, turning from junior to senior partner or even sole holder of power.

It is also true that a Communist victory in one country will almost necessarily stir up fears and provoke opposition from its neighbors. Second, even Communist parties in power cannot be entirely trusted by Moscow unless these Communists depend on Moscow's support for their very survival. If Third World Communist parties should come to power, this will be mainly owing to their own efforts, not as a result of Soviet help. These Communists will remember that the Soviet Union was dealing with their enemies, the former rulers, for years—and frequently against their interests. This will not normally make for great mutual trust. The cases of China, Yugoslavia, and Albania have shown that independent Communism is most likely to occur where victory came without Soviet help. There is reason to assume that this will still be true in the future.

FRONT ORGANIZATIONS AND THE MOVEMENT OF NONALIGNED COUNTRIES

Front organizations, public bodies ostensibly nonpartisan, but de facto manipulated by the Communists. have been a crucial part of Soviet strategy in the West since the 1930s. These bodies have included organizations such as the Partisans of Peace founded soon after World War II, and international associations of democratic lawyers, students, and scientific workers. Their heyday was in the 1950s; almost all of them still exist, but now their importance is minimal. In the Third World they were never very important in the first place. Various reasons account for this lack of success: the negative impact of the divisions inside the Communist camp on the world movement, the innately fraudulent character of these "fronts," and the fact that they were not what they pretended to be impaired their long-term chances. The Partisans of Peace had a limited appeal in Western Europe and North America because of the deeply ingrained pacifism in these areas.

But this is not so in the Third World. Most of these countries are ruled by the military, which has little compunction about splurging on defense. Many Third World countries have been involved in wars of one sort or another, and there are no pacifist movements to speak of. The aim of the front organization is to influence public opinion in democratic countries through manifestos and publications in a free press. Such opportunities do not exist (or barely exist) in most Third World countries. For these reasons as well as some others, European-style "fronts" have been, on the whole, unsuitable in the Third World context. There have been some specific Third World fronts such as the Afro-Asian Peoples Solidarity Organization, but they are different in character from the typical Western "front" inasmuch as no great effort has ever been made to camouflage their real character.

Communist tactics have changed in recent years in the West as well. Far more attention has been paid to home-grown pacifist movements than to the old (and discredited) Partisans of Peace. Soviet efforts in the Third World have been primarily concentrated on the nonaligned movement. To be sure, what the pacifist movement in the West and the nonaligned in the Third World have in common is that neither came into existence as the result of Soviet initiatives. On the contrary, some of their actions are undesirable from the Soviet point of view. Yet the general thrust of their activities fits the aims of Soviet foreign policy beautifully. In the view of Moscow, they deserve all possible support, discreet and, on occasion, not so discreet.

The nonaligned movement made its debut with a membership of 25 countries; today it has 95, as well as an additional 20 with observer or guest status. What started as a genuinely neutral (or neutralist) movement, with some of its leaders openly anti-American but cautious of the Soviet Union, has undergone palpable changes since the early 1970s. Manipulation by pro-Soviet elements inside the nonaligned movement, above all Cuba, is largely responsible for this reorientation. The very fact that Cuba is unquestioningly accepted as a legitimate nonaligned country, and in 1978–82 served as chairman and main spokesman, accurately reflects the transformation of the movement.

Needless to say, this reality will appear preposterous to most Western observers. The Soviet attitude toward the nonaligned was initially one of indifference, but in the late 1950s this gave way to benevolence, and since the early 1970s the attempt has been made to explain to the nonaligned that the real division in the world is not between North and South, or rich and poor nations, but between "imperialism" and "socialism." It is deeply mistaken and utterly reactionary to equate the two superpowers, it was said. The pro-Soviet elements are pressing the demand to make the foreign policy of the nonaligned countries "more precise" and to develop it further. In practical terms this means, as Castro said at the Algiers conference (1973) regarding the Soviet Union as the "natural ally of the non-aligned," or as President Samora Machel of Mozambique put it more recently, "Imperialism is our enemy, our economic, military, political and cultural enemy." At the Havana meeting (1979) Pham Van Dong of Vietnam went even further, stating that the attempt to reduce the movement to its original targets was contrary to the interests of the anti-imperialist struggle.

The political offensive aiming at inducing the nonaligned to give maximum support to Soviet foreign policy has continued ever since, and is likely to continue in future. It has not succeeded across the board; there has been considerable opposition. But more often than not, these efforts have achieved their aims. The general tenor of the resolutions of nonaligned meetings in recent years is hostile to America on virtually every count. Following Camp David, the attempt was made to exclude Egypt; on the other hand, there is never a word of criticism of the Soviet Union. The pro-Soviet bloc in the nonaligned movement also succeeded in barring the seating of a delegation from Kampuchea following the Vietnamese invasion of that country. Castro successfully prevented any condemnation of the Soviet invasion of Afghanistan, arguing that this was a domestic issue and outsiders had no right to interfere.

But nonaligned solidarity was not sufficiently strong on the Afghanistan question: 57 countries voted for a resolution in the United Nations condemning the Soviet invasion. This was interpreted as a severe blow to Castro and the Soviets, but it is also true that the resolution was couched in the mildest and most considerate terms, and, furthermore, that 35 nonaligned either voted against the resolution or abstained or were absent. While a majority of the nonaligned certainly did not like the Soviet invasion, they did not want to make waves, let alone extend effective help to a fellow nonaligned country. There never was danger of a split in the movement; the issue was shelved, which of course was a Soviet victory, albeit a limited one. To a certain extent, the importance of the nonaligned movement has declined. For if it could not maintain a common front in the United Nations, there is probably even less hope for effective collaboration on more weighty issues.

The attempt of Soviet surrogates to deflect the nonaligned movement from its original aims shows once again that a determined minority can have disproportionate political influence when facing a divided majority. On the other hand, as so often in the past, such attempts at manipulation cause damage to the organization that is the target of the take-over. The majority, unable to put up effective resistance but unwilling to go along with resolutions it does not fully endorse, begins to take less interest in the enterprise. This brings up the question of how much importance should be accorded to the nonaligned as a political factor. There has been a tendency in the West to overrate the cohesion of the bloc. Insofar as military and political power is concerned, there should be no delusions. Most of the Third World governments are unstable, and most of the countries are rent by internal discord.

Notwithstanding OPEC, the political power of the Third World is largely mythical. But it is a powerful myth that, despite all the setbacks it has suffered, is far from spent. It is of no great consequence whether, in the United Nations, Third World countries favor or oppose the Soviet occupation of Afghanistan. Soviet actions will not be influenced by such votes. But Third Worldism as a mood, a psychological attitude, a feeling that the members of the bloc have something in common, is a factor of some political influence. It is important in an indirect way, influencing liberal and left-wing opinion in Western societies. It has an impact on the smaller Western countries; not only Cyprus and Malta are members, but Sweden, Finland, Portugal, Austria, Spain, and even Switzerland have participated as guests or observers in the meetings of the nonaligned movement in recent years. These delegations would not have attended the meetings unless they thought them of some importance.

Thus, in the final analysis it is not the intrinsic strength of the movement that counts, but the perception. The nonaligned movement is one of speeches and declarations, not of actions. But speeches and declarations help to create a certain political climate and expectations about rising and declining forces in world politics, the ascendancy of the Soviet Union, and the isolation of the West. For this reason it is of some importance that Third World language is now considerably closer to that of the Soviet bloc than to that of the West and that, generally speaking, the Soviet Union is on the offensive in these Third World organizations, whereas the West is not putting up a terrifically effective defense.

THE SURROGATES

The use of proxies is the most interesting, innovative, and, on the whole, most effective technique in the Soviet instrumentality used in the Third World. Western perceptions in this respect have lagged behind realities: while much attention has been devoted to the ideological attractions of Soviet Communism (which are minute) or the blandishments of economic aid and trade (which are not very significant either), the importance of the activities of Soviet surrogates have until quite recently not been fully appreciated even though the facts were known and never in dispute.

Imperial powers have frequently used others to do their work: the Romans made the *clientes* fight various enemies; in the 16th century, mercenaries (*Landsknechte*), mainly of German and Swiss origin, were assisting the highest bidder all over Europe. The British army had (and still has) its Gurkhas, and the French their spahis and their Foreign Legion. But the role of the Cubans and the East Germans is different in many respects, be it only because they act for their patron in peace as well as in war. Their role is as much political as military.

Why Cuba, why East Germany? Their choice is, of course, not accidental. Generally, in the Third World Cuba is dissociated from the industrial North—culturally, politically, and even ethnically.[4] East Germany, on the other hand, is not only one of the most faithful Soviet satellites but also the most competent, efficient, and probably the most ambitious. Neither Poles nor Czechs nor Hungarians are heirs to a global tradition or have any wishes to serve the cause of Communism (or any other cause) in places far from their homeland. Germany does have such a tradition; hence the greater willingness to impart the blessing of the Communist system to countries such as South Yemen and Ethiopia.

Political-military action through proxies has many undoubted advantages, above all on the psychological level. Everywhere in Asia and Africa there is a residue of suspicion against great powers; if Soviet, rather than Cuban, soldiers had fought in Africa, there would have been an outcry. The use of Cuban forces, on the other hand, seems innocuous. As a small country and part of the nonaligned bloc, Cuba's presence had legitimacy and is free from any imperialist taint. Cubans are much less visible in Africa than Russians or other Slavs. Thus President Sékou Touré of Guinea expelled the Soviets in 1961, but a few years later asked the Cubans to set up a people's militia and even staffed the presidential guard with Cubans. East Germany, while not exactly nonaligned, is also no superpower except in athletics.

These Communist missionary activities in the Third World have a beneficial psychological effect on Cuba and East Germany. They enhance their status in the world, making them appear more important than they really are. Having built a nearly perfect society at home, they are now called upon to share their experience with others, surely a sign of distinction. They are the model pupils among the satellites. Their motivation is certainly not economic: East Germany and Cuba are the two Communist countries with the lowest percentage of trade with the Third World (6 percent in the case of East Germany, less in the case of Cuba).

The economic interest of the satellites in some Third World countries is bound to increase in the years to come. They have been given to understand by the Soviet Union that they will have to fend for themselves, at least to a certain extent, as far as the purchase of vital raw materials is concerned. This interest relates above all to the rich, oil-producing countries, although the East German and Cuban presence is limited for the time being to poorer African countries that have little to offer. However, no secret is made of the fact that the Communist foothold in Africa south of the Zambezi will ultimately result in depriving "imperialism" of chrome, manganese, and the other strategic minerals found in the southern part of Africa.

Intervention by proxy on a massive scale is possible, on the whole, only in countries in which the local rulers are basically willing to enter the

Soviet orbit. Governments wishing to preserve their independence may still invite a few East German advisers, but they will not employ thousands of them in the most sensitive positions.

East Germany's activity has been limited in the main to Angola, Mozambique, Ethiopia, and South Yemen; in these "neuralgic points" in world affairs they appear (to use their own terminology) as "representatives of the bloc of socialist states." East German leaders are paying long visits to these countries, and these visits are reciprocated in due course. Thousands of East German experts are active in state administration, education, industry, health, and, above all, the security forces and the army. Since their nation is one of the world's leaders in sports, East German trainers are very much in demand; promising young Africans are invited to special institutions in East Germany where they receive both professional training and political indoctrination. Others are trained locally in special camps. The constitution of South Yemen has been copied from that of East Germany, and the secret police, the *Tanzim* (the main pillar of the regime), is entirely in the hands of emissaries from East Berlin.

Ethiopia and South Yemen are among the world's most murderous dictatorships, but they are offically described as the most progressive Marxist-Leninist regimes in Africa and the Middle East; their leaders, such as Mengistu, are acclaimed as men of peace and great humanists even if they happen to kill, and perhaps also to torture, their political rivals with their own hands. The East Germans have learned that an excess of flattery has never caused a political crisis; hence the bestowing of honorary doctorates of philosophy and other such compliments on gangsters and torturers. Western democratic leaders are also known to act with cynicism, but in this respect they cannot possibly compete successfully with the Communists.

There is an obvious division of labor between Cubans and East Germans: of the 40,000 Cubans operating in Africa, 80 percent are officers and soldiers on active duty, mainly in Ethiopia (13,000) and Angola (19,000), whereas the great majority of East Germans are civilians (admittedly including many police and intelligence experts).

Cubans troops played a decisive role in the victory of the MPLA in Angola, and they took an active (and probably decisive) part in the Ogaden campaign in 1978 against the Somalis. Since then, in the two countries they have been kept mainly on guard duty, to train the local military forces, and to free them for action against UNITA and the Somalis. At the same time they act as the main pillar of shaky governments that have no popular support.

Cuban operations, originally concentrated on Latin America, were extended and subsequently switched to Africa in the early 1960s. Under Nkrumah, guerrilla training bases were established in Ghana, and Cuban security advisers were at various times active in Algeria, Guinea, the Congo,

Libya, Benin, Somalia, and Sierra Leone, though not on a massive scale. Local security forces in Uganda (under Amin) and in Equatorial Guinea (under Nguema) were trained by Cubans. More recently the concentration has been on Angola and the Horn of Africa, and there has been a regular link with the South-West Africa People's Organization (SWAPO), fighting for the independence of Nambia.

Mention has been made of the fact that massive involvement of Soviet proxies has so far taken place only in countries in which a basic inclination already existed on the part of "radical" movements or military dictatorships. However, some progress has also been made in other circumstances by the Communist vanguard. Zambia originally had no predisposition toward Communism and Soviet influence; the (official) Zambian press wrote about the East Germans in the 1960s that they "cause unrest wherever they appear" and that they "carry out dirty work for their bosses." Ten years later Kenneth Kaunda went on the East Berlin pilgrimage, proclaiming undying friendship to his "only true friends" and expressing the hope that more help would be given. Kaunda has not been converted to Leninism, but he now has on his doorstep two pro-Communist regimes that required certain political adjustments. At the same time the economic situation has rapidly deteriorated (following the 1978 policy of "guns instead of butter"). Help from the West has been next to impossible to obtain, and Kaunda can no longer be choosy in his selection of friends. The Zambian situation may recur in other parts of Africa.

Cuban and East German activities in Africa have not always been successful and have on occasion provoked conflict. Wherever the Communist presence is on a large scale, there is bound to be tension with the local population: Cuban and East German advisers and soldiers enjoy a considerably higher standard of living, a fact resented by the locals.[5] East German experts have made themselves unpopular by showing a lack of tact and a lack of understanding of local customs and mentality. Expectations of major and rapid economic progress have nowhere been fulfilled. Busts of Marx and Lenin, cassettes of the Communist Manifesto (in 20 languages), and even equipment for sport clubs pale next to desperately needed economic aid.

Economic hardship has been a constant among countries of "socialist orientation," excepting only such special cases as the Sahel countries. Massive aid will not come from the Soviet bloc. Africans have not been slow in realizing this. Zambia's minister of justice, returning from a Moscow conference on "peace and social progress," reported that the participants had called on the Soviet Union to increase its aid to the African countries. Yet there is no such hope, and it seems that the Communist-oriented countries of Africa—as well as Cuba and Nicaragua—have been encouraged by Moscow to apply for Western economic aid without in any way lessening their political ties with the Soviet bloc and without reducing the Cuban and East German presence. The assumption is that aid can be obtained from the West without any political strings attached.

The Communists have committed political mistakes. On occasion they have supported the wrong candidate in the struggle for power. Their candidate in Zimbabwe was Joshua Nkomo rather than Robert Mugabe, but when they realized that Nkomo would lose, they quickly switched. No enduring harm was done to their interests.

The question has repeatedly been raised in recent years whether Cuba and East Germany are in fact surrogates of the Soviet Union, or whether they pursue objectives and interests of their own within the general parameters of Soviet political and military strategy. In other words, Cuba's role has been compared to that of a paladin rather than a surrogate.

The debate has caused a great deal of unnecessary confusion. It is based on a misunderstanding of the relationship between the Soviet Union and its clients. This relationship is, of course, more complicated than it was in Stalin's day. Perhaps the relationship between patron and client in ancient Rome is a more apt analogy. The patron has the power (*potestas*), and can expect obedience (*obsequium*) from the client in all circumstances. Yet the relationship is not-one sided, since the patron very much needs the clients to shore up his political ambitions. He has the duty to protect the clients, and if he should break faith (*fides*), he will have forfeited any claim to their allegiance. East Germany, one of the Soviet Union's most faithful allies, has shown feelings of superiority vis-à-vis Soviet inefficiency. This is based on the conviction that a mixture of Marxism-Leninism and German thoroughness is preferable to the Russian mixture of Marxism-Leninism and slovenliness.

East Germany can hardly be suspected of pursuing its own objectives in Africa and the Middle East. How real are these claims with regard to Cuba? The Cubans certainly think of themselves as "self-motivated international paladins." It is clear, furthermore, that in certain circumstances those who conduct Soviet policy in the Third World will listen to the Cubans and sometimes take their advice. The fact that Soviet financial support for Cuba has more than quadrupled in recent years shows that Cuba's role is greatly appreciated. Yet the idea that the Cuban tail has been wagging the Soviet dog is altogether fanciful. The Soviet Union has a global strategy, even if it is not always comprehensive and consistent; and while Cuba will be praised and rewarded for its active role, it will not be permitted to lead the Soviet Union into any venture of any importance unless it corresponds with Soviet interests. Thus, despite outward appearances, Cuba no more has a specific African policy than Bulgaria does. Or, if it has one, it is of no practical consequence. The possibilities of action for a small country (or even for a medium power) in the contemporary world are exceedingly narrow, as de Gaulle and Tito came to realize. Impressive gestures, defiant speeches, and the outward trappings of independence amount to little or nothing unless they are backed by real power, which a small country does not have.

Cuba's African policy is of importance in the domestic Cuban context: it certainly adds to Cuba's pride and self-esteem. It strengthens the feeling that the nation has a mission to fulfill in the world—at a time of economic failure at home and Castro's predictions that in this respect nothing much is likely to improve in the next 20 years. In these circumstances Cuba's foreign operations may well be a political and psychological necessity. Likewise, national pride makes it imperative that the Cubans persuade themselves that they are acting independently, and that their alliance with the Soviet Union is one between (more or less) equals.

It is not impossible that Cuba may one day want to dissociate itself to some degree from the Soviet Union; there may even be a break. In contrast with the Warsaw Pact countries, it has no common border with the Soviet Union, nor are very strong Soviet forces stationed there. Furthermore, as in the case of Bulgaria, a feeling of Pan-Slavic solidarity is lacking. On the other hand, it is precisely because of its geographical situation that Soviet domination is far less palpably felt than in Eastern Europe. There is economic dependence, but no danger of Soviet invasion if Cuba should dare to disobey its patron. In view of its proximity to America, Cuba's natural inclination may be to distrust the nearer superpower and to look for support from the more distant one, unless Soviet pressure should become offensive to Cuban pride or its demands exorbitant—or if Moscow should not live up to its obligations as a protector.

For the time being, the Soviet Union can count on the support of its proxies, which, in the interest of friendly relations, it may even treat as paladins.[6]

Cuba and East Germany apart, there is the fascinating case of Libya under Qaddafi, which, though not a Communist country, has been of much help in promoting the aims of Soviet foreign policy (the invasion of Chad, assistance to Idi Amin and to rebels in the Philippines and Central America, not to mention coups, plots, and assassination attempts against the leaders of many countries, and financial help to many "liberation movements"). The drawback, for Moscow, is primarily Libya's erratic and unreliable behavior. Its record as a proxy, furthermore, has not been very successful. Libya's services can be used for some purposes but not for others: for destabilization rather than for securing pro-Soviet regimes. The Libyans have the money and the weapons, but not the political know-how; they cannot teach Africans how to develop a state party and administration, let alone a secret police force. From the ideological point of view, the Libyans, while not a rival, must be regarded as agents of confusion.

The people's Democratic Republic of Yemen (PDRY; South Yemen) has not been very active as a proxy in the past, but is potentially of considerable importance as a base in the contest for the Arabian Peninsula.

To argue that the United States has surrogates, one could point to Morocco, which has intervened in Equatorial Guinea and elsewhere, and Egypt, which has threatened to intervene against Libyan aggression in several African countries. Britain has kept a small presence in Oman, and both nations intervened (together with the Senegalese) against a coup in Gambia. The French under Giscard kept some 14,000 soldiers in 30 African countries, and they have assisted 10 of them against various threats. The best-known case was the defense of Zaire's Shaba Province.

However, these operations by Western and pro-Western forces cannot possibly be compared in scale, scope, or character with the activities of Soviet proxies and "paladins." Under Mitterand, the French government has shown no enthusiasm for playing gendarme; the present French government prefers to act through the United Nations. Morocco has been preoccupied with domestic affairs, and so has Egypt. But even previously pro-Western operations in the Third World were purely defensive and reactive, in contrast with the activities of the Soviet proxies. Furthermore, they were limited almost entirely to military conflict, leaving systematic political action to the Cubans and the East Germans.

Some Western countries may still have the capability to engage in political missionary work and in small-scale military rescue operations in the Third World. But none has the missionary zeal, and this will give the Soviet Union and its allies an inestimable advantage for years to come.

THE ATTRACTIONS OF IDEOLOGY

Ideology—that is, Marxist-Leninist doctrine as currently interpreted in the Soviet Union—raises questions about Soviet-Third World relations in three different respects:

- To what extent are Soviet operations in the Third World motivated by it?
- How do Soviet policy makers and experts explain developments in the Third World in the light of Marxist-Leninist doctrine?
- Are Third World leaders and movements attracted by Soviet ideology, and how decisive is this for Soviet-Third World collaboration?

For the present investigation, only the third question is of crucial importance; the first will be discussed briefly elsewhere. In the 1950s it was the fashion in the West to overrate the importance of Communist ideology; ever since, the tendency has been to downplay it. The fact that Soviet ideology has no great power of attraction in the industrial societies of the West does not necessarily mean that it lacks such an appeal among the elite of the less-developed countries. The belittling of ideology by observers is a typical case of "mirror imaging"; because ideology, by and large, is no longer of paramount importance in Western politics, it is assumed that the same is true in other societies.

At first sight, Marxism-Leninism is an unlikely doctrine for providing spiritual guidance to the Third World. When Marx envisaged "the revolution," he had the most developed countries in mind, not the most backward, in which the preconditions for a socialist society did not exist. The same is true with regard to Lenin, even though in his time the concepts of the "weakest link" and the "revolution in the East" first appeared.

And yet, despite all incongruities, there are certain affinities between Marxism-Leninism and Third World thought that help to explain the sympathies for the Soviet Union in some circles of the Third World. This refers, above all, to the Leninist theory of imperialism, which, albeit in a vague and bowdlerized form, has been accepted even by non-Marxists in Asia and Africa. It is, of course, not true, as Lenin thought, that the sole (or main) reason for Western imperialist rule is economic: the extraction of cheap raw materials and the wish to find markets. Nor is it true, as he predicted, that the imperialist powers would collapse following decolonization. But domination by foreigners was, all the same, a deeply humiliating experience; and the decisive issue is not why the British, French, and Dutch came, but that they came, and stayed on. In this context the United States constitutes a difficult but not insoluble problem for the Leninists: it was not an imperialist power, at least not in Asia and Africa. Therefore, the concept of neocolonialism—exploitation through the multinational firms—is brought in.

The idea that the Soviet Union is an imperialist power does not find a responsive audience in Asia and Africa, for Soviet techniques of conquest have been different. The Soviet Union traditionally has affected adjacent countries that were eventually absorbed. That it has taken over the Baltic countries, eastern Poland, Bessarabia, and other countries may worry the Europeans, but it does not cause sleepless nights to Third World elites. Soviet advances in the Far East may concern the Chinese and Japanese, but not the Indians or the Arabs.

The theory of imperialism apart, Soviet ideology has a certain attraction among Third World activists, who see in it a prescription for modernization following a noncapitalist approach, a way to become rich and powerful (or at any rate richer and more powerful than they are now). The preconditions for capitalist development do not exist today in most African and the less-developed Asian countries, nor do the prerequisites for democratic rule. The Soviet model, on the other hand, seems to show how to run a more or less effective dictatorship and to plan the economy. There is no room in most Third World countries for a free press or for much freedom of any sort.

It is therefore not surprising that most of these countries should side with the Soviet bloc rather than with the West at U. N. conferences and on other occasions. Communist-inspired dictatorships in the Third World give almost unlimited power to a new administrative class: semi-intellectuals, army officers, the new bourgeoisie. It could plausibly be argued that it is in the class interest of Third World elites to establish a state in which their power will be maximized and made more secure. On the other hand, Third Worldism is also "populist" in inspiration, and populism is, in some important respects, related to Leninism, even though it may turn into a bitter enemy in the struggle for power.

Some Western observers who cannot possibly be suspected of sympathy for Marxism-Leninism have detected certain positive aspects in countries with a socialist orientation, such as Mozambique. To begin with, a capitalist alternative does not exist. The administrative class does not enrich itself to the same degree as the private capitalist class. Economic policy may be less efficient and the system is bad for human liberty, but it does, on the whole, generate greater equality, according to Peter Wiles. To be fair, comparisons should be made not with Switzerland or Denmark, but with North Yemen or Uganda or even Nigeria.

It is too early at this stage to draw up a final balance sheet. The economic record of the countries with a socialist orientation has ranged from poor to very poor, almost without exception. On the other hand, they have not been free from corruption or nepotism. Economic progress has been infinitely more pronounced in countries of nonsocialist orientation (Taiwan, South Korea, Ivory Coast).

Brief mention should be made of the divisive factors between Marxism-Leninism and Third Worldism as an ideology. Even most countries with a socialist orientation are not willing to follow the Soviet lead on religion, nationalism, and tribalism, and there has been a constant debate about a specific African or Asian "road to socialism," much to the chagrin of the Soviets. The Soviet idea of the class struggle is not applicable in Asia and Africa; the army (that is, the officer corps) and/or the intelligentsia take the place of the working class as a "revolutionary vanguard," and this causes endless ideological complications. There are other differences—for instance, with regard to the existence and the role of a Communist party in the Third World political system.

However, all that matters in the final analysis is that in the Third World there are at least some affinities with Communist (Soviet) doctrine, whereas it is difficult to think of much ideological kinship with the West. That ideology is no more than a contributing, and never a decisive, factor in this rapprochement goes without saying. For if ideology were decisive, the Chinese model would have been at least as attractive as the Soviet. The fact that this has not been the case points to the limitations of the importance of ideology as a link cementing Third World-Soviet cooperation.

Double Strategy: The Question of Islam

Involvement in the Third World means the necessity of choice. Ideally, the Soviet Union should be on good terms with all countries, and all social and political forces. Given the many Third World conflicts, this is frequently impossible. The Soviet Union cannot at the same time support India and Pakistan, Ethiopia and Somalia, Libya and Morocco, radical and moderate Arab countries—let alone the Arabs and Israel. Sometimes the choice may appear easy: the Soviet leadership assumed that the Arabs were many and the Israelis few, and that the former would inevitably prove more important. Similar thoughts influenced them in the India-Pakistan conflict. In other circumstances, making a choice may be highly undesirable; there is always the danger that the Soviet leaders may back the wrong horse. Furthermore, even in the case of victory, a price has to be paid. For this reason the Soviet Union has tried to play the role of the disinterested onlooker and, on occasion, of the arbiter ("the spirit of Tashkent"), the friend of both sides, eager to restore peace and to establish a common front against the real enemy: Western imperialism. The war between Iran and Iraq was an example; the Soviet Union was under pressure to take both sides, and it refrained from doing so.

At other times, staying aloof may be far more difficult. Mention has been made of the Soviet dilemma vis-à-vis Communist parties in the Third World. It cannot altogether dissociate itself from them, but it frequently has to make deals over their heads and against their best interests. Sometimes it may even have to sacrifice them.

Another example, of even greater political consequence, is the Soviet attitude toward Islam. As a leading North African commentator succinctly put it: "The Soviet Union has the friendliest of feelings and is the staunchest ally of Islam. On one solitary condition: That the Muslims do not live in the Soviet Union itself. . . ." This comment was made before the rebirth of militant Islam (Khomeinism, the Muslin Brotherhoods), which, from the Soviet point of view, has made the problem even more complicated, the opportunities greater, and the risks higher. It has been Soviet policy at least since 1960 to combat and isolate Islam at home and to woo Muslims abroad. On the whole, this policy has met with some success; a confrontation between Moscow and militant Muslim leaders such as Khomeini and Qaddafi has certainly been prevented.

MUSLIMS IN THE SOVIET UNION

The number of Soviet Muslims has been a bone of contention between Western and Soviet experts.[7] According to the former, there are 50 million Azerbaijanis, Uzbeks, Kazakhs, Tadzhiks, and others; according to Soviet sources, only 35–40 million, many of whom do not profess Islam in any case. Fifty million is probably too high a figure, but it is not a matter of dispute that the birthrate is considerably higher in the Muslim republics than elsewhere in the Soviet Union (3.1 percent in Tadzhikistan, 3.0 percent in Uzbekistan, 2.8 percent in Turkmenistan). It is true that by no means all of those classified as Muslims are believers. It is also true—and Soviet experts have admitted this—that Islam which is not just a religion but also a way of life, is more deeply rooted than any other faith in the Soviet Union. Antireligious propaganda, which has continued both openly and discreetly, has not had much effect. The more educated section of the Muslim population have been influenced, but they also want to preserve their ethnic identity. If "old-fashioned" religion has declined in this milieu, a more modern nationalism has replaced it.

There has been speculation, much of it farfetched, in recent years about the impact of the Islamic resurgence on Soviet Muslims. Some analysts have even explained the Soviet intervention in Afghanistan with reference to the Islamic renaissance. That there has been such an influence is undeniable, but its political importance should not be overrated. There is no common front of minorities in the Soviet Union, nor is such unity likely to arise. The Azerbaijanis may dislike the Russians, but they traditionally dislike their Armenian and Georgian neighbors even more. The Tadzhiks (who are Shiite and speak Persian) have little in common with Tartars and Kazakhs, who are Sunnite and speak Turkic languages. There is no Muslim clergy in the Soviet Union that can spread and organize the new gospel. The political and economic achievements of Pakistan, Afghanistan, Iran, or even the Arab countries hardly constitute a major attraction for Soviet Muslims, or a threat to Communist rule.

The coming years may well witness a strengthening of a new Muslim identity in the Soviet Union, and this trend, as well as the danger of the export of an "Islamic counterrevolution" (Brezhnev's phrase), will be followed by the Soviet leaders with a watchful eye. But it is most unlikely that this rise of Islam will in any way influence Soviet domestic and foreign policy.[8] On the contrary, Soviet propaganda has tried to make use of the strong anti-Western and collectivist element in the Islamic renaissance. Since, in Islamic perspective, Marxism is very much a Western secular ideology, and therefore reprehensible, left-wing Muslims (and some major non-Soviet Communists) have been trying to find common ground between the original social ideals of Islam, with the prophet Muhammad as a precursor of Karl Marx. Seen in historical light, this kind of argumentation is deeply fraudulent, but it has nevertheless had some effect, just as some Christians have found their way to Communism by way of the "socialist ideals" of early Christianity.

Of far greater importance is the fact that as far as its social composition is concerned, the Islamic revival is largely a radical protest movement of the lower classes against the rich and against foreign influences. It resembles populist movements in other parts of the world, and its specific in the Middle East is its religious character.

Soviet policy in the Middle East has tolerated ideological concessions toward Islam outside the Soviet Union since the early 1960s; perhaps the first to envisage an "Islamic Marxism" was Ali Yata, secretary-general of the Moroccan Communist Party. He was followed by some Iranian student leaders. Soviet commentators have argued that Communists in the Arab world are tactically correct in avoiding criticism of Islam altogether. This refers, however, only to countries in which Communists are not in power; in the People's Democratic Republic of Yemen, Muslim festivals, including the Prophet's birthday, are ignored, and children are given an antireligious education.

Reports of persecution of Islam in the Soviet Union are routinely contradicted by official Soviet Muslim spokesmen, such as the ubiquitous "Mufti" Babahanov, chairman of the Spiritual Administration of Central Asia and Kazakhstan. On his frequent visits abroad, he has spread the word that Islam has every possible freedom in the Soviet Union. Other, nonreligious Soviet spokesmen, including Brezhnev, have requested time and again that Marxists draw the basic dividing line not between believers and atheists but between exploiters and the exploited, and that Marxists would like to cooperate closely with the many millions of Muslims who actively participate in the struggle against imperialism in Asia and Africa.

That the Soviet dual strategy has worked reasonably well is shown by the Libyan example. Up to the spring of 1974, the Soviet Union was, for Qaddafi, as much an imperialist country as the United States; it merely wanted to take the place of the United States and gain a foothold in the area. At the Tripoli Islamic Conference in 1974, Qaddafi stated that Islam was more progressive than Communism, and had provided the guiding principles for the happiness of the individual and of society. Communism was a vanguard party of individuals who had one thing in common: "the lust for power."

Beginning in 1974, there was a reorientation that led to cooperation in the sphere of ideology. Both Muslims and Communists agreed to disagree, arguing that "that which unites us is far more important than the divisions." Such a statement was not surprising from a pragmatic politician such as Kosygin; that militant Muslims should have accepted it is noteworthy. The Soviet Union had at the time lost its foothold in Egypt and was looking for new allies. Libya, which had not been very successful in its attempts to gain leadership of the Arab world, was searching for powerful allies. In the case of Iran under Khomeini, Soviet progress was less spectacular but nonetheless not negligible, the result of both common interest and clever manipulation. True, in Iran there is traditional suspicion of the designs of the powerful neighbor to the north. But Soviet policy showed that these suspicions could be overcome by exploiting internal divisions in the Third World and between these countries and the West. It also showed that even extreme Muslim leaders are by no means impervious to realpolitik and that their fanaticism is not indiscriminate.

Unlike their Western counterparts, Soviet experts and policy makers have never underrated the attraction of Islam; they were aware of the strength of the Islamic revival in Iran in the mid-1970s, when most other observers tended to belittle it. On the other hand, they have not exaggerated it, as became the fashion in many Western circles after the fall of the shah. As far as Moscow is concerned, the Islamic revival is not the wave of the future, but a temporary manifestation of the general protest movement in backward societies.

Soviet experts assume that it will disappear following its failure to solve urgent economic and social problems. Pro-Soviet elements will try to take over the leadership of this inchoate radical movement, which, they assume, will gradually shed its Islamic coloring. But they also take into account that they may be mistaken, and they are moving with great caution.

DIPLOMACY

After three decades of inactivity, the Soviet Union has been more active diplomatically in the Third World than any other nation. These activities include the exploitation of regional conflicts as well as classical diplomacy, the formalization of its relationship with other countries through treaties and agreements.[9] No other country has been instrumental in arranging so many state visits and top-level conferences. No other nation has invested so much effort in cultural and quasi-cultural exchanges. The Soviet Union has tried on occasion to act as "honest broker" in conflicts between Third World nations. A large propaganda effort has been staged, Soviet periodicals and films are distributed by the embassies, local newspapers are subsidized, and Soviet radio stations beam broadcasts to the Third World in most Asian and African languages. This effort far exceeds the activities of the Western nations taken together.

THE EXPLOITATION OF CONFLICT SITUATIONS

It has been said that but for the India-China (and the India-Pakistan) conflict, for the Arab-Israeli confrontation, the dispute between Algeria and Morocco, and other endemic conflicts, the Soviet Union would not have been able to make much headway in Asia and Africa. There is a kernal of truth in this assertion: The Soviet penetration of the Arab world began with the arms deals with Egypt in 1955, as the Arab-Israeli conflict became more acute. The rapprochement with India was intensified after India's defeat in the war with China in 1962. However, exploitation of such opportunities can explain Soviet achievements in the Third World only up to a point. Neither India, Pakistan, Israel, nor the Arab "front-line" states have joined the Soviet camp. Those that entered the Soviet orbit have not done so as the result of a conflict with their neighbors.

Political help and military aid have created a climate of goodwill in India and the Arab world, but such goodwill can be translated into tangible support for the Soviet cause only to a limited extent. Among the Arab "front-line" states, only Syria has signed a treaty with Moscow that may give substantial military advantages to the Soviet Union. The goodwill has manifested itself mainly in anti-American rhetoric rather than in acceptance of the Soviet political and social model. It is quite likely that such anti-Americanism was unavoidable in any case, as far as the more radical Third World countries are concerned.

The Soviet Union has tried to be on good (or at least better-than-normal) terms with as many Third World countries as possible. Thus, it scrupulously refrained from taking sides in the war between Iraq and Iran. In other cases, such as Ethiopia and Somalia, it was clearly impossible to keep the goodwill of both sides, and the Soviet Union predictably switched its support to the side likely to prevail. This "inevitability of choice" has created dilemmas for the Soviet Union, and it will cause problems in future. Soviet clients have been defeated (Nasser in 1967), and this has necessitated deeper Soviet involvement than may have been thought prudent or cost-effective. The process of involvement has a momentum of its own. Unless the patron takes good care of his clients, he loses face, his reputation suffers, and other clients will be reluctant to entrust him with their fate.

Last, exploitation of conflict situations is not the monopoly of superpowers. Since time immemorial, small countries have played off one big power against another for their own purposes. Some have reached a degree of perfection in this field, changing sides fairly regularly, always on the lookout for the higher bidder. Europe in the age of wars of religion (the 16th and 17th centuries) is a perfect example of such practices, but they have, of course, been used in many places and at many times. While the Soviet Union has no wish to be used in such a way, it cannot entirely escape this practice. There has to be give and take; alliances cannot be one-way streets. The Soviet leaders will be fully aware (and will accept) that their partners pursue interests that have little or nothing in common with their own. They will still be willing to make concessions, since they assume that in the longer run their smaller allies will become more dependent on them and the junior partner will have to follow the lead of the senior partner.

FEAR AND "FALSE CONSCIOUSNESS"

In Third World diplomacy the Soviet Union makes full use of two syndromes widespread in Asia and Africa (and to a certain extent in Latin America): fear and "the-Soviet-Union-is-a-faraway-country" perception. While much (perhaps too much) has been said and written about ideology as a weapon, fear of the Soviet Union is, on the whole, an underrated factor. Whereas the Soviet Union may not be able to extend much help to Third World countries in the economic field and in other respects, the countries situated not far from the Soviet borders know that their powerful neighbor is capable of doing considerable harm to them. If they should act systematically against Soviet interests, the full blast of Communist propaganda will be directed against them, they may be subjected to various measures of destabilization, and Soviet displeasure will be felt in other ways.

The projection of Soviet military power and its political use ought to be mentioned here. The presence of the Soviet navy has limited the possibility of American intervention, and showing the flag has a psychological impact today as in the past. Thus, the need for military action is obviated ipso facto by the Soviet presence—the "demonstration effect." The same is true, a fortiori, with regard to the Soviet army vis-à-vis Russia's neighbors. Whatever its economic weaknesses, the Soviet Union is a military superpower, and it is conventional wisdom in the Third World that defiance is a risky business. The cautious behavior of Turkey facing Soviet (and proxy) intervention in its domestic affairs, Pakistan's submissiveness despite all-out Soviet support for India, the restraint vis-à-vis Russia shown even by Khomeini and his followers serve as illustrations.

On the other hand, in countries far from the Soviet borders, the opposite syndrome is frequently encountered: Since the Soviet Union is (or seems) so far away,[10] it cannot possibly constitute a danger, and therefore is a natural counterweight, a political ally against the other (and nearer) superpower. For this reason, for many Latin Americans the United States will always be the greater threat.

By the same geopolitical logic, the Asian and Middle Eastern countries situated near the Soviet borders should look for American support against the superpower that is nearer and more dynamic, and happens to have the greater appetite. Common sense should make them wary of excessively close ties with the Soviet Union and seek better relations with the United States as a counterweight. This is true as much for Communist countries wanting to maintain their independence (as the Yugoslav and Chinese examples show) as for non-Communists. Interestingly, some of the Marxists have shown greater realism in this respect than the non-Marxists. Whatever their domestic orientations and ideological preferences, all these countries want to preserve their independence and sovereignty. Yet frequently it is not self-interest or political savvy that dictates their behavior, but "false consciousness." Their policies are affected by various delusions and misconceptions.

The concept "false consciousness" was introduced by Marxist thinkers trying to explain the (to them) incomprehensible fact that many workers do not vote—or act—according to their class interest, but give their support to conservative parties (for instance, the "working-class Tories"). Whether "false consciousness" is applicable in a domestic context is not certain; political decisions clearly are not influenced by class interest alone, nor is it always possible to identify who belongs to a class. Be that as it may, "false consciousness" is certainly of help in explaining the otherwise inexplicable, the fact that countries in an exposed position, threatened by Soviet domination, and eager to maintain their independence, nevertheless may pursue a policy contrary to their own national interest.

It is understandable that such countries will refrain from provoking their powerful neighbor. It is not readily intelligible why they sometimes go out of their way to antagonize the other superpower that could redress the balance. Elementary logic seems to demand that they act to achieve a balance—unless, of course, they have reached the conclusion that the other superpower (the United States) is too weak to help them. But this is decidedly not the case: America's military power more frequently than not is overrated, rather than underestimated, in Third World countries. Another possible explanation for the illogical and possibly suicidal behavior of some Third World nations is the assumption that America is so strong that they have nothing to fear from the Soviet Union. For in the case of a Soviet encroachment, America would, more or less automatically, come to their help, however bad the relations had been previously. These assumptions are fairly widespread in Third World elites (and also among European neutrals and neutralists), but they alone cannot explain the seemingly paradoxical behavior described above.

This leads to the inevitable conclusion that Third World foreign policy is not guided mainly by logic or by self-interest, but that powerful emotions such as xenophobia, of the West in particular, have a greater impact. Is false consciousness a permanent condition or a temporary aberration?

Inasmuch as such behavior may lead to national suicide, and since societies, in contrast with individuals, rarely commit suicide, chances are that in the long run the facts of geopolitical life will prevail. But the emphasis should be on "in the long run," and it ought to be repeated that what has been said applies mainly to countries located near the Soviet borders. It certainly is not true with regard to Latin America or most of tropical Africa. In the view of Moscow, it is in the best interest of the Soviet Union to perpetuate this false consciousness even though irrational behavior on the part of neighbors and clients may cause problems for Russia.

CULTURAL DIPLOMACY AND EXCHANGES

The aim of the cultural policy of the Soviet Union, like that of every other nation, is to create interest in and sympathy for Soviet culture and the Soviet Union in general. This policy is pursued through countless local "friendship societies," radio programs, and exchanges in every conceivable field. Between 1957 and 1978, the Soviet Union signed some 40 agreements on cultural and scientific cooperation, the first ones (ironically) with Egypt (1957) and Guinea (1959). Russian-language teachers have been sent to most Third World countries; 2,000 arrive in Africa each year. Soviet ballet groups have visited the major Asian and African countries; there have been extensive academic exchanges and common botanical and zoological expeditions; Third World technical experts have been trained in the Soviet Union; Soviet institutes have helped to organize and develop scientific research in selected Third World countries. There is cooperation in the field of public health, Soviet trainers have helped Asians and Africans to develop their sports facilities, and Soviet soccer teams have visited most African countries. Soviet musicians, painters, and sculptors have toured the Third World and taken part in exhibitions; Soviet plays have been performed virtually everywhere; and selected Soviet movies are shown in remote villages.

It would be difficult to think of any field that has been omitted or neglected. In quantitative terms, the Soviet effort has been impressive; after decades of total isolation, tens of thousands of Third World citizens have stayed in the Soviet Union and other Communist bloc countries for varying periods, and the Soviet cultural, scientific, and technological presence in Asia and Africa has been very substantial.

Benefits that have accrued to the Soviet Union from these activities have been small, and sometimes the efforts have been counterproductive. The fact that so many Third World students have been exposed to Soviet realities has not turned most of them into ardent Communists. An inclement climate, strange surroundings, food they dislike, a closed society in which contact with foreigners is discouraged, covert racialism, the virtual impossibility of finding female company, the drabness of Soviet daily life, and many other circumstances act as a damper on enthusiasm. For different reasons, Soviet experts sent abroad find a prolonged stay in Asia and Africa less than congenial. Both groups—the Asian and African students and the Soviet experts—would greatly prefer American and Western Europe for a prolonged stay, and they regard their destination as a poor second best.

The KGB still finds a few recruits among the foreigners, and a few Africans and Asians, for unfathomable reasons, may come to like the Soviet way of life. But the great majority will not. The fault is by no means all on one side. Some of the demands of the foreigners are unrealistic or even preposterous, given the nature of Soviet society. At one time the Soviet tried to concentrate most Third World students in Patrice Lumumba University, whereupon the foreign visitors protested against being shut up in a ghetto. But their dispersal over Soviet institutes of higher learning also has not worked well, in view of linguistic and other handicaps. As a result of past experience, it has been Soviet policy in recent years not to expand exchanges much further, but to provide more on-the-spot training.[11] The Soviets have established various institutes in Asia and Africa. On the primary school level, Soviet influence has been more marked (for instance, in Algeria, Tanzania, and Guinea). But the political impact of such kinds of cultural exchanges has been minimal. For while the Soviets stress the superiority of socialist over "bourgeois" pedagogical models, the virtues of the socialist model are, in fact, those of yesterday's Western schools: stricter discipline and greater demands on pupils.

Soviet cultural propaganda has had few successes to its credit: Soviet exhibitions in the Third World attract little interest, and Soviet movies find few voluntary viewers (some are more highly appreciated in New York, London, and Paris). Soviet books are not widely read. In all these respects, Western imports are greatly preferred, even though their level may be deplorably low. Soviet culture is thought to be boring, not only by Third World highbrows but also on the grass roots level.

If the Soviet effort nevertheless has some effect, it is through its sheer size. Western books and periodicals are very expensive; Soviet books are far more readily available. The Indian and African student, schoolteacher, or scientist may know that the quality of Western professional literature is superior, but will not be able to buy it. Soviet radio programs attract no particular interest, but the stations are received loud and clear in English and the vernacular for many more hours than Western broadcasts. The endless repetition of the Soviet interpretation of world events is bound to have a cumulative effect. In short, if there are achievements in the field of Soviet cultural propaganda, they are the result of an investment that, in some respects, is much greater than that made by the West.[12] As in other fields, the Soviets have to overcome the handicap of inferior quality by sheer quantity and, in some instances, by cheaper prices.

SOVIET ECONOMIC AID AND TRADE

About Soviet economic relations with Third World countries, it can be said *grosso modo* that they were never very important, that they have decreased in relative importance since the early 1970s, and that this has not done any major political damage to the Soviet Union. Perhaps there has been less disappointment in the nonoil-producing Third World countries than should have been expected, because the Soviet leaders never made excessive promises. They always made it clear that their main contributions to Third World countries would be guidance rather than economic assistance. The Soviets are great believers in self-help; they say that they pulled themselves from backwardness by their own bootstraps (a comparison that is of doubtful value, for Russia in 1917 had a substantial industry, unlike most of Asia and all of Africa after World War II).

For a long time now, too much attention has been devoted in the West to Soviet aid and trade with the Third World. As recently as October 1980, a CIA study noted, "These long-term military and economic aid programs have enabled the U.S.S.R. to forward important strategic, geopolitical, and commercial objectives at low cost—particularly in the Middle East, North Africa, and South Asia." A congressional study published in 1981 said that in 1978, Soviet aid grants "skyrocketed" to a new record, and a semiofficial West German study (1980) claims that between 1968 and 1978, the amount of Soviet aid further increased.

Yet, in fact trade between the Soviet Union and the Third World decreased to 13 percent of the Soviet total in 1980 (from 15 percent in 1975), and Soviet economic aid disbursements fell from $1 billion in 1972 to half that sum in 1980. (This should be compared with $3–4 billion pumped into Cuba in 1982 alone.) What causes some confusion is that sometimes no distinction is made between economic and military aid. The latter has been substantial—more than $55 billion committed from 1954 to 1981—the former, perhaps less than $20 billion during the same period. Another reason for overrating the extent of Soviet aid is that no distinction is made between aid offered and aid actually disbursed, which was less than half of the former in that period. On other occasions, Soviet help to Cuba and Vietnam is included in the figures for Soviet aid to the less-developed countries (LDCs). Thus, $2.6 billion was pledged in 1979 to the Third World; disbursement amounted to $1.8 billion, of which the bulk went to Cuba and Vietnam. In the same year the Netherlands actively disbursed $1.8 billion in aid.

The reasons for the low (and declining) Soviet economic presence in the Third World are threefold. The Soviet Union is not one of the world's leaders in trade, and most of its foreign trade is (and will be) with the other Communist bloc and industrial countries; the choice of Soviet goods for export is limited; and the Soviet allies in Eastern Europe have suffered increasing difficulties in recent years that further limit Soviet capacity to extend aid elsewhere.[13] However, and perhaps most important, it is not Soviet policy even to try to compete with the West as far as aid to the Third World is concerned. Soviet leaders believe that development aid (in contrast with trade) is not to the Soviet advantage except in cases of an obvious political interest, as in Cuba and Vietnam. The Soviet Union favors resource transfer from North to South—but only for the Western "colonialist nations."[14] According to Soviet thought, the best contribution that the Soviet bloc can make to world economic development is to grow in strength. If aid is given, it will be given bilaterally, not through multilateral agencies, so as to gain maximum propaganda benefit. But, by and large, Soviet leaders do not believe that friendship and influence can be gained through extending more aid.

In the 1950s, the Soviet Union had higher hopes for political dividends from economic assistance and investments. During that period it concentrated on a few major projects, such as the Aswan Dam in Egypt and steelworks in India. Since then, the trend has been, on the whole, away from mammoth projects; one exception was the $2 billion grant to Morocco in 1978 for the development of the local phosphate industry, the largest deal ever signed between the Soviet Union and a Third World country. But deals of this kind are straightforward commercial deals, not acts of charity. Morocco will have to pay back the Soviet Union in phosphate, on terms considerably lower than the world market price. (A similar, albeit smaller, deal was concluded with Guinea concerning the production of bauxite: the first 12 years of production will go to repay Soviet credits.) To provide a few more illustrations; the Soviet Union pays less than the world market price for Afghan gas, for shoes from India, and for a variety of other raw materials or commodities, the production of which it helped to finance.

To what extent is Soviet aid directly serving political aims? The fact that many times more help has been given to Cuba and Vietnam than to countries of the Third World has been mentioned. The question thus arises for only a relatively small part of development aid. About three-quarters of this aid went to six countries: India, Egypt, Iran, Iraq, Turkey, and Afghanistan. In recent years, Morocco and Algeria were added to this list. In most cases, the political motivation is obvious: the decline in trade relations with Egypt after Nasser, and the disproportionate amount of aid given at one time to Chile and more recently to Nicaragua.

On the other hand, the reorientation in the Middle East from Egypt to the oil-producing countries also had commercial motives: the Soviet Union badly needed to increase its hard-currency reserves. Given Egypt's economic situation, it must have occurred to the Soviet leaders that a good case could be made for transferring their activities to countries that, in view of their natural resources, were likely to repay their debts in full and on time. Hence, for instance, the increase in trade in the 1970s with the shah's Iran and the relative decrease with Turkey. It could be argued that in some cases, aid was given to countries oriented toward the West (Turkey, Iran under the shah, Morocco) with the intention of weakening their ties with "imperialism" and "monopoly capitalism."

But if such intentions existed, which seems quite likely, they were only one motive among many, and certainly not the decisive one. If a country had made the jump into the Communist camp, as Cuba and Vietnam had done, political considerations were always paramount. But in relations with other Third World countries—friendly, unfriendly, and indifferent—economic motives have not been altogether absent. The Soviet Union wants to make both political and economic profits in its dealings with Third World countries, and this is likely to cause problems in the future.

Poor Soviet aid performance in the Third World has provoked criticism from Asian and African leaders. Among the specific complaints, the following have been repeatedly made:

- The Soviet bloc loan terms are frequently harder.
- Unlike the West, it seldom gives nonproject aid, such as raw materials, food, or fuel.
- Little access is provided to Soviet bloc markets.
- The goods supplied by the Soviet bloc are frequently of low quality; they could be unsalable elsewhere.
- The Soviet Union has sometimes been reluctant to grant repayment relief to countries in economic difficulty.
- Soviet voluntary payments to specialized U.N. agencies are small and are made in nonconvertible rubles.
- The exchange rate between North and Third World currencies has been changed to the latter's detriment.
- The Soviet bloc resells in the West products received from Third World countries ("switch trade").
- The Soviet bloc avoids international conferences at which specific pledges or donations to developing countries are made.

These and similar complaints are made, and as the Soviet aid programs expire, repayments of debts by Third World countries quite frequently exceed new grants. This is true not only of Egypt, but also of India.

Given the fact that Soviet capacity to remedy these complaints is limited (and that there would be other complaints even if they did), the overall policy has been to put Soviet interests first, to give the very minimum necessary, and to concentrate on military aid. True, there have been discussions inside the Soviet Union about a more sophisticated approach to the Soviet economic presence in the Third World. But in view of the limited trade and aid potential of the Soviet bloc, these have been largely academic.

But the salient fact is that a poor Soviet record has caused no major political damage. Similarly, the fact that the economic difficulties of nonoil-producing LDCs are substantially due to (or at least are aggravated by) OPEC policies has caused only mild protests in Third World capitals. How to explain this apparent paradox? The details about the economic situation are known to only a small elite in Third World countries. The media are induced to give little exposure to these facts. Much more is expected from the "rich" West than from the Soviet bloc. And last, despite the disappointments, a certain mental affinity is still felt with the Soviet bloc ("socialism") rather than with the West, and this, at least in the short run, weighs more heavily than the economic facts of life.

In the long run, needless to say, Soviet inability or unwillingness to offer greater help is having a negative effect on Third World attitudes. But the Soviet leaders also know that in their relations with the Third World, the economic dimension will never be decisive. They may be good Marxists-Leninists, but they clearly believe in the primacy of policy over economics in their Third World agenda. Ironically, Western capitalists adopt quasi-Marxist attitudes when dealing with the Third World, expecting dividends as the result of economic investment.

China has followed, in this respect at least, the Soviet example: Chinese disbursements to Third World countries have fallen steadily since 1976 and are now less than $100 billion, their lowest level since the 1960s. Most of this aid went to Pakistan, Burma, Sudan, and Djibouti, but loans were also offered to such East African countries as Tanzania, Kenya, and Zambia, in which China had a traditional, albeit small, interest.

ARMS TRANSFER AND THE MILITARY OPTION

Military transactions with the Third World have been one of the most important levers in Soviet policy, yet for many years these have been given hardly any publicity: the early Soviet arms deals (with Syria, Afghanistan, and Egypt in 1955/56) were systematically played down, the deal with Egypt being ostensibly carried out through Czechoslovakia. Having for decades denounced the "merchants of death," the Soviet Union found itself uncomfortable in the role of one of the world's leading arms suppliers. The Soviet leaders preferred to create the impression that their help to the Third

World was basically limited to disinterested fraternal advice: how to organize trade unions, to improve education and health services, and, of course, to help economic development in practical ways. But their capacity to render economic help was exceedingly limited, diverting resources to the Third World was never popular among the Soviet public, and the Soviet leaders soon realized that even major infusions of credit would not reap them much gratitude.

Ambitious Third World leaders such as Nasser and Sukarno wanted arms both for practical purposes and as status symbols. These could be obtained from the West only with difficulty and at relatively high cost. The Soviet arms industry, on the other hand, was capable of supplying great quantities of modern arms on terms that were far more acceptable from the LDCs' point of view (barter deals such as Egyptian cotton for MiGs and tanks). Gradually arms exports to the Third World became a substantial factor in the foreign trade of the USSR. While complete figures are not available, arms agreements with the Third World since 1956 are estimated at $55–60 billion, of which some $45 billion was actually delivered. Nonmilitary aid during the same period accounted for $20 billion, of which only $10 billion was disbursed—a striking discrepancy.[15] Total Soviet exports in 1977 were about $45 billion, of which some $6–7 billion went to the developing countries. Soviet arms exports to LDCs that year were $4 billion, the largest single item by far.

Most of the Soviet military assistance originally went to the Middle East, about half of the total to the Arab countries. In recent years, North Africa and tropical Africa also have emerged as major recipients. First, agreements were concluded with Somalia (1963), South Yemen (1969), and the Congo (1969). In the 1970s, Angola, Mozambique, and Ethiopia (1976) were added to this list. Today Libya, Iraq, Syria, and Algeria are among the leading recipients of Soviet arms. The great advantage from the LDCs' point of view was, as already indicated, that they could buy more arms for less money. The price of one U.S. F-15 was approximately equal to that of two Soviet MiG-23s, and for the price of one F-4 they could obtain three MiG-21s. While U.S. planes were superior in performance, it is not certain that they were substantially superior, and the same is true a fortiori with regard to less sophisticated weapons.

Exact prices, discounts from list prices, and forms of payment have been kept secret. We have it on the authority of the late Gamal Abdel Nasser, who, in an emotional speech expressing genuine gratitude, related how he had gone to Moscow after the Six Day War in 1967, and how the Soviet leaders offered him, virtually free of charge ("We would never have been able to pay for it"), far more weapons than he had dared to ask for. On the other hand, most of the Soviet arms trade in the 1970s was directed to the oil-rich countries of the Middle East and North Africa, and pressure has been exerted on not-so-rich recipients (including Benin, Congo, and Madagascar) to pay for previous deals. Thus, by the mid-1970s there was much reason to assume that Soviet "military aid" was, overall, commercially profitable.[16]

Soviet arms shipments to the Third World made recipients considerably dependent on the Soviets for advice, the supply of spare parts, and logistic support. True, it gave the Soviets, as in Egypt, access to air and naval bases. Yet, the more sophisticated the arms system, the greater the dependence, which raises the broader question of military and political benefits accruing to the Soviet Union from these arms deals.

Soviet leaders have, of course, long been aware that they could compete in this field with the West far more easily than in others and that they could, in fact, operate as arms dealers from a position of strength. Arms deals, as in the case of Egypt in 1955, have been the point of departure for many Soviet political initiatives in the Middle East. But it is also true that neither arms deals per se, nor the presence of Soviet military advisers, not the most favorable terms for payment have created a secure foundation for Soviet presence in the Third World. Military penetration in Egypt was very thorough, but not sufficient to prevent a reversal of Egypt's foreign policy. Being men of the world, the Soviet leaders must have known that gratitude is not a factor to be counted upon in world affairs. In Egypt, as elsewhere, complaints harped on the quality of Soviet arms and the behavior of Soviet military advisers.

The inability to pay in full and on time, among other bones of contention, have further dampened Soviet-Third World relations. In fact, 2,000 Cubans in an African country may have a far more potent political impact than the 20,000 Soviet advisers had in Egypt. Third World countries have tried for a variety of reasons (technological, political, and economic) to diversify their sources of arms and supplies.

In the overall balance, political and economic gains clearly outweigh losses in Soviet arms trade with and aid to the Third World. The supply of arms has not been a magic wand. The paramount question is not the supply of arms, but in whose hands political power resides. And since power in most Third World countries has come to rest in the hands of the military, directly or indirectly, the decisive issue, in the view of Moscow, is how to win over the officer corps in the Third World countries—or, if that should not be possible, how to help overthrow and replace them with more amenable candidates.

Soviet leaders remember that with the exception of the Allende government in Chile, committed pro-Soviet governments have never come to power through peaceful means, but always through violence, mainly military coups and civil wars. This is true of Egypt in the 1950s and Somalia in 1969; it applies to Iraq and Congo (Brazzaville) in 1968, to Benin in 1971, to Ethiopia in 1974, and of course to Angola, Mozambique, and Nicaragua. Likewise, Madagascar, Syria, Libya, and the little island of Grenada (even though the 1979 coup there was bloodless) can be included. True, in a few of these cases, the military leader (or the junta) was only gradually converted to more ardent pro-Sovietism; this was true of President Nasser and Qaddafi; Colonel Kérékou of Benin is a special case, since his various ideological conversions (to Marxism, to Islam) should be taken with some reserve. In one or two other cases, the attachment to the Soviet bloc came after a struggle within the leadership, as in the overthrow of President Rubay of South Yemen by Abdul Fattah Ismail in 1978.

In the 1960s, Soviet observers came to believe that since political parties were structurally too weak in most Third World countries, the Communists had little chance and the officer corps was bound to be propelled into a position of leadership. At about this time the concept of the "military intelligentsia" was first developed in Moscow. This did not, of course, imply that all officers were good bets from the Soviet point of view, only the *revoliutsionni demokrati pogonakh* (revolutionary democrats with epaulettes). This referred to sons of peasant or lower middle-class families, who felt the resentment of poor people against the rich (and of the army officer stationed in the province against the capital), who made common cause with the radical intelligentsia and were willing both to carry out far-reaching domestic reforms and to cooperate closely with the Soviet Union.

Soviet observers thought that in most Third World countries, power would pass into the hands of these radical-progressive officers within a number of years. But military rule was regarded only as a transient stage. For all their enthusiasm, the officers lacked the qualities needed for political work and organizational activity. They were (in the best case) patriots, devoted to duty, determined and disciplined. But they were not administrators, except on the lower and middle levels, and they could not mobilize the masses. This could be achieved only by an avant-garde political party, the Communists; and once such a party had come into being, these regimes would cease, in fact, to be military in character.

Events since 1970 have not borne out these Soviet assumptions. The army and the police are still the repositories of power, and there is no reason to assume that this situation will change in the foreseeable future. It could be argued that from the Soviet point of view, it does not greatly matter whether a certain country is run by a military junta or a small group of civilians, whether the dictator is a colonel or a doctor of philosophy, provided Moscow can more or less count on his loyalty. This is no doubt true particularly with regard to the diplomats and the KGB, if not to the ideologists who face difficulties of Leninist interpretation. But it also means that if power in a pro-Soviet country rests in a few hands, there is always the danger that these few will be killed or deposed if there is no mass party. A fairly substantial praetorian guard is needed, a native or "foreign" legion that remains loyal to the regime.

The Soviets originally assumed that pro-Soviet regimes could come to power as the result of decolonization and the "wars of liberation," without much assistance on the part of the Soviet Union. But decolonization has ended, and if the Soviets wish to install more reliable pro-Soviet regimes in the Third World, this can be done only through violent action.[17] The Afghani model—military occupation—seems impracticable for most Third World countries for the time being. Far more likely alternatives are coups d'etat instigated, engineered, or at least assisted by the Soviet Union and its proxies, and civil wars or other internal unrest, in which massive help is provided to the pro-Soviet party by Soviet surrogates.

The Soviet sphere of influence in the Third World will expand only as the result of a major effort. Everything points to the fact that the Soviet leaders are willing to make this effort; how much priority will be given will depend on the general orientation and the dynamism of the post-Brezhnev generation of Soviet policy makers. The capability to intervene exists—not everywhere, but in many countries—owing mainly to the presence of surrogates and the absence of such forces on the side of the West, the ability of the KGB to engage in covert action, and the West's very reduced capacity to undertake such action. The Soviet leaders will probably be careful not to intervene in places where the United States is heavily committed; this could lead to undesirable escalation of conflict. But the United States is not heavily committed in many places, and countries like Sudan and Zaire will remain obvious targets for destabilization and intervention. Moscow will continue to recognize inherent risks, but they may be acceptable.

There is another danger from the Soviet point of view: that following a pro-Soviet takeover in one country, there will be a negative reaction among its neighbors, just as an infection produces antibodies. The price that has to be paid for a Soviet advance may be too high. The ideal solution would be gradual (and necessarily slow) progress, on a broad front, toward pro-Sovietism in the Third World. In other words, it would be highly desirable if South Yemen were not the pioneer in the Middle East but if, instead, all Arab and North African countries gradually moved into the Soviet orbit. But this is illusory, because local conditions vary greatly and enmities exist between Arab and North African countries. Strong Soviet support for Libya is bound to antagonize Libya's neighbors.

Similarly, very close Soviet ties with Syria will not be like those elsewhere in the Arab world. This is a risk the Soviets have to take. Since the optimistic predictions of 1970 have not come true, they will, in all likelihood, concentrate their efforts on a limited number of countries—to consolidate their hold on those they have and to take over others, chosen for their intrinsic importance or because of a favorable prognosis for radical change.

THE KGB

The activities of Soviet intelligence in the Third World have seldom been paid sufficient attention, despite the fact that the KGB is an important tool in the penetration and consolidation of Soviet influence. Its tasks in the developing countries of Asia and Africa are different from their assignments in the West: there are no industrial secrets to be stolen, and the order of battle of the Cameroon army is of only limited interest to Soviet policy makers. On the other hand, Soviet operatives are very active in recruiting influence agents as well as establishing close relations with politicians and military men in key positions—or candidates for such positions. They can offer both money and support for their careers, and they have not, on the whole, been unsuccessful. On the other hand, Soviet intelligence has been involved in covert action in the Third World against governments and parties deemed insufficiently pro-Soviet. These activities range from the instigation of military coups and supply of arms to insurgents to provision of political, financial, and logistic help to pro-Soviet groups.

Since Soviet intelligence was apprehended in flagranti delicto more than once in the 1960s, there has been greater caution. A division of labor has been introduced, and many Soviet operations are now carried out by the Cuban DGI and the East German Ministry for State Security. However, the strong presence of the KGB in many Asian and African countries shows that Soviet intelligence by no means refrains from covert action even now.

The KGB has not been very subtle, to put it mildly, in its approach, but subtlety is frequently contraindicated in the Third World. In theory, Soviet intelligence operatives are much better prepared than their Western counterparts; their training, at least on paper, lasts much longer, and they should have greater familiarity with local conditions and languages. Yet, in practice, this is often not the case, perhaps because the KGB recruits frequently are not of high quality, or perhaps because the more accomplished Soviet agents are not sent to Asian and African countries. Another source of weakness is the frequent difficulty in adjusting to the mentality of foreign people, so different in customs, outlook, and general character from the usual product of Soviet society. The lack of tact, the inability to take local susceptibilities into account, and the open contempt frequently shown the "natives" are grave handicaps.

And yet, although Russians have not been popular in most Third World countries, they have not been ineffective. They have, to a certain extent, learned from their setbacks in the past. They operate with a little more tact than before, and they are, unlike their Western colleagues, on the offensive most of the time.

CONCLUSION

Soviet operations in the Third World raise several crucial questions: Are they part of a grand strategic design, or are they generated by political opportunism, by vacuums to be filled? Is the main purpose of Soviet penetration the acquisition of military bases to threaten Western lines of communication, and of mineral deposits both to be used by the Soviets and to be denied to the West? (This is known as the interdiction theory.) Does the Soviet Union practice something akin to a "counterimperialism"? To what extent can the Soviet Union rely on its allies and clients in the Third World—when is the point of no return reached, and a Soviet stronghold created?[18]

These questions, however vital, are outside the scope of this paper; so is the issue of Western countermeasures. Only the last of the issues mentioned, the question of irreversibility, has a direct bearing on the present investigation and should be mentioned at least in passing. In principle, the Soviet Union cannot be certain of maintaining its hold on a country unless it is in physical, military control or, at the very least, can count on the absolute loyalty of the local security forces (army and secret police).

Through its surrogates, the Soviet Union is in physical control of a very few countries, but in a greater number of countries, it has given absolute priority to infiltrating or even taking over the local security forces. How solid is this hold? The adherents of the "some you win, some you lose" theory claim that the Soviet hold is never secure, as shown by the fact that many countries deeply penetrated by the Soviet Union have managed to get rid of the Russians with relative ease. However, the examples given are neither many nor convincing (Indonesia, Ghana, Iraq), for Soviet presence in these countries was relatively small; neither the army nor the secret police had been taken over. The same is true, mutatis mutandis, with regard to Egypt after Nasser; there were Soviet agents in the Egyptian army and the *Mukhabarat* (the Egyptian political police), but not nearly enough to control them. Egypt, Ghana, and Guinea were, as Peter Wiles put it, simply allied to the Soviet Union; they had not proclaimed themselves Marxist-Leninist, persecuted religion, or founded or encouraged Communist parties.

What happened in these countries is of little or no relevance to the future of South Yemen or Mozambique. "The one that got away" (Barry Lynch's phrase) is Somalia, and its success shows "that you can't escape unless the U.S.S.R. virtually declares war on you."[19] To a considerable extent, everything depends on how much time the Soviet Union had for the penetration of the key positions; that some countries are more resistant then others goes without saying. All this does not mean that de-Sovietization of a Sovietized country cannot possibly happen in the Third World. It only means that it has become difficult, and has not yet happened.

Of the instrumentalities of Soviet policy in the Third World, economic aid and trade are the least important; cultural and other such exchanges are not significant; the local Communist parties are of help in some respects and a hindrance in others; the impact of ideology should not be overrated. What does matter are the operations of the surrogates, for which there is no Western equivalent, the "false consciousness" on the part of certain Third World countries, and military aid with all its implications.[20] Arms transfer and the training of Third World armies per se are no more a guarantee for the spread of Soviet influence than a treaty of friendship and cooperation. Only direct military commitment ("timely assistance by the socialist countries") can secure a foothold and maintain it.

The willingness and the capacity to make direct military commitments exist; one does not know how much priority will be given to Soviet forward strategy in the Third World by the post-Brezhnev leadership. At least in part, it will depend on the ability and the will of the United States to counteract Soviet bloc expansion in the Third World. In the struggle for influence in the Third World, the initiative so far has almost invariably been with the Soviet Union. American attitudes and those of other Western countries have been based on the assumption that, if Third World nations are left to their own devices, their intensely nationalist feelings will be the best guarantee for their independence in the years to come. In many ways an attractive vision, it had the added advantage that it did not necessitate any active policy on America's part. Unfortunately, events since the early 1970s showed that the assumption was overly optimistic.

NOTES

1. When the present writer began his work on Soviet influence and Communism in Asia and Africa in the early 1950s, he was told by some of his elders and betters not to waste his time on a nonexistent topic.

2. It has been argued that the Soviet Union was ready to intervene militarily in Iran in early November 1979. According to some close observers, it was preparing such intervention, but was deterred by the Iranian government's renunciation of both the defense treaty with the United States (signed in March 1959) and articles V and VI of the Soviet-Iranian treaty of February 1921, according to which the Soviet Union was permitted to intervene in case of an armed intervention by a third power.

The present writer does not believe that there was a serious Soviet intention to occupy Iran, in view of the incalculable consequences of such an action. But if there had been such determination, the Soviet leaders would not have been deterred by the renunciation of old treaties.

3. According to the "classical" Soviet definition, such a state must remove Western military bases from its territory, reduce Western economic influence, carry out far-reaching social reforms, grant freedom of organization and democratic rights to political parties, trade unions, and other such bodies. The demand for the removal of Western bases is naturally of basic importance, but it was accepted long ago that the demand of democratic rights in countries with one party (or no party) is unrealistic.

4. It is estimated that about 70 percent of the Cuban soldiers in Africa, but only 11 percent of the officers, are of African origin.

5. Cuban soldiers in Angola are said to be paid $600 a month. Average per capita income in Angola is $440 a year. East Germans are paid more than the Cubans.

6. Paladins are characterized in the standard works of reference as "knightly heroes, renowned champions, knights-errant." Seen in this light, Qaddafi could be regarded as a paladin because he is less dependent on the Russians.

7. Religion does not appear in the Soviet census.

8. Only in the framework of a general weakening of Soviet rule is a movement toward separatism even thinkable.

9. Little more than one year after Bangladesh became independent in 1971, the Soviet Union had concluded 13 agreements with the new state. (See Chapter 2.)

10. National leaders sometimes have strange geographical notions. The Egyptian leader, Nahas Pasha, claimed after World War II that "since the Soviet Union is 4000 miles away from Egypt its activities could not possibly jeopardize Egypt." In fact, the southern borders of the Soviet Union are nearer 1,000 than 4,000 miles from Suez.

11. In the mid-1970s there were some 12,000 African students in the Soviet Union. It is believed that their number has not increased significantly since then.

12. There are no accurate figures, but the following estimates will not be far off target. About 55,000 students from Third World countries were trained in Soviet bloc countries between the late 1950s and 1981, about two-thirds in the USSR and the rest in Eastern Europe. About 60,000 Third World military personnel were trained in the Soviet bloc, and about the same number of Soviet bloc military instructors have been stationed in Asia and Africa. (These figures do not include the Cuban and East German officers and men on more or less permanent duty.) More than 100,000 Soviet bloc technicians have visited Third World countries for varying periods since the mid-1950s; one-third of them have gone to Algeria and Libya.

13. In the present context, "Soviet aid to the Third World" refers to both Soviet and East European aid. Soviet aid amounts to about 60–70 percent of the total.

14. Until 1979, UNCTAD excepted the Soviet Union from such demands "in view of the many common links between the LDCs and the socialist countries"; since then it has been included.

15. According to some leading experts, the CIA figures for Soviet arms deliveries are too low. See, for instance, Peter Wiles, ed., *The New Communist Third World* (New York: St. Martin's Press, 1982), p. 376. The ACDA estimates are, broadly speaking, similar.

16. The value of Soviet arms delivered to Iraq and to Libya between 1975 and 1979 was about $5 billion in each case; Syria's arms imports were $3.6 billion. Gur Ofer, "Economic Aspects of Soviet Involvement," in Y. Roy, ed., *The Limits to Power* (London: St. Martin's Press, 1979), p. 78.

17. There is, at least in theory, another possibility: that South Yemen, Mozambique, Benin, and Grenada will be so successful in "building socialism" that overwhelming enthusiasm will be generated in the Third World to adopt and emulate these models—hardly a likely assumption.

18. There are many other issues, such as Sino-Soviet rivalry in the Third World, that have not been touched. While China practices neoisolationism at present, a more activist approach at some future time cannot be excluded.

19. Barry Lynch, "Ethiopia" Wiles, op. cit., p. 20.

20. It is interesting, though perhaps not very surprising, that there is an enormous Soviet literature on the nonissues in Soviet-Third World relations (ideology, cultural relations, economic aid), whereas the truly important issues are hardly ever discussed openly. A study of Soviet military thought on the Third World, by Mark N. Katz, notes that each successive step of Soviet military involvement is discussed by the military thinkers in Moscow only after it has occurred in practice. A similar observation was made by Raymond Garthoff in the 1960s. That a great deal of (unpublished) spade work has been done in recent years is revealed by such studies as *Vooruzhonnie sili v politicheskoi systeme* (Moscow: Soviet Academy of Sciences, 1981).

TWO

Soviet Diplomacy in the Third World
ARIEH EILAN

SOVIET MENTALITY AND THE THIRD WORLD

Diplomacy is only one of the tools employed by governments in furthering their aims abroad; this is particularly true of the Third World. Trade, aid, and military assistance (whether it is merely the supply of weapons or includes advisers and military personnel) go hand in hand with diplomacy, enhancing the diplomatic effort or sometimes creating problems that the diplomat is called upon to solve. Soviet diplomacy has sometimes paved the way for the acceptance by a Third World country of military assistance from the USSR, as was the case in India. Conversely, it may be a Third World country's need for Soviet military assistance that enables Soviet diplomacy to reap political benefits, as in Somalia.

In reviewing the effectiveness of Soviet diplomacy in the Third World, one has to take into account the activities of the KGB, which has been extremely successful, perhaps more so than Soviet diplomats, in making friends for the USSR and influencing political events in Asia and Africa. In stressing the importance of the KGB we are, of course, not referring to the departments that deal with espionage, but to those involved in the creation and maintenance of contacts with "liberation movements" such as SWAPO in Namibia, or in assistance to opposition groups that work against pro-Western governments in the Third World, such as the alleged support by the KGB of Al Zulfikar, a guerrilla organization in Pakistan, supposedly directed by Murtaza Bhutto, son of executed Prime Minister Ali Bhutto.

The establishment and maintenance of clandestine contacts with political groups and their leaders require, at times, much diplomatic ability, sensitivity, and adroitness. KGB officials engaged in such duties display all these qualities to a much higher degree than the rank-and-file Soviet diplomats. The KGB officer working on such an assignment seems to be entrusted with greater freedom of action than is his official counterpart in the Soviet diplomatic service. In addition, the decision-making process of the KGB seems to be less cumbersome and swifter than that of the Ministry of Foreign Affairs.

The large-scale employment of the KGB in Asia, and especially in Africa, in purely political tasks was a natural Soviet response to the political conditions prevailing in parts of the Third World in the two decades after decolonization. Political instability and frequent changes of government occurred in many of the newly independent states: Pakistan, Indonesia, Ghana, and Nigeria. There were also liberation movements actually fighting colonial regimes, as was the case in Angola, Mozambique, and Rhodesia, and is still the case in Namibia (South-West Africa). In such situations official diplomatic channels and techniques are of little use.

Although there is no written proof, one can assume (on the basis of conversations with Soviet émigrés and Third World diplomats) that one of the results of the KGB in Asia and Africa is the creation of an institutional momentum that sometimes propels the agency into ventures that have not always been foreseen, or even considered particularly desirable, by the Central Committee, the Ministry of Foreign Affairs, or the Politburo. Whether or not there is truth in these assumptions, one cannot disregard the role of the KGB if one reviews the Soviet political effort in the Third World.

As for Soviet diplomacy itself, and those who follow it and its political aims, attempts to discern a particular method or esoteric technique that is employed exclusively by Soviet diplomats present difficulties. If anything, the Russians, perhaps more than any other power in postcolonial Asia and Africa, have gone through periods of trial and error, sometimes repeating their mistakes and sometimes learning from them.

Like the Americans, Israelis, and Scandinavians, the Soviets were suffering from lack of familiarity with Asia and Africa. While the Russians today are somewhat more adept at dealing with Africans and Asians than they were in the 1950s and 1960s, they had, and still have, to overcome particular obstacles that stem from the Russian character and the Soviet way of life.

Russia's own national experience is one of massive uniformity. The enormous expanse of much of the Russian landscape, unbroken by the irregularity of hill and dale, induces in its people a sense of uniformity that they regard as the natural order of things. Throughout the length and breadth of European Russia (except the Ukraine and Byelorussia), there is little difference of accent between the Russian spoken near the Arctic Circle and that spoken in the subtropical Crimea. Russians have, therefore, always regarded small countries, such as England, where accents and sometimes even social customs are liable to change every 200 miles or so, with amusement and some contempt.

The innate Russian preference for uniformity has stood them in exceedingly bad stead in their dealings with Asians and Africans; on both continents the Russians have come up against a bewildering variety of regional, ethnic, religious, linguistic, and social characteristics that their diplomats have rejected and impatiently condemned as atavistic vestiges of a primitive past.

The Soviet way of life induces in every Soviet citizen a sense of vigilant suspicion against those around him or her. To lower one's guard in Stalin's days meant risking one's life or freedom; today it means risking one's job or chances of advancement. A Soviet diplomat is a product of his environment, and when brought into contact with a foreigner, he naturally behaves with exaggerated circumspection, which in turn causes the Asian, and especially the more extraverted African, to respond in kind.

All this has not stopped the Soviet Union from gaining a foothold in Angola and Mozambique, Ethiopia and South Yemen, to mention a few countries in Africa and the Middle East, or from exercising control over the nations of Indochina. However, the lack of trust the Russians generate has been a contributing factor in their ejection from Egypt, Guinea, Ghana, Indonesia, and Mali, and in their failures in Burma, Nigeria, Kenya, and Singapore.

On a practical level the performance of Soviet diplomacy has been mediocre. Leaders of the Third World have often been offended by the coldness and frank, even rough, manner of the Russians. Genuine trust almost never develops, relations are smoother in situations where the client's dependency is nearly total and ideological ties are close—Angola and Ethiopia are models here. Yet even Nito [Neto] and Mengistu were dismayed by the Soviet attempts to control or undermine them; the arrogance and condescending manners of Soviet advisers are also notorious in much of the world.

A review of the Soviet political effort in Asia and Africa, though devoted to the diplomatic aspect, cannot disregard the ideological banner the Russian diplomat, soldier, aid official, or KGB officer invariably carries wherever he goes, whatever he does. True, he may sometimes unfurl the banner or discreetly tuck it away, depending on the exigencies of the situation; the importance of the banner lies not only in its ideological message but also in the Asian or African perception of it, whether favorable or hostile.

The political realities of Asia and Africa in the two decades after decolonization are so dissimilar that it is very difficult to discuss Soviet policy on the two continents simultaneously. Though occasionally one can discern common denominators in the Soviet attitude to Asian and African problems, they are too few and far between to establish paradigms of Soviet political methods common to both continents.

The causes for this difference are numerous; we shall mention two of them.

First, in Asia both main contestants for supremacy, China and the Soviet Union, are situated on the continent itself and share a common border. However, China, Russia, and the United States are outsiders in Africa, and are regarded as such by the majority of Africans. Therefore, in Africa, all the superpowers have to operate from afar—a fact that causes special military and political problems for them.

Second, Soviet contact with Asia for the first 25 years after the Russian Revolution was carried out primarily on an ideological level. Only after 1955 did the Russians begin to employ diplomacy in Asia parallel with ideological conversion.

In Africa, on the other hand, with a few exceptions, there was no Soviet ideological penetration prior to independence. In the early 1960s, a multitude of black African countries were suddenly plunged into independence by the fiats of the colonial powers. The absence of an anticolonial struggle deprived the Soviets of the opportunity to exploit it for their own ideological purposes. Only in a minority of African countries, where independence was delayed—as in the case of Portuguese and Spanish colonies—did the Russians have time to educate cadres fit to take power; this was particularly true of FRELIMO in Mozambique and the MPLA in Angola. These and other differences between the Soviet involvement in Asia and Africa caused Moscow to apply different political strategies.

In Asia, especially in their relations with India and Pakistan, the Russians employed diplomacy in its widest sense to broaden the sphere of Soviet influence. In Africa, where conditions were much more unstable, the Russians were forced to make the most of military aid, intervention by Soviet surrogate forces, and clandestine recruitment rather than diplomacy.

The Soviet attitude toward Asia and Africa can be divided into four periods. First, the epoch of Lenin's revolutionary internationalism; then Stalin's catatonic isolationism; followed by Khrushchev's dramatic thrust into manifest commitment; the present period might be described as pragmatic adventurism.

Soviet Russia rarely creates conflicts, but often exploits existing ones. The postcolonial era, like the postimperial epochs of the past, gave rise to a multitude of small states, reviving ancient rivalries that had remained dormant under colonial rule. According to SIPRI, some 135 armed conflicts of all kinds have erupted since the end of World War II in what has come to be called the Third World. Not all of them have been exploited by the Soviets; nevertheless, if the Israel-Arab, India-Pakistan, and Ethiopia-Somali disputes were settled, and a solution found for the problems of Namibia and the Moroccan Sahara, Soviet diplomacy in Asia and Africa would be obliged to undergo fundamental reorientation.

SOVIET DIPLOMACY IN SOUTH ASIA

Asia has been the subject of intense Soviet interest since the early days of the Russian Revolution. Soviet Russia, like the Russia of the tsars, considers itself an Asian power. The Communists have changed the names of many cities in Russia, but Vladivostok, founded by the tsars, has retained its name under the Bolsheviks. *Vladi* is, in Russian, the imperative form of the verb "to rule," and vostok means "the East."

Until the mid-1950s, Soviet involvement in Asian affairs was carried out on a strictly party-to-party basis. Under Lenin and Stalin, the task of certain departments in the Central Committee was to foster the creation of Communist parties in various regions of Asia and to assist them in every way possible. Since our concern is Soviet diplomacy in Asia, however, the period under review will begin after the mid-1950s, when the first serious moves designed to further Soviet interests through diplomatic convention were made. However, even in this period one cannot afford to ignore the effects of the ideological affiliation between Soviet and Asian countries, both in offering the USSR ready tools for action and in the manner that the very existence of such parties influenced decision making in the Kremlin.

As far as this paper is concerned, the existence of Communist states in Asia, and of large Communist parties in some Asian states, is a political fact that, like strategic and economic considerations, influences the course of Soviet diplomacy. There is nothing in this situation that would be beyond the comprehension of Niccolo Machiavelli's 16th-century mind.

Russia's main preoccupation in Asia is China, and this governs Soviet moves and attitudes to much of what is happening throughout Asia. The second focal point of great-power rivalry is the competition with the United States for control of the Indian Ocean, with everything that this confrontation entails. In response to these two challenges, Soviet diplomatic and military goals have been twofold.

First, the Soviet Union had to do everything in its power to divert China's military attention from the 4,000 miles of common border by creating military and political divisions, a "second front" of sorts, south of China, in the area of Indochina, India, and Burma. At the same time, Soviet Russia intends to make the most of its enormous superiority over China in air and sea power by making its naval presence felt from the Sea of Japan down to the Indian Ocean.

Second, in the Indian Ocean, Russia's strategic aim is abundantly clear and is analyzed in detail in innumerable books and articles. Suffice it to say here that if Russia were ever to control vital choke points, such a Bab el Mandeb and the Straits of Hormuz, it not only would be able to deny the West access to Middle Eastern Oil fields, but would also be in a position to influence political events in East Africa, the Middle East, and East Asia. In fact, the Russians are reverting to the classical 19th-century British imperial concept, in accordance with which power can be projected onto the land-mass by control of vital waterways. The function of Soviet diplomacy in Asia (as in East Africa and the Middle East) is to create political conditions that will make it possible for Russia to achieve these aims.

Both of these Soviet preoccupations, China and the Indian Ocean, have a common pivotal point: the Indian subcontinent, consisting of India, Pakistan, and Bangladesh. Therefore, in a review of Soviet diplomacy in Asia, much attention will be focused on the USSR's relations with India, which have remained the central element in the Soviet diplomatic effort in Asia. Soviet involvement in Indonesia—which, though considerable, was not as geopolitically essential to the USSR as its relations with India—will not be discussed here.

India was chosen as the stage upon which Khrushchev made his debut in 1955, breaking 30 years of Stalinist isolation of the USSR. Leonid Brezhnev's visit to India in 1973 was his first visit to an Asian state after becoming CPSU general secretary in 1964. On the Soviet side, Brezhnev's visit was accompanied by an unusually heavy volume of press and broadcast publicity.

Friendly relations with a country are judged not only by the number of agreements signed with the USSR, but also by the number and level of official visits. Brezhnev visited India again in 1981; Kosygin made five visits; Gromyko is a frequent visitor. The Soviet defense establishment, including ministers of defense, marshals of the Red Army, air chief marshals, and admirals of the fleet, have visited India in one capacity or another almost every year since 1966.

Finally, India is the only non-Communist country in Asia to have signed a treaty of friendship and mutual assistance with the USSR. This is in addition to more than 200 routine agreements reached by the two countries.

Given the importance of India to Soviet diplomacy, that country's relations with Pakistan and China determine Soviet Russia's attitude to much of the Asian power game. India's conflicts with China and Pakistan are thus of interest here, inasmuch as they reflect on the diplomatic strategy of the USSR vis-à-vis India.

Moreover, the outcome of the crowning Soviet diplomatic initiative in Asia—the collective security pact—and the Soviet reaction to the India-sponsored proposal for the declaration of the Indian Ocean as a zone of peace were to some extent the result of the attitude of New Delhi to these proposals.

Political realities would probably have caused India to seek Russian friendship regardless of ideology or the political predisposition of the people in power in New Delhi. Nevertheless, the personal views of Nehru and his daughter, Indira Gandhi, have contributed considerably to the rapprochment between Russia and India.

Nehru's views on Russia in the 1930s were based on the old principle that "my enemy's enemy will be my friend." After India's independence, and in the course of the Cold War, Nehru maintained a neutral posture of noninvolvement that the Russians greatly appreciated at the time. The Kremlin noted with satisfaction that India refused to join SEATO in 1954. It appreciated much less Nehru's refusal to accede to the urgent demarches of the Soviet ambassador in New Delhi, voicing the Soviet Union's desire to participate in the Bandung Conference of 1955. Nehru remained a riddle to the Russians throughout his life. Publicly he proclaimed a foreign policy that the Russians supported because it charted a course of independence from the Western alliance. There were no parallel statements by Nehru of his desire to be independent of the Eastern bloc.

At the same time, a succession of Soviet diplomats found Nehru to be a reluctant colloquist with a disdainful manner, rather like a bored aristocrat who put up with listening to the presentation of the Soviet ambassador but was reluctant to maintain a dialogue.

Soviet diplomacy in India in the 1950s and 1960s cultivated the Indian political elite of the younger generation with a combination of uncharacteristic tact and typical Russian tenacity. Most prominent among the elite was the "Ginger Group," at the head of which were Indira Gandhi and Krishna Menon. This group was greatly influenced by the left wing of the British Labour Party, and by publications such as the *Tribune*, a left-wing British weekly. In addition to the radicalism of the British Left, the "Ginger Group" copied the rabid anti-Americanism of the British Socialist intellectuals. Anyone who had the opportunity to discuss world events with Mrs. Gandhi in the early 1960s would agree that her views appeared to be much more anti-American than actually pro-Soviet. Her apprehensiveness of the United States has not lessened as the years have passed. At the same time, her attitude toward the Soviet Union has matured from youthful adoration to the pragmatism of a marriage of convenience.

In much of Africa and Asia, the Soviet diplomat concentrates on cultivating the "ruling few," whoever they may be; in most countries of the Third World the educated elite is small and not necessarily from the strata of the population likely to produce political leadership. In Africa, for instance, army sergeants are more likely to become presidents than are schoolteachers. In India, however, with 120 universities annually graduating tens of thousands of students, Soviet diplomacy quite rightly devotes much effort to "spreading the word" over as large a section of India's educated class as possible.

The Soviet embassy in New Delhi and the consulates in Bombay, Calcutta, and Madras devote a great deal of time and effort to cultural propaganda. Soviet diplomatic missions are aided in pro-Soviet propaganda by the India-Soviet Study Center, established in 1973, the India-Soviet Cultural Society, and similar bodies.

In its attempt to create favorable attitudes among the Indian people and to direct pressure at the Indian government from internal sources, the Soviet Union has built up a large propaganda effort, estimated in 1968 to cost $15 million annually. One analyst has estimated that one million words per month flow from the Information Department of the Soviet Embassy in New Delhi. Periodicals or other publications distributed by Communist missions in India had a combined yearly total circulation in 1972 in excess of 23 million. Over two score journals are distributed by the Soviet Embassy, compared with less than half that number published by the U.S. government. In addition, indigenous Soviet and pro-Communist newspapers and periodicals taking a pro-Soviet line (many directly or indirectly subsidized by the Soviets) have a circulation of well over 10 million. Radio Moscow and Radio Peace and Progress have, in recent years, broadcast to India over 125 hours per week.[1]

In 1973, a Soviet-Indian protocol on cooperation in television and radio was signed. The agreement called for the exchange of professional personnel in the field of communications.

Soviet diplomats have been active in promoting the placement of pro-Soviet and anti-American articles in the Indian press. They are also known to have interceded with Indian authorities to prevent the publication or the distribution of anti-Soviet articles and books printed in the West. Soviet diplomats pay special attention to university departments of political science and international relations. They have been known to intervene by protesting the employment of Western lecturers and the use of Western, particularly American, books dealing with Sovietology.

Resentment on the part of some Indians against Soviet interference is frequently counterbalanced by the support given to it by powerful Communist and leftist elements. The Soviet diplomat in India takes pains to distance himself from both of the Communist parties. However, Indian Communist elements are being used by the Soviet embassy in New Delhi to help the Soviet diplomat in his performance of certain specific assignments.

Of whatever shade, the party has sympathizers all over the country, in every walk of life, and particularly in educational institutions, both in the faculty and the student community. The two have frequent contacts with wholetime Communist workers who also advise them on the kind of activity they should take up; it may be to counter criticism of Soviet action in Afghanistan, or it may be to explain the situation in Poland. The view, of course, is as projected from the Kremlin. There could be some conscientious objectors with awkward questions, but they are to be pushed aside or thrown out. Wholetimers decide who should be "eliminated" and who should occupy which position.[2]

The Calcutta-based *Statesman,* describing the Soviet lobby in the Indian government, says: "There are some nervous men in India's Foreign Office who at the slightest suggestion of Russian displeasure will send Moscow reassurances of India's undying love."[3]

The investment of so much of the Soviet effort in India in the field of media control, involving considerable financial outlays, is unparalleled anywhere in the Third World. For lack of a more precise term, what one might call the process of "Finlandization" of the Indian public media proves that the Soviets do not wish to repeat the mistakes they made in Indonesia, Ghana, Egypt, Algeria, and Zimbabwe by relying entirely on the pro-Soviet sympathies of an individual national leader, or even on the exclusive allegiance to Moscow of Communist parties. In India, the Russians are taking a long-term view by trying to secure a pro-Soviet attitude among a large section of Indian public opinion, but progressive and right-wing.

Although such facts are hard to determine with exactitude, it appears that the Soviet political propaganda in India has succeeded over the years in establishing a "pro-Russian party" that, regardless of ideological orientation, favors the continuation of the "special relationship" between the two countries. The USSR is perceived as a "reliable friend in need."

SOVIET DIPLOMACY: CONFLICT SITUATIONS AND TREATIES

The preceding brief review of Soviet propaganda efforts in India affords an idea of the depth of the USSR's commitment in the Indian subcontinent. We shall now consider the two main methods used separately and together to further the Soviets' interests.

The Soviet Union managed to exploit India's endemic conflict with Pakistan and the border dispute with China to its own advantage and to the detriment of the United States and China. At the same time, the Soviet Union sought to isolate China and establish a *pax sovietica* in Asia by means of bilateral and multilateral treaties, and by bringing warring sides to the negotiating table under the aegis of Soviet diplomacy. In reviewing the first method, the exploitation of conflict situations, let us first deal with the Sino-Indian dispute.

The Use of Conflict Situations

The Sino-Indian Conflict

After India's defeat in the Sino-Indian war of 1962, and the open break between Peking and Moscow a year or two later, Soviet diplomacy skillfully exploited India's most pressing need to its advantage by establishing close working cooperation between the Red Army and the Indian army, which was then undergoing a thorough reorganization.

Rightly or wrongly, the Indians blamed their defeat at the hands of the Chinese on having slavishly applied the British military model, and therefore Indian army generals were only too happy to send promising young Indian officers to the Frunze military academy. The Indian military intelligence was almost exclusively Pakistan-oriented, and lacked essential information about the Chinese army. Again the Russians were willing and well able to help, since most Chinese military equipment was of Soviet design. In addition, GUR (Soviet military intelligence) was probably the world's most knowledgeable source for the Chinese order of battle and Chinese training methods. The Indians appreciated both the USSR's willingness to help and its discretion. Soviet diplomats made it a point never to refer to the cooperation between the two armies, thus scoring high in the esteem of Indian officials.

Perhaps because of this, Indian diplomats were prepared to accept at face value the highly biased political information about Chinese designs to conquer further strategic strong points in the Aksai-Chin that were transmitted by the Soviets to the Indian Ministry of External Affairs.

The cooperation between the two military intelligence services paved the way for the gradual change in India's military procurement from Britain, as a main foreign supplier, to the Soviet Union. Indian pilots were routinely sent to Moscow for training, and the Red Army would see to it that Indian trainees were not exposed to ideological proselytizing.

Arms transfers to India became, in the course of time, one of the most important tools of Soviet diplomacy. The Indians found in the USSR not only a very reliable, but also a very cheap, source of sophisticated armament. Most important of all, Soviet Russia's readiness to accept Indian imports as part payment secured for the Soviets a continuation of a relationship that both sides found profitable. Although by 1977, 2,075 Indians had been trained in the USSR, there is no evidence that Indian trainees had become a pro-Soviet element in the Indian army. On the other hand, the arms transfers strengthened the image of the USSR in India as that of a reliable ally. The utilization by the Russians of the Sino-Indian conflict represents Soviet diplomacy at its best. It knew how to seize the diplomatic initiative and further its aim with tact and much patience.

The Soviet position in the Sino-Indian dispute was, and is, essentially weak, owing to the very nature of the conflict. India's border disagreement with China is highly localized and plainly solvable if both sides so desire. The struggle for military advantage in the strategic mountain ranges of the disputed Himalayan region of Aksai-Chin can be resolved by territorial trade-offs. The Russians are painfully aware that to achieve this, India does not need Soviet help. In fact, the power constellation that is now emerging in Asia, after the Soviet invasion of Afghanistan, has caused the Chinese and the Indians to think of normalizing their relations.

Chinese Foreign Minister Huang Hua's visit to India in June 1981, the proposed trip of Mrs. Gandhi to Peking, and the agreement to set up the necessary diplomatic machinery to negotiate the border problems must be viewed as signs that both Peking and New Delhi have decided the time has come to resolve the conflict. Huang Hua's visit to New Delhi was reported in the Soviet press without comment or cheer. Basically, Soviet diplomacy cannot depend on the continuation of the Sino-Indian dispute as an aid to its own conflict with China. This may be one of the important considerations that moved Brezhnev to make a bid for understanding with Peking.

The USSR and the Indo-Pakistan Conflict

Ever since 1953, when the United States initiated diplomatic consultations with Pakistan, with a view toward enlisting it in a system of alliances later known as SEATO and CENTO, Pakistan has been thought of as pro-Western. However, there were long intervals of cool relations between Washington and Islamabad. After the 1965 Indo-Pakistan war, the Soviet Union courted Pakistan, and relations between the two countries were sufficiently friendly to cause anxiety in New Delhi.

It has been said of Soviet diplomacy in the Middle East that had Israel not existed, Moscow would have had to invent it. Political parallels are always slippery, but it can be said that Russian diplomacy has used India's distrust and fear of Pakistan in a manner similar to Soviet reliance on Arab hostility toward Israel to further its aims in the Middle East.

India's fear of Pakistan is difficult for an outsider to comprehend. Being so much the stronger of the two, and having defeated Pakistan in two wars, one might have thought that, especially after the breaking away of East Pakistan, India could have taken a more confident view of its own military superiority.

Whether the roots of Indian apprehension are buried in the Hindus' traditional fear of the Muslin conqueror or in a civil war mentality is immaterial. Soviet diplomacy has, since 1955, been extremely successful in "stoking the furnace" in New Delhi, accomplishing by this not only the maintenance of a conflict situation favorable to the Soviet Union, but also the insurance of India's distrust of the United States for its role as Pakistan's occasional ally.

The Pakistan initiative in proposing that India sign a nonaggression pact caught the Russians off guard. During February and March 1982, Soviet diplomats told their Indian counterparts that the signing of a treaty of nonaggression with Pakistan might contradict Indian obligations under the 1971 treaty with the USSR. The Russians went so far as to warn their Indian colleagues of the danger of American military intervention in Pakistan, if that country ever considered itself endangered by the USSR. This, of course, is sheer nonsense, but the voicing of such possibilities by the Russians is indicative of their nervousness as India seems to be mending its fences with both China and Pakistan.

A more official demonstration of Soviet jitters was provided by the visit to New Delhi of Marshal Dimitri F. Ustinov, the Soviet minister of defense, in March 1982. This was the first such visit by Ustinov to a non-Communist country; he was accompanied by 16 senior officers, among them Soviet Admiral of the Fleet Sergei G. Gorshakov and Air Chief Marshal Pavel S. Kulakhov. Never before has so much top Soviet brass descended on any part of the globe. This visit serves to emphasize the importance that the Soviet Union, rightly or wrongly, attaches to its ties with India.

The *New York Times* explained Ustinov's visit as evidence of the concern felt by the Russians over the diversification of arms purchases by the Indians, especially the order for submarines in West Germany, the manufacture of the British Jaguar jet fighter in India, and ongoing negotiations with the French for a new Mirage fighter.[4]

Although India's attempt to buy arms from Western Europe, or to negotiate production rights of European weapons, may cause some fears in the military-industrial complex in Moscow, it could not, in the opinion of this writer, account for the "showing of the flag" by Ustinov and company. After all, Soviet exports account for only 15 percent of India's arms production. The visit of the three heads of the Soviet armed forces to New Delhi should be seen in the light of a deeper and more serious anxiety felt in Moscow: that by mending its fences with Pakistan and China, New Delhi is depriving Soviet Russia of its main leverage in the relationship between the two countries, thereby changing the balance of power in Asia to Russia's disadvantage.

New Delhi's reaction to the post-Afghanistan situation is another source of Soviet concern. Although Indira Gandhi and Indian diplomats have been enigmatic in their comments on the Soviet invasion of Afghanistan, it now appears that the Soviet determination to stay on in Kabul indefinitely caused the Indian establishment to review the basic geopolitical assumptions that have hitherto guided Indian policy towards the Soviet Union. The "natural ally" theory received a severe jolt when, as a result of the Soviet presence in Afghanistan, it gradually became apparent to the Indians that Soviet proximity also meant a change in the relationship between the two countries. Before the Soviet invasion of Afghanistan the Indians were conscious of being able to negotiate with the Russians from a position of diplomatic advantage; however this would no longer be the case after the Red Army had established its presence on Pakistan's borders.

Therefore, these days, New Delhi is vitally interested in the continued existence of a stable Pakistan as a buffer between India and Soviet controlled Afghanistan. In the course of Marshal Ustinov's visit to New Delhi in March of '82, the Indians informed the Soviet generals that any Soviet moves aimed at the destabilization of Pakistan would have an adverse effect on Soviet-Indian relations. This warning was repeatedly related through diplomatic channels.

Indira Gandhi's 1982 visit to Washington may appear as the London *Economist* described it, a "signal" to the United States. Nevertheless, it should not be construed as an indication of an impending change of India's relationship with the U.S.S.R.; this will continue to be friendly but perhaps not quite as cordial as before.

Soviet diplomacy has repeatedly tried, and failed, to establish a foothold in Islamabad. The reasons for the Soviet failure to develop closer links with Pakistan are interesting because they demonstrate the kind of obstacles Soviet diplomacy finds it difficult to overcome. To begin with, the Communist Party in Pakistan has always been small, ineffectual, and clandestine. The Russians lacked, therefore, the kind of back-up support that the Indian Communist Party and its sympathizers have been able to give Soviet diplomacy from time to time. In fact, in the conditions of Pakistan, the pro-Communist elements have been an obstacle to Soviet diplomacy because they have raised the fear of a Communist conspiracy. Many rulers of Muslim Pakistan have been army generals who did not share the intellectual and ideological inclinations of Nehru or Indira Gandhi. Throughout the Third World, Soviet diplomacy has always relied heavily on cooperation with a national leader; in this it failed in Pakistan, even when Bhutto, an intellectual with radical leanings, was prime minister. Gromyko is reported to have described Bhutto as an "unstable hothead." For whatever reasons, Communist agitators and Soviet diplomats have failed to display in Pakistan the flexibility required to recruit friends.

Pakistan's strategic importance, before and after the Russian invasion of Afghanistan, poses certain problems that the USSR may try to solve by destabilizing Pakistan, thereby putting an end to Pakistani support (however limited) of the Afghan rebels. One way of achieving this might be to encourage the irredentist aspirations of Baluchi tribes in Pakistan and Afghanistan. The KGB reportedly is supporting Al Zulfikar, a guerrilla organization allegedly led by Murtaza Bhutto, son of the executed prime minister.

The Use of Treaties and Agreements

Soviet diplomacy has always put much faith in the formalization of the USSR's relationship with other countries through treaties and agreements. An Asian diplomat once described the Soviet love of signed agreements as "Russian Treatomania." When Bangladesh became independent in 1971, the Soviet Union rushed in and arranged for 13 agreements to be signed between February 1972 and August 1973.

The Soviets have felt the need to give legal sanction to their relationships with allies and friends in the Third World by means of a variety of treaties with client states, such as Cuba, Vietnam, and South Yemen, and the allies of varying degrees of political affinity, such as Iraq, Syria, Nasser's Egypt, and India.

Soviet Russia's endeavors to establish its supremacy in Asia by diplomatic means can be separated into three categories: the wish to act as an arbitrator of disputes between Asian states; the wish to formalize through treaties relations with countries friendly to the USSR, such as India; the wish to attempt, by means of a multilateral treaty of Asian states, to isolate China and give formal confirmation of the Soviet Union's position as an Asian state. Again using India as a focal point, we shall review examples from each category.

Tashkent

The Soviet Union succeeded in bringing the 1965 war between India and Pakistan to an end when Kosygin invited the president of Pakistan, Ayub Khan, and the prime minister of India, Lal Shastri, to a peace conference in the city of Tashkent. The choice of venue was deliberate. The capital of the Kirghiz Soviet Republic is close to China and Pakistan; convening a conference there on Asian matters was meant to emphasize Russia's "Asian face."

The declaration of Tashkent in January 1966 was perhaps Soviet diplomacy's outstanding success in South Asia. In the words of a Pakistan commentator, "The document was neither a victory for Pakistan nor for India. It was, however, a triumph for the Soviet Prime Minister,"[5] In spite of strenuous efforts, the Russians failed to repeat their successful role as arbitrator in the Indo-Pakistan war of 1971. The Indians declined to accept the good offices of the USSR and instead conducted direct negotiations with Pakistan, culminating with the Simla Agreement.

Essentially, there is no contradiction between the role of peacemaker so ardently pursued by Soviet diplomacy and the exploitation and instigation of conflicts. The choice the Russians present to the Indians and Pakistanis is simple: either endure continued conflict with your neighbor or allow the Soviet Union to arbitrate. If the USSR had its way, it would probably prefer the role of arbitrator of conflicts to that of inciter, because it might then establish a *pax sovietica* in South Asia while preventing China from capitalizing on these conflicts in the future

The Soviet-Indian Friendship Treaty

The Russians succeeded in convincing the Indians to sign a treaty of friendship and cooperation in August 1971. Under the conditions prevailing at that time, the treaty gave India Soviet backing for action against

Pakistan. The Russians, on the other hand, were interested in signing a formal treaty with India at a time when Henry Kissinger was initiating the first American contacts with China. The treaty does not amount to much in terms of the actual obligations assumed by each side. It states that "India respects the peace-loving policy of the Union of Soviet Socialist Republics" and that the USSR "respects India's policy of non-alignment."

There are the usual provisions for nonaggression. Article 8 stipulates that "each of the High contracting parties . . . shall not enter into or participate in any military alliances directed against the other party." Article 9 states that both parties are to refrain from giving assistance to a third party engaged in a conflict with either signatory of the agreement. Article 10 stipulates that in the event of an attack or threat directed toward either by a third party, both sides pledge to start mutual consultation immediately, with a view to eliminating the threat.

Basically, the treaty was drafted in a manner that did not automatically obligate either side. It did not cost the Russians much to sign it, but it did provide Russian diplomacy with precisely what it seeks—a formal and juridical announcement of a mutuality of interests between the USSR and an Asian non-Communist power.

In 1981, Indira Gandhi was invited to go to Moscow to celebrate the tenth anniversary of the treaty. She politely refused, and sent a member of the cabinet instead. Moscow celebrated the anniversary with great pomp. In New Delhi the celebrations were more restrained.

Much of New Delhi's diminished enthusiasm can be attributed to the Soviet invasion of Afghanistan. It was also a reaction to Soviet diplomatic clumsiness. The Russians had been the initiators of the treaty of friendship and cooperation, which had been discussed for two years prior to 1971, with little progress being made in the face of continued diplomatic procrastination by the Indians. The Russians finally succeeded when India needed Soviet support in the 1971 war against Pakistan. Ten years later, however, the situation in East Asia had changed, and the Soviet embassy in New Delhi must have failed to convey the change of mood to Moscow.

The Asian Collective Security Pact

The Soviet initiative for an Asian "Helsinki Agreement" was Moscow's most ambitious diplomatic enterprise in Asia, and it totally aborted because the Soviet Union failed to perceive that the idea essentially rested on a false premise: that Asian states could be induced or cajoled into signing an anti-Chinese document drafted in Moscow.

It is difficult to believe that Soviet diplomats in Asia did not foresee the inevitable fiasco. One has to assume that since the idea originated at the very top of the Soviet leadership, ambassadors of the USSR in Asian capitals had no option but to voice optimism in their reports to Moscow.

At the world conference of Communist parties at Moscow in June 1969, Leonid Brezhnev, after stressing the importance of achieving a conference on European security, went on to say, "We believe the course of events is also placing on the agenda the task of creating a system of collective security in Asia."[6] Quite likely it was a trial balloon, but the ensuing wave of speculation in the world press apparently encouraged the Russians to go ahead.

Russian diplomacy is extraordinarily tenacious in its pursuit of declared diplomatic objectives. The Soviets are sometimes quite content to allow their initiatives to lie fallow temporarily, if the situation so demands, and to revive them at the earliest possible opportunity. There were periods when most observers in Europe believed that the Russians had finally abandoned their idea for a treaty of collective security and cooperation in Europe. They were proved wrong.

Japan and the states that make up ASEAN reacted with an unambiguous refusal to consider the Soviet idea. The Indians played a more subtle game of qualified support: Mrs. Gandhi announced that she would endorse the idea of economic cooperation among Asia states; this was followed by contradictory statements made by successive Indian foreign ministers; and during Mrs. Gandhi's visit to Moscow in 1976, she decisively poured cold water over the Soviet initiative.

Russian diplomacy also had to cope with a competing idea put forward by the prime minister of Malaysia in July 1971, which proposed that Southeast Asia be neutralized under the guarantee of the "great powers": China, the Soviet Union, and the United States, in that order. This initiative was calculated as an Asian response to the Soviet proposal to exclude China by putting it on a par with the USSR and the United States as guarantors of Asian stability.

Quite likely the Russians, in proposing an Asian collective security pact, were carried away by their desire to exploit opportunities that seemed to present themselves to the strategists in the Kremlin at the end of the 1960s and the beginning of the 1970s.

The Nixon Doctrine assured the Russians that the Americans had no intention of stepping into British shoes as the guarantors of peace and freedom of navigation in the Indian Ocean and its waterways. The Nixon administration obviously intended to end the war in Vietnam, which meant a reduced American presence in Asia. The British and Americans were leaving, and the Russians, seeking to take their place in Asia, wanted a document that would give legitimacy to their presence. They failed to realize that in Asia they were still regarded as intruders, white men who had come from the east instead of the west.

The Indian Ocean

Although the subject of the Indian Ocean does not properly belong to the part of this paper devoted to the use of treaties and agreements by Soviet diplomacy in Asia, the informal understanding reached between the USSR and India on this subject is of considerable importance to the Soviet stance in this much-contested part of the world.

Since the mid-1960s Soviet diplomacy has had a dual aim to pursue in New Delhi concerning the Indian Ocean. Foremost was Russia's urgent need to secure for the Soviet fleet, sailing from distant Vladivostok, naval servicing facilities in the Bay of Bengal and in the Indian Ocean. Rumors that such facilities have been granted to the Russians at Vizakapatam and the Laccadive Islands have been categorically denied by the Indians. The need for these facilities is not quite as critical to the Soviet Union now that it has acquired the right to use Vietnamese airfields and ports at Cam Ranh Bay and Danang. Nevertheless, a Soviet presence in the Laccadive Islands would greatly strengthen the Soviet naval deployment in the Indian Ocean. It is, however, very doubtful that even Indira Gandhi's government would wish to risk further deterioration of its relationship with Washington by giving the Russians an additional edge over the Americans in the Indian Ocean. Also, the growing Indian navy is reported to have voiced strong objections to a Soviet presence in what it regards as its own waters.

Moscow's second diplomatic objective in New Delhi regarding the Indian Ocean concerned a divergence between the Indian and Soviet positions on this matter at the United Nations. In the General Assembly, the initiative to declare the Indian Ocean a zone of peace was originally tabled by Sri Lanka in 1972, but was generally understood to have strong Indian support. The resolution called upon the great powers to "enter into consultations with the littoral states with a view to halting the escalation of their military presence in the Indian Ocean and eliminating bases, military installations, logistical supply facilities, nuclear weapons, and any other manifestations of great power military presence." It also called on the permanent members of the Security Council and other maritime powers to enter into consultation with states of the region for the purpose of insuring that military forces in the area not threaten the sovereignty or the terrritorial integrity of the littoral and hinterland states. Subject to these provisions and to the norms of international law, the right to free and unimpeded access by vessels of all nations would not be abridged.[7]

From the very start, the Americans and the Soviets entertained severe reservations about the resolution, and consequently abstained on the vote. Whatever their formal reasons, both great powers feared that a declaration, or perhaps an accession to an international convention, would put constraints on freedom of navigation for their navies.

During Brezhnev's visit to New Delhi in 1973, the Russians explained to the Indians that as long as the Americans had a base on Diego Garcia, the Russians felt obliged to maintain a naval presence in the Indian Ocean. It is not necessary to follow each move of the diplomatic see-saw between the two powers on this particular matter. Suffice it to say that Soviet diplomacy was in trouble, not only opposing the Indians but also going against the decisions of the heads of state conferences of the nonaligned on this matter, which supported the Sri Lanka initiative.

The problem was solved in a twofold manner. Mrs. Gandhi, on her visit to the USSR in 1976, declared at a press conference in Moscow: "There is a difference between ships passing by and a permanent base, especially if it is a nuclear one." Thus, by denouncing the upgrading of the American base at Diego Garcia, the Indian prime minister was excusing the passage of ships of the Soviet navy. On the other hand, in 1977, the Soviet Union changed its vote and began supporting the Sri Lanka resolution on the Indian Ocean, and thus made it easier for the Indians "to appear in Soviet company" at the United Nations. In actual fact, the Soviet support for the resolution of the General Assembly and Mrs. Gandhi's statement in Moscow are of only marginal value. Important is the refusal of the Indian government to allow Soviet naval facilities on Indian shores.

Thus, in the Soviet-Indian quid pro quo on the subject of the Indian Ocean, the Russians have achieved unanimity with the Indians in the realm of declaratory diplomacy, but have failed to obtain the military advantage they had hoped to gain from their special relationship with India.[8]

SOVIET POLICY IN BLACK AFRICA

We shall select a limited number of case studies that serve to illustrate various phases and types of Soviet involvement: the Soviet learning process in Ghana, Kenya, and Nigeria; the scope and circumstances of Soviet intervention in Angola and Ethiopia; and Zaire and Sudan as likely targets for future Soviet action. The case study method is constructive because, although Soviet aims in Africa are patently clear, the Russians have been guided and misguided by circumstances as they have arisen since the early 1960s.

The Soviet Learning Process

Ghana

When Kwame Nkrumah was proclaimed prime minister of an independent Ghana in 1957, the Soviet Union, as well as the United States and most of the Western world, were completely unprepared for the headlong rush to independence of so many African states south of the Sahara. Within four years, 17 African countries became independent, and the chancelleries of the West and the East were busily looking for people to manage their African departments.

Today few people care to remember or admit that in the opinion of most international experts in the mid-1950s, Africa was not due for independence for another two or three decades. This attitude was not restricted to "reactionary Western circles." It was shared by most participants in the Bandung Conference. Whenever Africa was mentioned, the reference was mostly to North Africa, and especially to Algeria. Though pious lip service was paid to Africa south of the Sahara, almost the sole topic of discussion at Bandung was the future of Asia in the struggle between the United States and the USSR.

All Soviet research on Asia and Africa was concentrated in the Oriental Institute (Institut Vostokovedinya), which in 1957 was still under the direction of an old-fashioned Bolshevik named Potekhin, who did not believe that there was much sense in developing relations with Asian or African leaders who were not outright Communists. When Ghana became independent, Moscow sent a low-level delegation to the independence celebration at Accra. The Russians, and especially Potekhin, were highly suspicious of Nkrumah, who seemed to them to be too pro-Western. After several weeks in Accra, Potekhin returned to Moscow and gave grudging agreement to a number of measures that were to pave the way for the Soviet Union's first major involvement in African affairs.

The leader of the new Africa was undoubtedly Nkrumah, although Sékou Touré of Guinea and Modibo Keita of Mali were not only partners in Africa's surge toward independence, but also sometimes evidenced a more radical attitude toward the solution of Africa's many problems.

The Soviet Union, after initial hesitation, decided to go all out in its support for these three West African countries and their leaders. There was little in Russia's Asian experience at that time—with Indonesia, North Korea, North Vietnam, and India—to guide it in its dealings with Africans. The absence in Africa of ideological affinity with the Soviet Union and of an established pattern of diplomatic negotiations posed problems to Soviet diplomacy for which there were no prefabricated solutions. The small group of "African experts" in Moscow at that time was hammering out ideological justifications for the Soviet support of countries that lacked a Communist movement. This was accomplished by stating that, notwithstanding an absence of a bourgeois class, Ghana, Guinea, and Mali already possessed the subjective preconditions for socialism.

The Soviet diplomats, however, were painfully aware that each of the three leaders meant something different when he urged his people to emulate the Soviet example. Nkrumah had been greatly influenced by George Padmore, a West Indian ex-Communist who, in his book *Communism or Pan Africanism,* preached the creed of "African Socialism," pure heresy to the Russians.[9] Yet the Russians had no alternative but to "grin and bear it." They saw in Ghana their gateway to Africa.

A conferenece of independent African states was convened at Accra, Ghana, in 1958, and in the same year Ghana played host to the first All-African People's Conference, which brought together many of Africa's new and future leaders. Both conferences adopted numerous anticolonial resolutions couched in clearly anti-Western slogans. Soviet diplomacy could not miss this bandwagon because of a difference in ideological terminology.

The Russians were rightly concerned with the stability of the regimes of their newly found friends and also worried about the political reliability of leaders who were not orthodox Marxists. In Guinea, the Russians made the fatal mistake of "rushing it," and apparently plotted to have Sékou Touré replaced by a more obedient politician. In Touré's words, the Soviet ambassador, Solod, was "caught red-handed" and immediately expelled.[10] Consequently, Touré never made Nkrumah's mistake of entrusting his security arrangements entirely to the Soviets and the East Germans; although he had to survive several abortive coups, he managed to stay in power, never abandoning his radical *cri de guerre* but never trusting the Russians beyond accepting limited Soviet technical assistance and repaying it with a low-key support of the Soviet Union in international arenas.

In Ghana, after a short flirtation with parliamentary democracy, Nkrumah came to realize that without concentrating power in his own hands and building a political machine to help him maintain that power, he could not hope to achieve his political ambitions. The USSR was prepared to give him the wherewithal for a power apparatus, and the East Germans were called upon to organize the secret service and special police units to guard Nkrumah, a role they were to perform many times in other African nations.

Nkrumah's total reliance on foreign protection cost him dearly. One morning in February 1966, Kwame Nkrumah was deposed, the East Germans and a multitude of Soviet advisers were told to leave Ghana, and eight years of intense Soviet involvement in an African country that was regarded as being in the vanguard of African independence was brought to nothing.

The Russian debacle in Ghana is known to have caused much heat in Moscow. Today it might be argued that had 10,000 Cubans been stationed in Ghana in 1966, Nkrumah might still be in power. The Russians came to realize that without strong ideological identification with Soviet Communism, African regimes could not be expected to permit the USSR to exert the kind of control over them that the Kremlin demands of its allies. The other lesson the USSR learned with the downfall of Nkrumah was that Soviet control of the security apparatus alone is not sufficient to protect its political investments. Later, in Angola, Mozambique, and Ethiopia both these mistakes were corrected. The political leadership of the MPLA, FRELIMO, and the Derg are as solidly Marxist as the African dislike of ideological orthodoxy permits, and the presence of Cuban troops ensures that the events of February 1966 in Ghana do not recur.

In Ghana, the Soviet Union also began to reassess realistically the nature and effectiveness of its technical assistance. Although technical assistance is not the subject of this paper, it cannot be ignored because, if desired, it can become an important tool that the donor country can use to bolster its diplomatic effort in a Third World country. Suffice it to say that after the experience with Ghana, Guinea, Mali, Tanzania, Kenya, and Nigeria, the Russians had to admit to themselves that their aid was inferior to that of the West, and that even with East German and Czech assistance, they had no chance of competing with capitalist countries. In the course of time, however, whatever fears the Soviets may have had in this respect were dispelled by the realization that, generally speaking, Western aid to African countries carried virtually no political strings. By the end of the 1960s, and certainly in the 1980s, the Soviets may be found, however discreetly, urging their African friends to accept as much Western and multilateral aid as possible (except military) because this saves the Russians from facing African demands they cannot, or are unwilling, to meet.

Having succeeded in relieving the Communist countries of any moral obligation to help the Third World, and not being an accessory to the "crime of colonialism," the Soviet contribution to multilateral aid is minimal. There are signs that some Africans are beginning to be critical of these Russian tactics. The secretary-general of the Organization of African Trade Union Unity, Akumo, said that ". . . while the socialist countries are less generous to developing countries, particularly in Africa, they insist on buying African minerals like gold, at the same imperialist manipulated prices."[11]

Kenya

As Colim Legum points out, "Virtually no nation states yet exist in Africa. The continental political systems are at different stages of evolution towards becoming or failing to become viable national states . . . all African regimes are essentially temporary and transitional since with very few exceptions they do not operate within an established framework of viable and widely based institutions."[12] The temptation for the fledgling Soviet diplomacy in the 1960s to support certain tribes against others was, therefore, considerable.

In Kenya, the Soviets found themselves supporting a minority tribal group, the Lous, headed by Oginga Odinga, against Jomo Kenyatta, president of the republic, who was the head of Kenya's largest tribe, the Kikuyu. Kenyatta had visited the Soviet Union in the 1930s, but soon left it, disappointed with the dependent status of a member of a Soviet kolkhoz.[13] Russian diplomacy, therefore, could not repeat in Kenya its performance in

Ghana, where, in one way or another, the modus operandi depended almost entirely on cooperation with the national leader. Oginga Odinga, however, proved to be a poor investment. His attempts to stage a coup were thwarted on several occasions. A Soviet ship, the *Fizik Lebedev,* carrying arms to Odinga, was intercepted at Mombasa in April 1965, and Odinga's star began to wane. Subsequently, Russian diplomats and Tass correspondents were expelled from Kenya on short notice. In later years, the Russians became very wary of involvement in Africa's tribal politics.

Nigeria

If the Soviet experiment with Kenya was a textbook example of how diplomacy should not be conducted in Africa, Soviet assistance to Nigeria secured for the USSR a reputation in Africa of a reliable friend. Before the outbreak of the Biafra civil war, the Soviets had been cautiously (after the Kenya experience) exploring the intricacies of Nigerian politics, and had wisely decided to stay out. When the Ibos of the Eastern Region rose in revolt in 1968, and after the West had refused to sell arms to the federal government, a Nigerian delegation went to Moscow and procured the required assistance.

The Soviet Union offered the most generous terms for credit, but the Nigerians politely declined, saying that they would pay in cash or in cocoa (this was before the major oil boom). The Czechs, who had been helping the Biafrans, had to be told by Moscow to stop forthwith. After the victory of the central government over Biafra, there was a brief period of euphoria in the relations between the two countries, but it soon died down because the Nigerian Northern Region (Moslem and conservative) discouraged close relations between Lagos and Moscow.

Nevertheless, Soviet diplomacy in Africa had been helped enormously. In the decade of Soviet inactivity in Africa that followed the civil war in Nigeria, Russia's prompt assistance to the Nigerian central government was frequently praised by African political leaders who, because of Africa's internal divisions, were particularly appreciative of Soviet help to prevent secession.

Soviet Military Interventions

Angola

The Soviet military intervention in Angola, aided by Cuban troops and East German military and security specialists, has been analyzed ably, realistically, and in detail elsewhere. There is no need, therefore, in this paper to recall the course of events. In 1982, and after an equally costly intervention in the Horn of Africa, Russia's involvement in Angola still stands out as its boldest military venture into a region of the globe extremely remote from the widest possible periphery of a Soviet sphere of interest.

The lesson of the Soviet debacle in Ghana a decade before must have played its part in Moscow's decision to go all out in Angola. In 1975, the Russians saw their tireless investment of some 15 years of support for the MPLA in danger of dissolving because on power struggles within the movement, and as a result of the popularity in Angola of the two rival liberation movements, the FNLA and UNITA, which had Chinese and American support, respectively.

For a number of reasons the MPLA was Moscow's only hope to gain and keep control of Angola. After a decade and a half of African experience, the Russians had become painfully aware of the African reluctance to embrace the dogmas of ideology. In the many years of training Angolans at the Patrice Lumumba University, it became apparent that *mesticos* (mixed blood) and *assimilados* (Africans who were given Portuguese citizenship because of their literacy and knowledge of the Portuguese language) were among the most eager to accept Marxism. The MPLA was largely dependent on the *mesticos* and *assimilados* for support, along with a sprinkling of Angolans who belonged to the Kimbundu tribe.

Thus, by supporting the MPLA, the Russians were aware from the start that they were choosing a minority group as their mainstay in Angola. This assured the Soviets control of the ruling elite of the future independent Angola; on the other hand, it deprived them of a wider tribal grass roots support. The events in Kenya a decade before were in danger of repeating themselves. However, another lesson had been learned from Ghana and Indonesia; Augustinho Neto was considered (especially before independence) a loyal supporter of the USSR, but the Russians were not banking on the loyalties of one man alone. The Politburo of the MPLA, in spite of internal rivalries, was, on the whole, solidly pro-Soviet, and it proved its allegiance to the USSR after Neto's death.

Without going into the complexities of the power struggle among the various political movements that led up to the 1975–76 war, suffice it to say that the Soviet Union was not prepared to allow either the results of democratic elections or the fortunes of an African war to decide the fate of a pro-Soviet political party. It did not wish to leave to chance the installation of such a party in Luanda, nor its capacity to stay in power without being deposed by a coup, as so many African leaders have been. The dispatch of surrogate forces became inevitable in Moscow's eyes, as soon as the MPLA's victory became questionable.

By 1974—before the revolution in Portugal—the Russians had already spent $54 million on supporting the MPLA. They had a further year to decide and prepare for the possibility of military intervention. The speed with which specially trained Cuban troops seem to have been available for transport to Angola, and the efficiency of the Soviet airlift, certainly suggest long-term planning. The intervention was therefore the fruit of a long-standing Soviet conception of the crucial importance of Angola: its strategic assets in terms of the South Atlantic sea routes, its mineral resources, and its value as a staging ground for the support of SWAPO in Namibia.

It is not unlikely that the Russians underestimated the strength of the American reaction to their dispatch of Cuban troops to Angola. The Kremlin relies heavily on what is sometimes called "smoke signal diplomacy." The United States had not sent up serious warning signals when the Russians installed the pro-Soviet governments of FRELIMO in Mozambique and Paigc in Guinea-Bissau. In addition, the Russians might easily have been led to believe that the United States would quietly acquiesce in the takeover in Angola because of the attitude displayed by the Americans at the U.N. General Assembly, where the situation in Angola had been an item on the agenda since the mid-1960s. Representatives of the MPLA, FRELIMO, and other liberation movements traveled to New York, appeared as petitioners before the General Assembly's Fourth Committee, made statements couched in the phraseology of a Communist pamphlet, and received public support from the delegates of the Soviet bloc. All of this occurred without much opposition or criticism on the part of the U.S. delegation, which was extremely well briefed on the extent of Soviet penetration of the liberation movements in the Portuguese colonies.

Whether or not the Russians had miscalculated, they now have to underwrite an Angola to which they are bound by a 20-year treaty of friendship and mutual assistance, and that has a government that, without Cuban help, cannot stand up to the challenge of UNITA's control of much of the countryside.

Even though Angola's profits from Gulf Oil defray much of the cost of maintaining the Cuban troops in a state of battle readiness, most of the country's economy is in shambles. The Soviet Union and its allies are unable to restore Angola to the level of prosperity it enjoyed under Portuguese rule.

Visiting American businessmen have often been told by Angola officials that they would welcome closer economic ties with the United States. There can be little doubt of the sincerity of the Angolans, who, like many Africans, have come to terms with the limitations of Soviet aid. Even solidly pro-Soviet Angolans would doubtless be interested in an infusion of Western capital and know-how, especially since this does not oblige them to alter their political course or cease their support for the USSR. Nevertheless, the Russians, who traditionally suffer from excessive suspicion, warned a visiting Angolan delegation in Moscow of an American plot to return the African nation to the American sphere of influence. The warning was given in January 1982, at a Kremlin luncheon hosted by Premier Nikolai Tikhonov less than a week after the American assistant secretary of state for African affairs, Chester A. Crocker, held a meeting in Paris with Paulo Jorge, the Angolan foreign minister.

The *New York Times* report of the Moscow luncheon further mentions that the Angolan group, led by Lucio Lara, a member of the Politburo of the MPLA, was said to have been empowered "to tell the Russians that their interest in the Angolan and Namibian situations would not be prejudiced by the American contacts."[14] Mr. Lara took pains to stress Angola's loyalty to and friendship for Moscow, and its continuing hostility toward the United States.

Whatever the real feelings of the MPLA's leadership may be, there is no alternative for them but to continue with their pro-Soviet policy because the present government cannot survive without Cuban support.

The more the present government in Angola may have second thoughts about the "blessings" of an alliance with the USSR, the less the Soviets can contemplate a reduction of the Cuban presence in Angola. Also, the Cubans have an additional role to play in helping SWAPO in its activities in Namibia, a situation that is likely to continue for quite some time. Thus, the MPLA, the Russians, and the Cubans find themselves in a situation in which none can afford to let go of the others, whatever the cost.

For Soviet Russia, a defeat of its proxies in Angola would be such a staggering blow to its policies in Africa that it can be expected to go to any lengths to prevent such a loss. It is worth recalling that as the Angolan civil war was entering a crucial phase in 1976, a Kotlin-class destroyer, a Krista-class cruiser, and an amphibious vessel carrying Soviet sea infantry were cruising off Angola.

Somalia-Ethiopia

The Soviet military presence in Somalia in 1971–77 demands no speculative expansionist world power seeking to control vital waterways and other strategically important areas of convergence between Africa and the Middle East.

Soviet diplomacy did not have to exert much effort to gain a foothold in Somalia. President Siad Barre's government more or less invited the Russians to come in, and in 1972, they gained unrestricted access to the port of Berbera. In addition to naval servicing facilities, the Somalis agreed to the installation of a long-range communications station and the Soviet right to stage maritime reconnaissance flights from Somali airfields.

Although the Somalis professed ideological admiration of the Soviet Union, there was little pretense about the nature of the Soviet-Somali deal. In exchange for bases, the Somalis wanted Soviet weapons and Soviet military instruction. The Russians were completely aware of the Somalis' intention to use their newly acquired military strength to conquer the Ogaden from Ethiopia.

The border between the two countries, though defined by an agreement between Ethiopia and the European colonial powers in 1897 and 1908, was never demarcated (with the exception of 18 miles), and the continuous border dispute postponed the proclamation of Somalia's independence until 1960. The Somalis agreed most unwillingly to a border settlement that left much of the Ogaden on the Ethiopian side, in order not to give Ethiopia a pretext for demanding a further postponement of Somalia's independence.

The intention to annex the Ogaden was an openly proclaimed aim of each subsequent Somali government. Although the Russians had never officially supported Somalia's territorial claims, they were very much aware, in 1972, of the inevitable Somali intention to use Soviet arms to attack Ethiopia. As in so many other parts of the Third World, the USSR was using a local dispute to further its imperial goals. Quite likely, Moscow was not just considering the acquisition of an important naval base well worth the risks of an entanglement in a Somali-Ethiopian war; at the beginning of the 1970s, it was not averse to the prospect of a pro-Western Ethiopia being attacked by African protégés of the USSR.

The Soviet decision in 1976 to support the Derg (Ethiopia's radical military government after the overthrow of the emperor) could not have been taken lightly. It must have been an agonizing choice, even if the Russians had seriously entertained hopes of stemming the hostilities between Somalia and Ethiopia by acting as arbitrators and by proclaiming a pax-sovietica in a kind of African Tashkent agreement. One must, of course, remember that the risk of losing Berbera was made easier for the Soviets by the gradual improvement of Soviet military installations in Aden and Socotra, and their hopes of gaining naval bases at Massawa and Assab. Nevertheless, in 1977 the loss of an alliance with Somalia, which revoked the 1974 friendship agreement with Moscow, at a time when Sadat, having expelled the Russians, was making his way toward the Camp David Agreement with the approval of Sudan's ruler, Numeiry, must have caused considerable uneasiness in Moscow.

If anything, the loss of Soviet influence in Egypt and Sudan must have given the Russians additional reasons to seek a compensatory foothold in Ethiopia. In their drive for control of the Horn of Africa, the Russians, having gambled, had no choice but to make sure that their new ally would decisively gain the upper hand. This the Derg did, and the cost of airlifting 16,000 Cuban troops, plus heavy equipment, must have been enormous.

The expulsion of Somalia's invading armies from Ogaden, with the help of Cuban and East German armed forces, reestablished Soviet prestige in Africa and the Middle East, and Soviet Russia is now perceived as the only superpower (with the possible exception of France) able and willing to throw the full weight of its might behind its allies.

The continued presence of the Cubans in Ogaden has been justified by the Soviets as a measure necessary to protect the inhabitants against the Ethiopians, and as a means to prevent the Ethiopians from crossing the Somali border. There is probably some truth in the last assertion. If Mogadishu wishes to come to some kind of terms with Ethiopia, it can now turn only to the Soviet Union for help. The original Soviet aim of acting as an arbitrator in the conflict on the Horn of Africa is now a distinct possibility

In the meantime, the Russians are beginning to experience predictable difficulties in their partnership with the Derg, as Colonel Mengistu and his friends are finding it more and more difficult to run the country. Ethiopia, more than twice the size of France, has an extremely varied topography—from high mountain plateaus, impassable mountain gorges, and untamed rivers to malarial swamps and very few roads. All this favors the existence of regional fiefdoms, and the emperor rarely managed to exercise more than nominal control over local chiefs and divergent ethnic, linguistic, and religious groups. Since it was never a colony (with the exception of a brief period of Italian rule), there is no detailed land survey of Ethiopia. The rulers in Addis Ababa, be they emperors or commissars, have no exact knowledge of the natural resources and food-growing potentials of the country.

Ethiopia is one of the ten poorest countries in the world, but in the opinion of some Israeli agricultural experts who worked there before 1973, the country not only could, under proper management, be self-sufficient in food supplies but also could become a large exporter of industrial crops. This would require enormous outlays of capital and know-how, and also would take many years of concentrated effort. No doubt this is what Mengistu would like the Soviets to help him accomplish; however, Moscow has other priorities, such as retrieving at least part of the cost of airlifting military equipment and the two divisions of Cubans and East Germans into Ethiopia, conducting a war against Somalia, and maintaining the surrogate forces in a state of battle readiness in the inhospitable desert regions of Ogaden. All that Ethiopia can offer as repayment is an excellent quality of coffee beans.

Consequently, tensions between Ethiopia and the USSR are inevitable, and in December 1981, the Soviet ambassador, Boris Y. Kirnovski, was asked to pack his bags. Ethiopian officials characterized the ambassador's behavior "as being abrupt to the point of condescension."[15] Mr. Kirnovski is not the first Soviet ambassador who has had to leave an African country in a hurry, nor is he likely to be the last. Had Lieutenant Colonel Mengistu Haile Mariam consulted the late Augustinho Neto of

Angola or Samora Machel of Mozambique, they would, in comparing notes, have come to the conclusion that a change in behavior inevitably ensues when a Soviet ambassador begins to see himself as an imperial proconsul.

Difficulties in the close relationship between the USSR and its African protégés should not, however, lead American observers to hope that the day is near when the Russians will be told to clear out, as they were in Egypt and Sudan. In Egypt, Sadat saw a clear alternative to subservience to Moscow, and the Egyptian army was strong enough to use force against the Russians, if necessary.

There was no danger of an attack by Israel; Sadat, therefore, could not be blackmailed by Moscow. Sudan is not involved in any conflict the Russians could exploit, and Numeiry's only fear was that the Soviet embassy would finally succeed in engineering a coup against him. In contrast with the situations in Egypt and Sudan, both the MPLA in Angola and the Derg in Ethiopia will continue to be dependent on Soviet support, and both are unlikely to possess the military strength to force the Cubans to leave, if ever they so wish.

The USSR obviously plans a long stay in the Horn of Africa. The Treaty of Friendship and Cooperation Between Socialist Ethiopia, the People's Democratic Republic of Yemen and the Socialist People's Libyan Arab Jamahiriya of August 19, 1981, stipulates in Article 16:

> In the event of aggression against any one of the Contracting Parties, the other Contracting Parties, regarding it as an aggression against all, shall in the exercise of their right of individual and collective self-defense, defend together, the party so aggressed, with all means necessary.

In Article 17, the contracting parties undertake to promote military and security cooperation "on the basis of signed agreements among themselves."

There is no unclassified information on whether similar additional agreements have been signed among the three signatories. The wording of the treaty is of no great importance, and does not oblige the parties to follow a definite course of action in the several conflict situations in which each of the signatories was involved at the time of signing.

Since two of the three signatories are close allies of the USSR, there can be no doubt whatsoever that this treaty was inspired by Moscow. Mu'amar al-Qaddafi signed because the agreement purports to establish an anti-Egyptian, anti-Sudanese alliance that the colonel supports. It may also be seen as a desire by Moscow to establish a formal framework for cooperation between two Soviet allies, Ethiopia and Southern Yemen, which control the Gulf of Aden and the entrance to the Suez Canal.

Likely Targets: Zaire and Sudan

What is sometimes described as the "imperial impetus" is perhaps better expressed colloquially: "One thing leads to another." In the heyday of their empire, the British were not interested in conquering what is now known as Nigeria; they were quite happy controlling the Gold Coast (Ghana). However, the enormous expanse of land north of the Gold Coast, as yet unclaimed by any European power, must have worried some strategists in the Colonial Office, so the British moved reluctantly into what was then called the "white man's grave."

There are no exact historical parallels, but one might safely say that the Soviet Union could easily refrain from seeking control over Zaire and Sudan without that restraint's impinging in the least on the status of the Soviet Union as a great power, or even without its affecting Russia's standing in Africa.

However, there are without doubt African interest groups in the Politburo, the Central Committee, and the KGB that can point out that Zaire's enormous mineral resources are essential to Western economies, and therefore important to the Soviet policy of mineral denial. A cursory glance at the map is enough to explain Sudan's importance to whatever great power is interested in controlling the underpinnings of the Horn of Africa.

Having committed so much money and political effort in their interventions in Angola and Ethiopia, the Soviets may quite reasonably come to the conclusion that it would be "penny wise and pound foolish" to abstain from an additional, relatively minor effort that would secure them more comprehensive control over Africa's mineral resources, and over the strategic African approaches to Egypt and the Middle East. There may also be minds in the Soviet capital that fully understand the relative ease with which Zaire and Sudan may be destabilized, as opposed to the much more difficult task of subsequently exercising effective control over these two largest countries on the African continent. The Russians are most likely to be guided in their decisions by opportunities as they arise, and by situations that they themselves have been instrumental in creating.

Zaire

Formerly the Belgian Congo, Zaire was the scene of one of Soviet Russia's earliest fiascos when the USSR, supporting the erratic Patrice Lumumba, lost to the West and to the then secretary-general of the United Nations, Dag Hammerskjold who genuinely believed that the United Nations would be able to act as a "third force" in the bipolar struggle over the future of postcolonial Africa. The Russians were more successful in installing themselves across the river from Kinshasa, in Congo (Brazzaville). Although unimportant in terms of mineral resources, Congo (Brazzaville) provides the KGB with an excellent listening post and a possible staging platform for an anti-Mobutu revolution in Zaire. The Russians have twice tried, and failed, to detach Zaire's copper-rich province of Shaba (Katanga) from Zaire—in 1977 and 1978—by armed incursion from Angola. Had it not been for the prompt interventions of France and Morocco, the Cubans would today be in control of Shaba, and perhaps of the whole of Zaire.

The pro-Western ruler of Zaire, Mobutu Sese Seko, is one of Africa's most corrupt and profligate dictators, and his extravagances have become notorious, even in Africa. His personal fortune is estimated at more than $3 billion, at a time when Zaire is on the verge of bankruptcy and thousands are dying of malnutrition in what should be one of the richest countries in Africa.

This situation cannot last, and the United States is faced, not for the first time, with a dilemma for which there is no simple solution. On one hand, Zaire not only is rich in copper, but is also the world's principal exporter of industrial diamonds and the supplier of between 60 and 70 percent of the world's cobalt. On the other hand, Mobutu, who relies for support on a complex coalition of tribal and personal loyalties, cannot be easily removed by the West without creating the kind of chaos the Russians, watching the scene from Brazzaville and Angola, are hopefully expecting.

It has been suggested that Nguza Karl I. Bond, the former foreign minister of Zaire, now residing in Europe and challenging Mobutu's authority, should be supported by the United States. Whether this is feasible is not a simple question, but something had better be done quickly.

Sudan

To understand Sudan's importance in terms of African political geography, it should be remembered that it borders on Egypt, Libya, Chad, Central African Republic, Zaire, Uganda, and Ethiopia. In terms of the political alignments of the 1980s it borders on a pro-American Egypt, and was one of the very few Arab states to support Sadat. Sudan's borders with Libya and Ethiopia make it a target of a possible Soviet-inspired Libya-Ethiopia conspiracy, in conformity with the treaty of August 1981.

The results of a Soviet coup against Numeiry, with the help of its proxies, would be incalculable. With Soviet control of Ethiopia and Sudan, Upper Egypt would be exposed to Soviet harassment; large stretches of the Nile would be under Soviet control, and the Egyptian army would be called upon to protect Egypt's "soft underbelly." Under those circumstances, it is very doubtful that any regime in Cairo could long maintain a pro-American orientation. The effects of such a turn of events on the Middle East and the Egyptian peace treaty with Israel are too obvious to require elaboration. In addition, since Sudan reaches into the heart of Africa, Zaire's future could not be unaffected for long.

Sudan, like most African countries, has its full share of regional and tribal difficulties ready to be exploited by whoever may be interested in doing so. President Jaafar al-Numeiry said in February 1982 that he believed Quaddafi would use the treaty of August 1981 to infiltrate agents along the Sudanese-Ethiopian border and "buy Sudanese" to stir up trouble.[16] The civil war between South and North Sudan, fought for 17 years and formally ended, has left enough unsettled problems to make it very easy for the Russians and Qaddafi to exploit the situation. Sudan once possessed the best-organized Communist party in Black Africa, and although Numeiry has liquidated its leaders, one must assume that it has been driven underground and is still active. There is also the now familiar potpourri of revolutionists, consisting of left-wing university students, Islamic fundamentalists, dissatisfied army generals, and corrupt government officials. The United States has a high profile in the Sudan: stepped-up American military aid worth $100 million has begun to arrive, and U.S. economic aid in 1983 totals $180 million, Washington's biggest aid package in Africa, apart from its support for Egypt.[17]

Again one is faced with the old question of what else, if anything, can be done to protect an unpopular leader in a country having chronic instability. If Numeiry were to go, quite likely every leader who followed him would suffer a similar fate. The Soviet solution to such problems in Ethiopia and Angola is the presence of Cuban battalions protecting Soviet investments. The United States, unfortunately, has no proxies it could install even if this was thought desirable.

There is no smooth solution to the protection of American interests in the quicksands of African politics. Neither butter alone nor guns, nor a combination of the two, can guarantee success. The only way may be to exploit opportunities as they arise, to abandon the pursuit of outworn methods, to give Africans the feeling that the United States will support its friends, but will no longer stand by leaders who have become unpopular. This demands the employment of highly specialized experts who, keeping a low profile, can act swiftly and decisively. It also requires a more realistic understanding by the media of a situation in which there are few "good guys" and a host of very "bad" ones.

Alternative Soviet Targets in Africa

There are now 37 independent black countries on the mainland of Africa; 32 of them maintain diplomatic relations with the Union of Soviet Socialist Republics.[18] Only the Central African Republic, the Ivory Coast, Lesotho, Malawi, and Swaziland have no Soviet embassy in their capitals, either because diplomatic relations with the Soviet Union have been severed or because they were never established.

Are all of these 37 newly established independent African countries potential targets for Soviet penetration and control? It is safe to assume that if all and each of them were suddenly to beg Moscow to manage their affairs, the Russians would be in real trouble.

Twelve of these African countries were formerly French colonies, and with the exception of Guinea and Mali, which passed through a brief period of close cooperation with the Soviet Union in the 1960s—and of Benin and Congo (Brazzaville), which came under Soviet influence—most of French-speaking Africa was left untouched by Soviet ambitions. The reason for this Soviet restraint was Moscow's clear realization that France was prepared to intervene militarily to protect nations friendly to it—and that they enjoyed considerable French economic support. Many French-speaking African states have defense treaties with their former colonial masters that are reinforced by the presence of some 8,000 French troops on the continent. The French units are highly mobile and can be quickly moved to a potential trouble spot. A well-developed network of intelligence and security agents in all of French-speaking Africa provides the French with an efficient advance warning system.

Zaire, formerly a Belgian colony, is now protected by the French writ. Without French help, Angola's MPLA would have conquered Shaba province. The French have, with varying degrees of success, intervened in the civil wars in Chad and Niger.

Moscow must also have realized that undue interference in the affairs of France's African allies might have a negative influence on Soviet-French relations, especially in the periods of de Gaulle and Valery Giscard d'Estaing, when France's European policies found great favor in the Kremlin. President Omar Bongo of Gabon, who is reputed to possess the most luxurious palace on the African continent, may not be the ideological soul mate of a socialist like Mitterand, but Gabon's fabulous mineral wealth guarantees continued French protection of the existing regime.

Are the Russians likely to intervene in Africa whenever an opportunity presents itself? The cases of Ghana and Gambia offer insight to the contrary. On December 31, 1981, Flight Lieutenant Jerry John Rawlings seized power in Ghana. He did so for the second time in two years, having abdicated 112 days before in favor of the elected civilian government of President Hilla Limann. The usual ills of high inflation, corruption, and disorder followed, and Rawlings decided to return to power to put the house in order. In a sense, it was an African tragedy. Ghana was the first African country to become independent in the late 1950s; the British left it fully solvent, with a considerable foreign-currency reserve and a class of educated Africans, well able to administer the government and the country. Twenty-five years later, and after several coups, the country was bankrupt, the educated class having left long ago to seek employment elsewhere. Rawlings, an admirer of Colonel Qaddafi, invited the Libyans to reopen their embassy in Accra and help Ghana find its way to prosperity. In the United Nations, African diplomats maintain that Rawlings had also sought Soviet assistance, but that he was coolly turned down.

If this is true, it makes good sense, because the Russians don't really need Ghana any more. They have no interest in repeating their performance with Nkrumah and finding themselves again evicted, with no way to recoup their losses. Today, the Russians have their hands full, and they can afford to pick and choose their African friends.

Not only did the Soviets decide not to get involved in Ghana, but they also displayed no interest in the abortive left-wing coup in Gambia. There, on July 30, 1981,

> a mixed group comprising some civilians and some members of the Gambia paramilitary Field Force using the guns of the latter, took control of certain key points in and around the capital, Banjul, including the radio station. From here they broadcast that they had overthrown the government of President Dawda Jawara and proclaimed a "dictatorship of the proletariat" under the leadership of a twelve-man "National Revolutionary Council."[19]

The rebellion was suppressed, and subsequently Gambia merged with Senegal. Although no official information exists as to reasons for the revolt, there is no reason to suspect that it was Soviet-instigated. Had the revolution succeeded, the Russians would doubtless have responded with official joy, but probably would have remained extremely niggardly in extending military or economic aid to the newest propagators of the "dictatorship of the proletariat" on the African continent.

Were a pro-Soviet coup to take place where Russia had some interest, such as Zambia, Zimbabwe, Zaire, Sudan, or Cameroon, the Soviets would become "peddlers of power," selling a "political-security" machine to African countries whose friendship they have reasons to cultivate.

The area of Soviet interest and involvement, actual and potential, in Africa is enormous. It consists of Tanzania, Zambia, Zimbabwe, Angola, and Mozambique, the "confrontation states" in the conflict with South Africa, which possess enormous mineral wealth, the denial of which to Japan and the West is a recognized aim of Soviet diplomacy in Africa. Soviet publications speak constantly of the exploitation of Africa's mineral wealth by the greedy bourgeois imperialists. The conflict with South Africa is likely to continue for decades, and the Soviets can therefore rely on making the most of a situation in which the West, for strategic and economic reasons, may have no alternative but to protect the regime of apartheid

Even if some agreement about the future of Namibia is reached, it is not likely to last, given SWAPO's pro-Soviet leanings and South Africa's determination to keep control over the territory.

The Kremlin will need all of its pragmatic adventures, in addition to the continued availability of its Cuban proxies, to project and maintain Soviet power over such a vast expanse of territory and in the face of so many inter-African disputes. The Chinese may be sitting on the sidelines, waiting to exploit Soviet failures. They have succeeded to some extent in Tanzania, Mozambique, and Zimbabwe. Most Africans are aware, however, that in the near future Peking cannot provide them with the equivalent of either a Soviet-made "power package" or Western aid.

The best way to illustrate the difference between the character of Soviet involvement in Africa south of the Sahara and its involvement in Europe or Asia is to imagine a "worst case" scenario, from the Soviet point of view. If, for some reason, the Soviet Union were to lose all its military and diplomatic leverage in Europe or in Asia, one could assume that it would conclude that its vital defense interests were seriously imperiled. If, on the other hand, the Soviet Union were to suffer a similar setback in Africa south of the Sahara, this would leave Soviet defense arrangements intact, and would still allow a considerable, although somewhat more limited, Soviet offensive posture as a great power.

Africa, from the Soviet point of view, is therefore an area where the Soviet Union stakes its right to exercise influence as a great power that may intervene militarily, far beyond the requirements of national defense.

Consequently, Soviet intervention in Angola and Ethiopia, through its proxies, has to be seen in the light of Russia's global ambitions, much more so than its support for Vietnam in Cambodia, for instance, which may still be viewed as part of a defensive move against China.

The Russians were not, of course, planning a timetable for their imperial expansion, but responding to opportunities whenever and wherever they presented themselves. They were practicing "pragmatic adventurism." Quite likely, had the Kremlin been able to control the timing of the revolutions in Portugal and Ethiopia, they might have preferred to postpone these events for a year or two in order to reap the full benefits of détente, including the ratification of SALT II and the postponement of American rearmament.

All of this is, of course, pure speculation. However, one can safely say that had events in Portugal and Ethiopia taken place a decade earlier, the Soviet Union could not have responded to them as it did in the 1970s, because then it did not possess the military ability to transport large masses of men and matériel over vast distances.

Consequently, Soviet diplomacy in Africa south of the Sahara in the 1970s and 1980s is in a position to present an image of a power that is capable of fulfilling what it regards as its mission in Africa and, above all, to give full support to its African allies.

What of the African perception of the Soviet Union? After two decades of political naiveté, it now appears that most Africans have sized up Soviet policy in very realistic terms. President Kaunda of Zambia incurred Soviet wrath by his statement in which he compared the Cuban presence in Angola to a "plundering tiger with cubs." On the other hand, Kaunda, if he sees no alternative, may well decide to turn to the Soviet Union, hoping to keep his options open.

At the time of writing, five African states south of the Sahara—Angola, Mozambique, Ethiopia, Benin, and Congo (Brazzaville)—are allied to the Soviet Union both formally, by virtue of treaties, and actually, by supporting the Soviet Union in Africa as well as in the United Nations and at meetings of the nonaligned nations. The United States does not possess a single formal ally in sub-Saharan Africa, although Kenya, Somalia, Sudan, and Zaire are enjoying American support and can, in certain circumstances, be expected to assist the United States.

Both the Russians and the French have learned that because of the inherent instability of African regimes, whatever their ideology, the only way to protect one's African allies against coups is the use of highly mobile military units, such as the Cubans or the French Foreign Legion.

No one can prognosticate how long Cuban troops will be available to perform guard duty for the Soviet Union. Their availability means, however, that in addition to furthering Soviet goals in Latin America, Castro's Cuba has acquired a new role in Soviet designs on Africa that make it an indispensable ally of the Kremlin.

French-speaking African states that enjoy the military protection of France and benefit from its economic assistance fully realize that the price of both is political loyalty to France. Outside the French zone of influence, and apart from African countries allied to the Soviet Union, the situation is highly unstable. The likely dream of an African dictator, after seizing power, would be to have the protection of the Soviet "power package" and, at the same time, benefit from Western, and especially American, aid and trade without political strings. It is doubtful that this sort of arrangement would serve American interests because the United States would, in such cases, in effect be subsidizing a Soviet presence.

On the other hand, African leaders who, like Robert Mugabe of Zimbabwe, profess radical views should not automatically be rejected by the United States, because many Africans fully realize the constraints on their freedom that the Soviet "power package" entails and may, in spite of their views, welcome not only American help but also American political and military assistance.

In Africa in the 1980s there are no ready-made solutions to cover all contingencies. The United States may do worse than to adopt some of the advice given by Anatoly Gromyko (the son of the foreign minister), head of Moscow's African Institute, to Soviet "Africanists":

> Soviet specialists in African affairs will be required to study the differences in the stages of development of individual countries . . . to follow their conduct in international forums, their foreign policy profiles . . . and pay special attention to influential countries like Nigeria.[20]

This advice is a far cry from the rigidity of Soviet thinking in the 1950s and 1960s, and displays the flexibility required for the pursuit of a successful policy in Africa. It also implies that the Kremlin will judge African countries according to their conduct in matters of foreign policy. Should the United States be less insistent?

CONCLUDING REMARKS

How successful has Soviet diplomacy been in achieving some or all of the strategic and political goals described at the beginning of this paper? Before attempting to answer this question, we must bear in mind the difference between the achievements of Soviet diplomacy and those of Communist ideology.

Communist ideology has been propagated in Asia in one way or another since the early 1920s. Soviet diplomacy arrived on the Asian scene as recently as 1955. Russia's most solid success in Asia—the alignment of Vietnam with the Soviet Union—was more the result of Ho Chi Minh's (and his successor's) doctrinaire allegiance to Moscow, Vietnamese reaction against U.S. intervention, and the revival of the ancient enmity between China and Vietnam than it was the fruit of Soviet diplomacy: this is not meant, however, to detract from the skill of Russian diplomacy in creating and maintaining a special relationship with India, which resulted in Kosygin's presiding over the India-Pakistan peace talks at Tashkent in 1965, and in the signing of a treaty of friendship and mutual assistance with India in 1971.

Some of this success has been somewhat ephemeral. The Indians refused to allow the Russians to arbitrate between them and the Pakistanis a second time, after the war of 1971, and the Simla Agreement came about without Soviet participation. The Indo-Soviet treaty is unique in that part of Asia, but it does little to prevent India from pursuing an independent policy toward China and Pakistan. In the ongoing relationship between Moscow and New Delhi, the Russians are generally the supplicant—fearing the inevitable normalization of relations between India and Pakistan. The main goal of Soviet diplomacy—to have India ally itself with Russia against China—has not been attained, and is not likely to be reached in the foreseeable future.

By supporting India against Pakistan at the Security Council in 1965 and in 1971, and through the supply to India of advanced weaponry, the USSR has succeeded in projecting the image of a reliable friend, and thus has widened the circle of its supporters in India beyond the limits of ideological sympathies.

Soviet diplomacy has failed to secure naval servicing facilities for the USSR in Indian ports. This has become somewhat less vital for the Soviet Union because it can contest American power in the Indian Ocean from its bases in Vietnam and South Yemen.

No doubt Moscow is looking forward to a change of regime in Pakistan that would deprive the United States of an ally on Afghanistan's border and would not permit the Afghan refugee camps on the Pakistani side of the border to be used as recruiting grounds for anti-Soviet guerrillas. If the Soviets were to succeed in destabilizing Pakistan, they would greatly strengthen their bargaining position vis-à-vis New Delhi, even at the risk of straining their relations with India, and would help them pacify Afghanistan. Quite likely, this is the only move left to the Russians in Asia, where it now finds itself in a state of diplomatic immobility.

The Soviet ties with Indonesia, once so close, have been broken, and show no evidence of being renewed as long as Suharto is in power.

Soviet Russia's major diplomatic venture in Asia was the proposed Asian Collective Security Pact. This was a dismal failure, and must have convinced the Kremlin that with the exception of Vietnam and states under its control, no Asian government is now willing to enter into a bilateral or multilateral arrangement aimed against Peking.

In Burma, Soviet diplomacy has tried, but failed, to supplant the Americans in arms delivery, and has not succeeded in persuading Ne Win to ask the Russians for help against Chinese incursions into Burmese territory.

If one reviews Soviet relations with the countries of Asia, it would appear that more was achieved by Communist ideological propaganda than by diplomatic persuasion. However, the schism between Moscow and Peking deprived the Russians of profit from the spread of Communism in Asia. Therefore, in the 1980s, the Kremlin is not looking forward to the coming to power of the Communist parties in Indonesia, Malaysia, Burma, Thailand, and Sri Lanka, because in all likelihood these Communist parties would take their orders from Peking rather than Moscow, or they might become embroiled in such internecine struggles that any geopolitical gain in ideological orientation would be obviated.

At the time of Khrushchev's visit to India in 1955, Asia may have looked like a chessboard with innumerable possibilities for favorable moves for the Russian side; nearly 30 years later, the Russian chess player in Asia can hope for a draw at best. There is little tactical mobility for Soviet diplomacy in Asia these days; unlike Africa, no strategic gains can be secured by the dispatch of several thousand Cubans.

The main task of Soviet diplomacy in Asia now is not so much to conquer new positions as it is to contain expansion of Chinese influence.

In South Asia, there is little perception of Soviet power, although there is acute awareness of China's future role on the continent. Even fear of Vietnam, a Soviet proxy, does not enhance Soviet prestige. Bangkok and Rangoon prefer to negotiate directly with Hanoi, rather than act through Moscow.

On the other hand, the growing role of the Soviet navy worries the defense establishments of some Asian states, especially those that make up ASEAN. Their hope is for rearmament of Japan.

Mr. Thanat, the Thai Deputy Prime Minister has declared that it is time for Japan to do more than rely on the U.S. umbrella for security. If Japan only defended the immediate area, he declared, Soviet forces deployed in Asia would be tied down instead of prowling the Pacific and Indian Oceans.

It would appear that where Soviet diplomacy and Communist propaganda have failed, the Russian navy may be the means by which the USSR leaves its impact on Asia.

NOTES

1. Robert N. Donaldson, *The Soviet-Indian Alignment: Quest for Influence* (Denver: University of Denver Press, 1979).

2. "The Soviet Connection," *Seminar* (New Delhi), September 1981, p. 265.

3. Hasan Askari Rizvi, *The Soviet Union & the Indo-Pakistan Sub-Continent* (Lahore: Progressive Publishers, 1974).

4. Quoted in *New York Times,* March 16, 1982.

5. Rizvi, op. cit.

6. *New York Times,* op. cit.

7. Ibid.

8. In 1980, during Brezhnev's visit to New Delhi, the Russians laid forth a five-point proposal for the demilitarization of the Indian Ocean. It was drafted in a manner gauged to find favor with Indira Gandhi. In this, Moscow succeeded, but it is doubtful that the Soviets ever perceived it as anything more than a move to improve relations with India. The United States, Japan, and the ASEAN countries rejected this Soviet proposal because it would have prevented the United States from projecting its own power into the Persian Gulf.

9. African countries later allied to the Soviet Union, such as Congo (Brazzaville), Benin, Angola, Mozambique, and Ethiopia, claim to practice "scientific socialism."

10. William Atwood, *The Reds and the Blacks* (New York: Harper and Row, 1967).

11. Report of a statement by the secretary-general of the Organization of African Trade Union Unity, broadcast by Radio Accra, April 12, 1981, *Africa Currents* 24 (July 1981).

12. Colin Legum, *Africa in the 1980s* (Council on Foreign Relations).

13. Conversation with Kenyatta, sometime in 1975.

14. "Soviet Warns Angolans on U.S.," *New York Times,* January 22, 1982.

15. "Ethiopians' Links To Soviets Strained," *New York Times,* December 17, 1981.

16. "Regional Dispute Divides Sudan," *New York Times,* February 22, 1982.

17. "Clamor for Change Is Sounding Across the Sudan," *New York Times,* February 17, 1982.

18. For the purposes of this paper, I'm not referring to the Soviet-oriented regimes on islands such as Seychelles, and Cape Verde.

19. "Revolt in Gambia," *The Round Table,* October 1981.

20. *Narody Azii Afriki* (1981), no. 4: 6. A free translation by the writer.

BIBLIOGRAPHY

In addition to sources mentioned in the notes, I've drawn on the following publications:

Donaldson, Robert H., ed. *The Soviet Union in the Third World: Successes and Failures.* Boulder, Colo.: Westview Press, 1982.

Hinton, *Three and a Half Powers.* Bloomington: Indiana University Press, 1975.

Horelick, Arnold L., *The Soviet Union's Asian Collective Security Proposal.* RAND Papers series. Santa Monica, Calif.: RAND, 1974.

Indorf, Hans H., *ASEAN: Problems, Prospects.* Singapore: Institute of Southeast Asian Studies.

Menon, Rajan. "China and the Soviet Union in Asia." *Current History,* October 1981.

Scalapino, Robert A., *Asia and the Major Powers.*

THREE

The Soviet Union in India
ROBERT H. DONALDSON

INTRODUCTION

The purpose of this paper is to analyze the nature and extent of Soviet influence in India, as manifested in the political, economic, commercial, and cultural fields. When one state seeks to influence another, it is attempting through various acts or signals to change or sustain the behavior of that state. The observable result of a successful Soviet attempt at influence would be India's doing something (or refraining from something, or continuing something) that it would likely not have done in the absence of the Soviet attempt. Clearly, the realization of Soviet objectives is more likely insofar as those objectives are compatible with India's (as perceived by the latter's governing elite).

But certain actions taken by the Indian government that favor the realization of Soviet objectives may not result from an application of Soviet influence, to the extent that these actions are perceived by the Indians as contributing to their own objectives. If Moscow and New Delhi appear to be acting in tandem on a number of issues, it may not necessarily be a result of Soviet influence on India, or of Indian influence on the Soviet Union, but of a common but independent perception by policy makers in the two states that their interests lie in a similar direction. On the other hand, if the Soviets request Indian action on an issue of little moment to the Indians—in which they perceive scant vital interest of their own—or if Moscow seeks to alter or sustain Indian behavior in a matter on which New Delhi's objectives run counter to those of the Soviets, then the degree of Soviet influence is indeed being put to the test. A favorable Indian response in the latter case would of course signal greater strength of Soviet influence than in the former instance, in which Indian compliance could be achieved at a much smaller cost to New Delhi.

Moreover, an influence relationship rarely is completely one-sided; there is often a feedback effect that must be taken into account. Thus, the

Soviets might influence the Indians to take a particular action, while the Indians at the same time influence the Soviets to act in a manner favorable to the achievement of New Delhi's goals on a separate issue.

An important determinant of the degree of influence one state is able to exert on another in pursuit of its objectives is the type and quantity of capabilities it can muster in trying to affect the behavior of the target state. It is important to realize, however, that the mere existence of resources is in itself sufficient; a state's willingness to exert its capabilities, and the skill and credibility with which it does so, are also very important factors.

But quantity and credibility of capabilities and the degree of skill with which they are brought to bear are not just correlated with actual influence. Also important is the extent to which there is dependence between two countries in an influence relationship. A country that needs something from another is vulnerable to the latter's exercise of influence. Thus, in this case, the more dependent India is upon the Soviet Union, the more likely it is that Moscow's efforts will succeed in changing or sustaining New Delhi's behavior. But we should also consider the degree to which the Soviet Union needs India. To the extent that Soviet dependence on India approaches or surpasses Indian dependence on the USSR, there may well be a reduction in the Soviet potential to exert influence on New Delhi.

In addition to availability of resources and perception of need, another variable determining the degree of influence is the target state's responsiveness—its willingness to be influenced. Are the Indians, at either the elite or the mass level, disposed to receive Soviet requests with sympathy? An examination of the attitudes both of government officials and of members of the Indian public toward the Soviet Union can aid in assessing the likely weight of this factor in the Soviet-Indian relationship.

In evaluating Soviet successes and failures in India, this paper examines specific instances of Soviet-Indian interaction in the diplomatic, propaganda, military, and economic fields in order to arrive at an empirically based understanding of the actual extent of Soviet influence in India.

SOVIET-INDIAN FRIENDSHIP: OBJECTIVES AND LIMITATIONS

Leonid Brezhnev arrived in New Delhi in December 1980 as the champion of "reliable friendship" between the Soviet Union and India. The trip was his second to India in eight years—a record made more notable by the fact that India is the only non-Communist Third World country that Brezhnev had visited even once in the more than 17 years since he assumed the leadership of the Communist Party of the Soviet Union. Clearly, the Soviet leaders highly value their country's friendship with India, a theme

Brezhnev stressed in his first speech in New Delhi: "It may be said without fear of exaggeration that the Soviet people and their leaders are friends India can rely upon. Friends in good times and in hard times, in clear weather and in bad weather."[1]

Welcoming Brezhnev upon his arrival was a familiar partner in these periodic demonstrations of state-to-state friendship, Indira Gandhi, prime minister again after a hiatus of almost three years. Mrs. Gandhi, Brezhnev's hostess on his previous visit, had made three formal visits to Moscow. Brezhnev's words might thus have rung familiar, since they echoed a statement he had made when she was welcomed to the USSR on her last visit there, in June 1976: "In this connection may I repeat again: the Soviet Union has been and remains a reliable friend of India and the Indian people."[2] Prime Minister Gandhi was widely perceived as a special friend of Moscow, but the expressions of India's trust and confidence in the relationship of these two powers were not the product of a particular individual's preferences. Indeed, the Janata Party government of Morarji Desai, which had held power in New Delhi during the closing years of the 1970s, had disappointed some observers who had expected that Mrs. Gandhi's departure would produce a distinct reorientation of India's diplomatic, economic, and military ties away from the USSR. Atal Bihari Vajpayee, the Janata government's foreign minister and prominent politician from the right wing of India's political spectrum, had seemed no less ardent than his Congress Party predecessors when, in welcoming a Soviet parliamentary delegation in April 1978, he used the very phrase of which Brezhnev was so fond: through various trials and tests, Vajpayee said, "our country always found the only reliable friend in the Soviet Union alone."[3]

On occasions too numerous to detail here, both Soviet and Indian leaders have cited the stability of their friendship as the key to the maintenance of peace in the region. And as they are at pains to repeat, the notion of reliability is central in their perception of the relationship. Both India and the Soviet Union have worked carefully since the early 1970s to foster this perception of reliability. The two states calculate that their objectives are best served if regional and global rivals are led to conclude that New Delhi and Moscow can count on each other's support, without fear of abandonment or betrayal.

An examination of the record shows that neither side has trusted in their formal ties alone—including most prominently the 1971 treaty of peace, friendship, and cooperation—as the sure guarantors of a durable relationship. Diplomats in both capitals have recognized that such treaties cannot endure if either partner loses its sensitivity to the other's needs or ceases to work at limiting the damage that results from inevitable differences. As we shall see, the Soviet leaders, in particular, aware of the shambles that had been made of similar treaties concluded with Egypt and Somalia, have shown in their dealings with India that they know the value of continued efforts to cultivate a reputation as a reliable friend.

The preservation of a stable bilateral relationship is not seen in New Delhi or Moscow as an end in itself, but as the means by which each side is able to promote its own particular foreign policy objectives. It is important to examine these objectives, as they might be inferred on the basis of each state's pronouncements and behaviors in recent years, so that in understanding the extent to which they converge and differ, we might anticipate the points at which either compatibility or strain might be expected.

The most important Soviet objective in South Asia, pursued ardently for most of the period since the early 1960s and likely to persist for the foreseeable future, is the enlisting of Indian participation as a counterweight to China in the Asian "balance of power" game. Attainment of this objective requires exclusion of Chinese influence from India and Bangladesh, and minimization of Chinese influence in Pakistan. Thus, Moscow's friendly posture toward the Indians has had to be balanced by the maintenance and even strengthening of its ties with Pakistan and Bangladesh. Given traditional Indo-Pakistani enmity, this has required a delicate balancing act, generally guided by the calculation that efforts to stabilize the situation in the subcontinent best promote Soviet security. From the Soviet viewpoint, India's role in this enterprise of deterring Chinese military action and containing Chinese influence in South Asia is furthered by its visible partnership with the USSR in "collective security" efforts. The greater the public Indian enlistment in this anti-China campaign, the more confident Moscow can be of the permanence of the hostility between New Delhi and Beijing.

Though China is at present viewed by the Soviets as the greatest threat to their security, Moscow has a second major adversary in Asia—the United States—and India's participation is also sought in the limitation of American presence and influence in the region. Thus, the Soviets encourage New Delhi to take diplomatic and commercial decisions that help to lessen American and Western influence, just as they seek India's support and practical assistance in projecting their own capabilities, particularly in the key areas of the Indian Ocean and Persian Gulf.

A third Soviet objective is to encourage the Indian government, as a leader in the Third World, to take positions on international issues as close as possible to those of the Soviet Union. In both its public pronouncements and its behavior in international bodies, India's support is sought by the USSR. For Moscow, the image of a Soviet-Indian identity of views is valued both for its impact in Washington and Beijing and for its influence on the rest of the Third World.

Their Marxist convictions lead the Soviets to believe that India's reliable friendship can best be ensured if its domestic politics and policies reflect an orientation in the direction of a socialist economy (the "noncapitalist path") and a "progressive" polity (the "national-democratic state"). Not since the early years of Khrushchev's leadership have the Soviets viewed the creation of a Communist government in India as a realizable near-term objective; in recent years, in fact, they have demonstrated their awareness that such a development may create more problems than it would solve. After working rather contentedly with Mrs. Gandhi's "national bourgeois" government for many years, the Soviet leaders shuddered at her defeat in the 1977 elections. Nevertheless, they soon showed their willingness to cooperate with a Janata Party they had labeled reactionary, so long as it continued a foreign policy acceptable to Moscow.

As intermediate goals that help in the pursuit of the aforementioned objectives, the Soviets have sought to build strong and lasting commercial ties with India—both as a way of weakening the fabric of "imperialist" economies and as a useful partner for their own economy—and, through propaganda and cultural exchange, to create attitudes among the Indian elite and masses that are favorable to the USSR. Instrumental in the creation of such attitudes is the fostering of a sense of need among the Indians, a feeling that continued Soviet support and assistance are vital to the realization of India's objectives.

In the area of security and regional alignments, there appear to be, for the present at least, certain parallels in Indian and Soviet objectives. But there are also certain incompatibilities that raise doubts that the Indo-Soviet relationship will be either permanent or free of tension. Thus, we would expect that the Indians would desire more balance in their relations with the "great-power triangle" than the Soviets would like, and that the Soviets would hope to maintain more balance in their own relations in the subcontinent than the Indians would like.

In this arena there is the greatest likelihood that one side's actions might arouse suspicions and feelings of betrayal in the other. For example, we would expect to find some Indian resentment of the Soviet Union's attempts to strengthen its influence in Pakistan and Bangladesh, and Soviet nervousness over Indian efforts to improve relations with Beijing and Washington. We would expect that the Indians would be suspicious of Soviet-American dealings that appear to be aimed toward a superpower condominium, and specifically that New Delhi would take a different position on superpower activities in the Indian Ocean than would Moscow. We would also expect a more generalized tension arising from India's desires to maximize its freedom of action, minimize its dependence, and build up self-sufficiency in the security field, in contrast with Moscow's desires to construct a reliable anti-China security system in Asia, and its opposition to further proliferation of nuclear weapons.

With respect to Soviet and Indian positions on other international issues, there is also a large degree of parallelism, most prominently in the area of opposition to colonial and neocolonial activities in the Third World. But the Indians clearly wish to avoid the appearance of following the Soviet lead; rather, New Delhi wants to stake out its own positions, which, in the case of North-South issues, may well put an antisuperpower gloss on the issue.

In commercial relations it is not surprising that both sides perceive continuing benefits in their strengthened trade ties. The Indians, however, are pressing for Moscow to purchase more Indian manufactured goods and to make available more raw materials and nonproject assistance than the Soviets would like. And finally, with respect to India's internal development and political processes, the two sides' objectives are sufficiently different that it is not unexpected to find some tension resulting from Soviet propaganda and from efforts to create in India lobbies that pressure the Indian government to move in a more "progressive" direction.

Although the compatibility of some of their objectives might in itself provide a basis for Soviet-Indian friendship and cooperation, this is not a sufficient foundation on which to build a friendship that can endure "in clear weather and in bad weather." Far more important in motivating the two states to form a "reliable friendship" is the existence on each side of a sense of dependence upon or need for the other. A country that needs something from another is more vulnerable to its exercise of influence—more likely to change (or sustain) its behavior in a direction that it would not have taken had the other state not desired it—and thus more predictably cooperative and loyal.[4] It is important to assess the degree to which India and the USSR perceive themselves to be dependent upon each other.

In the military sphere, India relies both upon Soviet assistance in the event of an attack from Pakistan and China, and upon the military equipment that Moscow has proved willing to supply. The effect of the long-standing American arms embargo on the subcontinent—extending from 1965 to 1975, with a "one time exception" in 1970—was compounded by the apparent U.S. decision (as manifested in 1971) to abstain from pledging assistance to India in the event it became embroiled in hostilities with China. In these circumstances, India's need for Soviet help became even greater. In fact, there have been occasional indications that India is willing to accede to certain otherwise undesirable aspects of its relationship with Moscow in order not to jeopardize its source of reliable military assistance.

But there are definite limits to India's defense needs from the Soviet Union. The vow of Soviet support in the event of attack has already been formalized and proclaimed through the 1971 Indo-Soviet treaty. In the wake of India's victory in the December war and the breakup of Pakistan, which not only demonstrated its military superiority on the subcontinent but also substantially reduced the immediate threat to its security, India's sense of need has greatly lessened.

India's dependence upon the Soviets for supply of arms is also limited, to the extent that the end of the U.S. embargo (announced in February 1975) and greater availability of foreign exchange now make arms from the West more accessible, and to the degree that it succeeds in achieving self-sufficiency in domestic production of military equipment at the earliest possible date. Economically, India continues to rely upon external assistance. Its available foreign exchange resources remain limited even though they have expanded in recent years, due largely to remittances from Indians working in the Persian Gulf countries. A large portion of India's trade has been reoriented toward the Soviet Union and the CMEA bloc, and India will continue to require the imports that it can currently acquire from Communist sources without the expenditure of foreign exchange. It has incurred a massive debt with the Soviets, the repayment of which (expected to reach an annual rate of $325 million by 1980) will require a continued flow of exports to the USSR for many years to come.

Here again, however, there is evidence of a limitation on India's perception of the need for the Soviets. In the mid-1970s, Mrs. Gandhi flatly and publicly denied that India planned to join the Soviet trading bloc. Government trading representatives have in recent years sought to expand India's commercial relations with the Common Market, in recognition of India's inability to satisfy its needs through trade with Eastern Europe. There are also obvious limitations to the Soviets' willingness or ability to greatly expand their commercial and aid relationship with India. The Soviets have proved quite unwilling to adjust certain prices to India's liking or to supply certain raw materials that New Delhi requires.

In the political-diplomatic sphere, although India has occasionally relied upon a Soviet veto in the Security Council to protect its interests, and although it enjoys certain leverage and status in dealings with the West and the nonaligned world by virtue of its relationship with Moscow, the limits of dependence are even more evident. India's determination to retain independence of action and to preserve nonaligned credentials underlines a sensitivity to political dependence and a desire to maintain a balanced relationship with outside powers while not undermining its beneficial ties with the Soviets.

Even though this attitude had become increasingly evident in the final years of Mrs. Gandhi's first period in office, it was more forcefully articulated by the successor Janata administration. Within an hour of assuming office, Prime Minister Desai declared: "The foreign policy of nonalignment should be fully nonaligned, with no suspicion of alignment with anybody."[5] In contrast with Mrs. Gandhi, who often spoke of India's "special relationship" to the USSR, Desai insisted that "we won't have special relationships with other countries."[6] A few months later, Foreign Minister Vajpayee put it more bluntly: "Mrs. Gandhi committed the blunder of making India too much dependent on Soviet Russia. But now . . . a new chapter has opened."[7]

In its attempt to create favorable attitudes among the Indian people and to direct pressure upon the Indian government from internal sources, the Soviet Union has built up a large propaganda effort. One analyst has estimated that 1 million words per month flow from the Information Department of the Soviet embassy in New Delhi.[8] Periodicals and other publications distributed by Communist missions in India had a combined yearly total circulation in 1972 in excess of 23 million. Over two score journals are distributed by the Soviet embassy, compared with less than half that number published by the U.S. government. In addition, indigenous Communist and pro-Communist newspapers and periodicals taking a pro-Soviet line (many directly or indirectly subsidized by the Soviets) have a circulation of well over 10 million. Radio Moscow and Radio Peace and Progress have in recent years broadcast to India over 125 hours per week.

In the allied area of cultural activity, powerful assistance to the official Soviet effort is given by the Indo-Soviet Cultural Society, which has over 800 branches and 100,000 members in India. Through these and other auspices, numerous nonofficial exchanges are conducted; for example, in 1971–72 a total of 18 Indian delegations traveled to the Soviet Union and 23 Soviet delegations toured India.

A significant role in this sphere is played by the Communist Party of India, which voices an undeviating pro-Soviet line. In addition, there are about a dozen Indian branches of international Communist front organizations, all of which contribute to the propaganda effort and serve as pro-Soviet lobbies on the internal Indian political scene. The combined effect of all this activity is a substantial aggregate influence on public opinion.

In light of this impressive array of capabilities that the Soviets are able to bring to bear in the pursuit of their objectives in India, it is worth reiterating that the skill with which these resources are applied can be an important, and even a decisive, factor in determining the degree of Soviet influence. Apparent advantages brought about by the sheer quantity of resources can be canceled by the ostentatious display of these resources or by a heavy-handed exercise in arm twisting. Talent also is required in the proper matching of capabilities and objectives. Although the Soviets have in general been sufficiently cautious not to arouse Indian sensitivities, the record of recent years contains instances in which Soviet capabilities have been nullified by a clumsy approach.

A revealing study of the limits to the Soviet impact on the thinking and behavior of the Indian elite was published in 1973 by Canadian political scientist Stephen Clarkson.[9] Based on interviews with 100 Indian officials, journalists, scholars, and businessmen conducted during March and April 1972, Clarkson's article concluded that "neither in theory nor in practice have the Soviets had any noticeable impact on the Indian elite's ways of thinking or acting in governmental affairs." This conclusion he found surprising, in view of his expectation that there would be considerable Soviet intellectual and policy influence on the Indian elite, given the correspondence between Soviet doctrine and the views of the bulk of Indian intellectuals concerning the importance of national economic independence, the imperialism of American foreign policy, and the need for state control of the private sector.

Instead Clarkson found warm and even enthusiastic attitudes toward Soviet foreign policy existing side by side with great distrust of the political bias of Soviet scholars and the low quality of Soviet writing on these subjects. As he put it, the attitudes of those Indian intellectuals who could a priori be expected to be most familiar with Soviet thinking "can best be presented in three dimensions: little information, low credibility, and poor personal contact." Even among Communist Party intellectuals he found only "weak" Soviet scholarly influence. Few Indians speak Russian, and the preponderance of Soviet books in English available in India are technical and scientific texts rather than works on political economy.

In sum, Clarkson found no evidence at all of any policy spin-off from the excellent economic and diplomatic relations between Moscow and New Delhi. Among the elite there was both great friendliness and underlying distrust. Thus, though attitudes toward the Soviet Union as an international power "are warm and friendly, attitudes toward the Soviet system and ideology are hostile and suspicious."

The regular surveys by the Indian Institute of Public Opinion of public attitudes toward the Soviet Union and the United States enable us to assess the trends in popular responsiveness to these countries. The institute's survey is conducted among 1,000 literate adults, randomly selected from the election lists and evenly distributed among the four largest cities of India: Bombay, Calcutta, New Delhi, and Madras.[10] An examination of recent surveys shows that Indian opinion of the Soviet Union shortly after the 1971 war surpassed the previous post-Tashkent high, while opinion of the United States had sharply declined. (In April 1972, the weighted score of the United States was even lower than that of the People's Republic of China.) A year later, while American popularity had risen sharply, Soviet popularity, slipping slightly, continued to be quite high.

The opinion rating of the United States declined again in the spring of 1975, following Washington's announcement of readiness to resume arms sales to the subcontinent. But a year and a half later, the opinion of the United States had improved markedly, returning to pre-1971 levels. And in the August 1977 survey, with the Janata government's return to true nonalignment, the end of the Indochina war, and the accession of a Democratic administration in Washington, the United States outscored the Soviet Union in the survey for the first time in over a decade. However, this did not signal a growth in negative opinion toward the USSR; of those surveyed, 77 percent found Indo-Soviet relations "satisfactory," and 60 percent (compared with 57 percent for the United States) agreed that the "basic interests" of the two countries were in agreement.

The fluctuations could be attributed to international activity, especially as it relates to the subcontinent, of the two superpowers and to the perceived health of bilateral relations; there does not seem to be any correlation between the volume of propaganda activity within India and the public attitude toward either country. What the surveys do not tell us is the precise effect of public attitudes upon the behavior of the Indian governments—that is, whether the favorable opinion of the Soviet Union is passively permissive in nature or whether it can be translated more directly into acutal public pressure in favor of a particular foreign policy stance. At the very least, however, we may conclude that Indian public opinion does not stand as an obstacle to the achievement of Soviet influence in India.

SINO–INDIAN RELATIONS: SOVIET REACTION

Ironically, much of the Soviet Union's effort to woo Indian opinion reveals a certain degree of Soviet need for Indian support. India's position as the strongest power in South Asia and the only other mainland Asian power that can act as a counterweight to China creates a lasting Soviet need for Indian support in its effort to contain China. If India were to become hostile or indifferent to the Soviets, Moscow would be left with no major ally in the area. If New Delhi's strained relationship with the United States and China can be judged less irreparable than Moscow's conflict with Beijing, then it would appear that India has greater flexibility in its external ties than does the Soviet Union, and that it may be less "reliable" for Moscow than Moscow is for New Delhi.

The importance of China in shaping Soviet perceptions of India has been sharply underscored in recent years. Sino-Indian relations had been exacerbated in 1974 and 1975 by India's nuclear testing, its annexation of Sikkim, and China's growing influence in Bangladesh following the coup that removed Sheikh Mujibur Rahman. In the summer and fall of 1975, there were reports, ostentatiously reprinted in the Soviet press, of incidents on the Sino-Indian border.

In 1976, however, relations between Beijing and New Delhi showed signs of thaw, as the Chinese began to pursue a more active diplomacy. In January, China suggested that Sino-Indian diplomatic relations be upgraded, and within six months an Indian ambassador had been dispatched to Beijing, ending a 14-year break. Just prior to the ambassador's arrival. Mrs. Gandhi was in Moscow, and though the communiqué was silent on the question of China, the Indian prime misiter told a press conference in the Soviet capital that "when we discuss the international situation we cannot leave out a country like China, but India's decision to send an ambassador to China will not stand in the way of Indian-Soviet friendship."[11]

The movement toward normalization appeared to quicken with the accession of the Janata government. Foreign Minister Vajpayee told an interviewer in October 1977 that "we are willing to take such steps as are necessary to further the process of normalization." Acknowledging that the border dispute would not be easily solved, he stated that the best course would be to "keep it frozen" for the time being, seek other avenues for establishing trust, and, once the general climate had improved, return to "more serious problems." Although it was probably of little comfort to listeners in Moscow, Vajpayee took pains to state that normalization between India and China should not be at the cost of India's friendship with any country.[12]

Prime Minister Desai reportedly repeated these assurances to Brezhnev during a visit to the USSR later that month, but the Soviets nevertheless remained nervous. Their worries were doubtless heightened by Vice-Premier Deng Xiaoping's visits to Burma and Nepal early in 1978, during which he reiterated Beijing's hope for better relations with India. According to one report, other signs that China was seeking to curb Soviet influence in South Asia—including the expansion of trade ties with India, the dispatch of a delegation to New Delhi for a goodwill visit, and the issuance of an invitation to Vajpayee to visit Beijing—prompted Soviet embassy officials to make discreet inquiries of the government regarding the contemplated scope of Sino-Indian normalization.[13]

After one postponement, Vajpayee made his visit to Beijing in February 1979. Hoping to reopen negotiations on the border conflict, he claimed that the visit brought progress by helping to win China's assent to preservation of tranquillity along the Sino-Indian frontier. For its part, China was eager to display Vajpayee's visit as a sign of India's willingness to loosen its close ties with Moscow. But the cause of Sino-Indian rapprochement was not aided by China's choice of this moment to launch its punitive attack on Vietnam, nor by Deng Xiaoping's ill-advised reference to the attack as analogous to the 1962 border war with India.

China's seeming blunder and the early departure of Vajpayee came as a welcome relief to the Soviets in the face of their fears that New Delhi would drift toward neutrality in the Sino-Soviet conflict. Although these Soviet fears were clearly exaggerated, relief over the interruption in the Sino-Indian dialogue proved to be temporary. An Indian diplomat again traveled to Beijing in June 1980 for talks on the border issue. And although the Chinese angrily postponed a scheduled return visit of Foreign Minister Huang Hua, in the wake of India's recognition of the Heng Samrin regime in Kampuchea, Huang's visit finally took place in June 1981, much to Moscow's consternation. Huang publicly agreed to the opening of official talks on the border questions, but Soviet press commentaries sought to temper any Indian hopes that Sino-Indian relations might actually improve. Indeed, when the first round of border talks at Beijing in December 1981, and the second round at New Delhi in May 1981, adjourned without visible progress, the Soviets again displayed relief.

Further confirmation of the Soviet sense of need of India is available. Through their actions in the 1971 crisis, the Soviets made it clear that the preservation of their relationship with India was more important to them than their interest in seeking to prevent a potentially destabilizing war in the area. Earlier in the same year, the Soviets had demonstrated that their interest in preserving their ties with the Congress government overrode any potential benefit they might have seen in the victory of an anti-Congress coalition in the India parliamentary elections; the Soviets were not interested in change in India if this would bring uncertainty and instability. Brezhnev's direct praise of the Congress Party and its program during his November 1973 speech at the Red Fort in Delhi amounted to Soviet certification of the progressive credentials of Mrs. Gandhi's government. This endorsement further diminished the ability of the Communist Party of India to criticize the ruling party's policies as insufficiently radical. Brezhnev's statement left some Indian observers concluding that the Soviet stake in Mrs. Gandhi's Congress Party had heightened, making the Communist Party a redundant appendage in Indian politics.[14]

The 1975 political crisis in India, culminating in Mrs. Gandhi's proclamation of emergency rule in June, was initially welcomed by the Soviets for its seeming reversal of a mounting reactionary tide. But the period of the emergency freed Mrs. Gandhi of any parliamentary dependence on the Communist Party, and the harsh restrictions on political freedom limited the capabilities of the Communists as well as other parties. But Moscow saw no viable alternative to the Congress Party, viewing the opposition Janata Party as "the direct tool of extreme reaction . . . and the defender of the interests of landowners, usurers, and the local foreign monopolies." Its foreign policy platform was characterized as opposed to India's traditions, as well as to "such achievements as India's friendship and cooperation" with the USSR.[15]

Soviet fears of a sharp reversal in Indian foreign policy, in the wake of Mrs. Gandhi's surprising defeat in the 1977 elections, were soon allayed. The warm sentiments expressed by Foreign Minister Gromyko on his first visit with the new government in April 1977—that friendly Indo-Soviet relations "are not the result of transitory circumstances of expediency"—were reciprocated by the Indian leadership.[16] The Soviet press, elatedly hailing the "important political results" of Gromyko's trip, showed its relief that "the high hopes of the imperialist forces that Soviet-Indian relations would deteriorate were not justified."[17] Although their worst fears were not realized, Soviet commentators nevertheless continued to assume a cautious, even nervous, stance toward the Desai regime, regarding it as a far less reliable ally than its predecessor.[18]

BALANCE OF INFLUENCE: SOVIET ASSISTANCE AND INDIAN SUPPORT

In the record of Indo-Soviet relations since the early 1970s, there are many instances in which each side has demonstrated to the other (and to the world) the steadfastness of its commitment and its willingness to cooperate. Examples abound of "fair weather friendship," when cooperation is relatively painless or mutually beneficial. But of greater interest in documenting the existence of a particularly firm bond of friendship are occasions on which giving support to one's partner is done only at significant cost to one's own resources or interests.

In the context of India's security problem, one valuable resource the Soviets command is the ability to pledge their assistance in the event of an attack on India. The usefulness of this promise is, of course, as great in its deterrence value as in the case of actual hostilities.

Though lacking in specificity and not of a binding nature, such pledges of support could be highly valued by the Indians in the face of the prospect of a joint attack from Pakistan and China. Fearing such a contingency in the summer of 1971—compounded by an American message of nonsupport in the case of Sino-Indian hostilities—the Indians and Soviets agreed to make a public declaration of Moscow's support. The Indian government's perceived sense of need of the Soviets was clearly high at this point, and the Soviets were seeking to utilize this in their effort to encourage New Delhi not to take action that might precipitate military conflict on the subcontinent. The objectives of both sides were thus served by the conclusion of the Indo-Soviet treaty in August 1971.

For the Indians, the pressures of the civil war in Pakistan, and consequent refugee flood into India, were catalytic in reviving the idea of a treaty, discussions about which had actually begun two years before. Another important factor in the calculations of both sides was the revelation by

President Nixon in July that presidential adviser Henry Kissinger had traveled to Beijing to arrange a visit by Nixon in 1972. A detail of special interest to the Indians was Pakistan's role in facilitating Kissinger's secret journey. Thus, with the cooperation of India's sworn enemy, the American president was making overtures for a new relationship with China, India's second major antagonist in Asia.

In its two wars in the 1960s, India had enjoyed first the support and assistance of the United States against China, and then its strict neutrality in the 1965 war with Pakistan. As India faced the prospect of another round with Pakistan—supported by China—in 1971, could it even count on American neutrality? Indeed, reports were circulating that Kissinger had warned Mrs. Gandhi in the summer of 1971 that China might not remain aloof from a war in the subcontinent, and that the United States might not give New Delhi its support as it had in the Sino-Indian war of 1962.[19] In this context, the public promise of Soviet support was particularly welcome in India.

The Soviets, no less concerned over the prospect of a Sino-American rapprochement, saw India's dilemma as an opportunity both to gain influence in New Delhi and to deter another enervating conflict in the subcontinent. A large-scale Indo-Pakistani war could only intensify the drain on India's resources, thus likely wasting not only the Soviet economic investment in India but substantial Soviet arms investments as well.

The actual obligations the Soviets incurred from the treaty were minimal. Apart from pledges to strengthen economic, scientific, and cultural cooperation, and to continue regular contacts on international problems, each party to the treaty promised not to enter into any alliance or commit any aggression against the other (Article 8); not to undertake any commitment incompatible with the treaty (Article 10); and, in the event of an attack or threat directed toward either by a third party, immediately to start mutual consultations with a view to eliminating this threat (Article 9).

From the Soviet point of view, the treaty's main purpose was to formalize and extend Russian influence for the immediate end of stabilizing the situation in South Asia, both by deterring the Pakistanis and their Chinese patrons and by providing a psychological crutch for the Indians, designed to forestall an emotional drift toward early recognition of Bangladesh, and consequent war, on the part of New Delhi. Technically, the Soviets were under no greater obligation to give material assistance to India in case of attack than they had been prior to the treaty's signing. India, on the other hand, while not denying itself the option of unilateral military action against Pakistan, had solemnly declared its intention to consult the Soviets in the event of any threatened attack, thus formalizing and displaying for the benefit of third parties the strong Soviet interest in subcontinent affairs.

The official Indian view of the advantages brought by the treaty stressed not only the deterrence of hostile powers through Soviet support but also a gain in India's credibility and flexibility in the world. Soviet support of India's positions on Bangladesh and Kashmir was said to be assured, and Article 10 was read in New Delhi as prohibiting further Soviet supply of arms to Pakistan.

When war came in December, the Soviet provision of military and diplomatic support to India proved of great value. In the latter sphere, Ambassador Yakov Malik used his vetoes in the Security Council to block cease-fire resolutions while the Indians completed their military operations in East Pakistan. The Soviet position in the aftermath of the December war was anomalous. Though the Soviets had failed to bring about the removal of the refugee burden from India by peaceful means, they had at least played a major role in India's victory, while their American and Chinese rivals had both lined up on the side of the loser.

They might well have expected India's gratitude to produce even greater Soviet influence in New Delhi. But, as Mrs. Gandhi has said, "one of our faults is that we are unable to display gratitude in any tangible sense for anything."[20] Ironically, the Soviets, by helping India to eliminate an effective military threat from its main antagonist for nearly a quarter of a century, had thereby reduced India's need of the Soviets and, perhaps, its chances of enlarging the Soviet potential for influence. A militarily stronger and more confident India would therefore prove to be a mixed blessing for Moscow.

On the other hand, although the Soviets set about attempting to rebuild their relations with Pakistan so as not to leave it to the blandishments of Washington and Beijing, the Soviet Union now needed India more than ever, for it had become an even more valuable asset in the effort to outflank China. In addition, the Soviets were likely to be faced with a greater burden of both military and economic aid in an area in which prospects for stability had by no means been enhanced. But there seemed to be no alternative open to the Soviet Union except to shoulder the greater burden as the price of the hoped-for greater influence, for the maintenance of this influence still seemed to require that the Soviets seek stability in South Asia.

The ability of the Soviet Union to supply advanced weapons and training in their use to the Indian military, as well as to assist India in the development of its domestic defense industry, is an important pledge of Moscow's friendship. The value of the Soviet supply relationship, which amounted to $3.6 billion at the end of 1977 and was enlarged with a new $1.6 billion deal in 1980, is heightened by the fact that the United States, at least until the lifting of the arms embargo, had refused to act as an alternative supplier to the Indians. As Prime Minister Desai expressed it in an interview given to an American periodical, "If we buy more from the Soviet Union, it is the fault of the Western countries for not selling to us."[21]

For a period of several years, then, the Soviet Union has been the major supplier of weapons to India, providing roughly four-fifths of New Delhi's total military imports since 1965. Important to the Indians is the fact that these arms are purchased without the direct expenditure of foreign exchange; rather, they are paid for with Indian exports through the Soviets' rupee account. On most purchases, 10 percent down payment is required, with the balance covered by nine- or ten-year credits at 2 percent interest.

Moscow's reliability as a supplier of military equipment is matched by its importance to India as a steady source of economic assistance and trade. Between 1950–51 and 1971–72, India's trade with the USSR and Communist Eastern Europe rose from 0.5 percent to 20 percent of its total exports, and from a negligible amount to 11 percent of its imports. Although the volume of Soviet-Indian trade continued to rise in the 1970s, the relative weight of Soviet imports and exports in the total Indian trade picture fell from the peak years of the late 1960s and early 1970s. Although some instances of friction have accompanied this decline, it is still clear that Soviet trade is important to India both in drastically reducing its economic dependence on the West and in allowing it to make important purchases without the expenditure of scarce foreign currency.

Prior to 1977, when a new $340 million Soviet credit was announced, the total amount of Soviet economic aid to India since 1954 had been $1.943 billion in credits. Of this amount, over $450 million had not been drawn by the end of 1976. The decline in India's aid drawdowns, and consequently in Indian imports of Soviet products, is largely a result of Moscow's reluctance to shift away from the traditional pattern of public-sector project aid, involving primarily credits for heavy industrial equipment, and toward nonproject aid and the provision of raw materials—both of which are increasingly desired by the Indians as their own industrial capacity expands. Nevertheless, the undeniable fact is that Soviet aid and trade have been an important element in India's economy, thus making the Soviet Union's reliability more important as a source of economic cooperation.

Especially timely and valuable signs of Moscow's devotion were several Soviet actions designed to relieve India's burdens in the arena of energy resources. During the energy crisis of 1974, the USSR agreed to deliver to India 1 million tons of kerosene and 100,000 tons of diesel fuel. More important, the Soviets agreed in December 1976 to a long-term pertroleum supply relationship with India that, for the first time, obligated Moscow to supply New Delhi with crude oil on a barter basis. The four-year trade protocol called for the Russians to deliver 5.5 million metric tons of crude oil in return for Indian pig iron. The foreign exchange savings for India—and the consequent loss of hard currency earnings for the USSR—were indeed significant.[22]

In 1979, Soviet assistance was again critical in alleviating a serious shortfall in India's crude oil imports in the wake of the Iranian revolution.

During Premier Kosygin's March 1979 visit the Russians announced that an additional 600,000 tons of Soviet crude oil would be bartered that year for Indian rice (which Moscow reportedly planned to send to Vietnam). And in the course of Brezhnev's 1980 visit, agreements were signed that called for generous Soviet assistance to India in the fields of coal mining, oil exploration and refining, and power plant construction.[23]

One other agreement, also announced at the time of the 1976 oil deal, was in the politically sensitive area of nuclear fuel supplies. Prior to India's detonation of a nuclear explosion in May 1974, the United States and Canada had served as its sources of supply for heavy water and enriched uranium. But these sources were at least temporarily cut off by the adverse Canadian and American reactions to India's nuclear test, and as 1976 drew to a close, the Indians badly needed a supply of heavy water to recharge their reactor in Rajasthan. It was announced in December that the USSR had agreed to sell India 240 tons of heavy water, 25 percent of which would be shipped immediately, subject only to an Indian pledge that it would not be used in the production of plutonium for explosive devices.

The Soviet sale was seen in the West as a departure from Moscow's rigid nonproliferation stance, for there was no indication that the Indians would be required to agree to international safeguards on all their nuclear reactors. New Delhi had previously refused to do this in its dealings with North American suppliers. The Soviet Union, however, apparently did try to avoid diluting its nonproliferation principles for the prospect of a political gain in New Delhi, and it sought to apply its influence in a case where India's need to achieve a modification of the Indian position was strong.

In the end, however, the Soviets apparently had to compromise, managing to win Indian assent only to safeguards that were limited to the time and place that the Soviet heavy water was actually used. That the Indians refused to accept the original Soviet conditions, even in the face of Moscow's strong interest in effective safeguards and its heavy pressure on New Delhi, is an instructive illustration of the current "balance of influence" in the relationship, as well as an indication of the extent to which the Soviets are willing to go to demonstrate their commitment to India.[24]

Lacking great wealth and material resources, the Indians can best demonstrate their loyalty and friendship to the Soviet Union by giving Moscow less tangible assistance: diplomatic support for key Soviet actions or initiatives. On some occasions, this has taken the form not of praise and backing for Soviet behavior, but of silence and abstention from criticism at a time when the USSR is being widely attacked for its actions. To look at the most dramatic examples, on each of the three occasions since the mid-1950s when the Soviet Union had invaded a neighboring country, India has responded with its own peculiar blend of an expression of regret and a refusal to join in international condemnation of the Soviet actions. Although the Soviet Union would undoubtedly have preferred active support of its actions, it has shown that it recognizes India's refusals to condemn the Soviet invasions as friendly gestures.

In 1956, even though Indian leaders gave an estimate of the Soviet attack on Hungary that differed from that of the socialist camp, they still failed to support the Western position. Indeed, V. K. Krishna Menon's was one of only two non-Communist votes in the United Nations against the resolution calling for free elections in Hungary; he had earlier abstained on the U.S.-sponsored resolution calling for a withdrawal of Soviet forces. Preoccupied at the time with the Suez question, India seemed to prefer to take its stand on clear-cut cases of "imperialist aggression" against non-Western countries and to sit on the sidelines when Soviet aggression in Eastern Europe was at issue.

Perhaps the clearest example of an Indian statement framed with an eye toward its possible effect in Moscow occurred in 1968, at the time of the Soviet invasion of Czechoslovakia. And yet the Indian statement, while couched in milder terms than the United States would have liked, could have been phrased in a way that would have pleased the Soviets even more. Mrs. Gandhi's apparent compromise was to issue a statement that viewed the events in Prague with a "heavy heart" and "profound concern and anguish." Her statement explicitly took note of India's "close and many-sided" relations with Moscow, which New Delhi wished to "preserve and extend."[25] The Indian government instructed its delegate to abstain on the Security Council resolution that sought to condemn the Soviet action. This behavior, which caused an uproar in the Indian Parliament, clearly demonstrated India's unwillingness in 1968 to jeopardize its relations with the Soviet Union.

In reacting to a Soviet military intervention that occurred much closer to home—the December 1979 invasion of Afghanistan—the Indian government concocted a similar blend: public statements of regret and concern balanced by polite acknowledgments of the Soviet version of events and adamant refusal to be drawn into international condemnations of the Soviet action. On the eve of the 1980 elections, Mrs. Gandhi issued a statement on the Soviet invasion: "I am strongly against any interference. But in Afghanistan, the Soviet interference is not one-sided. Other interferences were going on there."[26] Abstaining from the U.N. vote condemning the Soviet action, the Indian representatives said that "we have no reason to doubt assurances, particularly from a friendly country like the Soviet Union" that Russian troops had intervened in Afghanistan at the request of the government there.[27] Privately, the Indians have told the Soviets on many occasions that they would prefer that Soviet troops be withdrawn from Afghanistan. But they have not publicly disputed the Soviet line that

Moscow was "provoked" to protect its interests when anti-Soviet rebels in Afghanistan received aid from Pakistan, China, and the U.S. Central Intelligence Agency.[28]

Joint declarations issued on the occasions of visits to Moscow by the India president and foreign minister in 1980 signaled the inability of the two countries to agree on a common position on Afghanistan by simply omitting any mention of the issue.[29] Similarly, there was no direct reference to Afghanistan in the joint declaration that was issued in December, following the visit to India of Soviet President Brezhnev. There was, however, a paragraph dealing with Southwest Asia, which said that "India and the Soviet Union reiterate their opposition to all forms of outside interference in the internal affairs of the countries in that region." Both sides, it says, "are confident that a negotiated political solution alone can guarantee a durable settlement of the existing problems of the region."[30] This formula was consistent with the public positions of both sides, yet committed neither one to endorsement of the other's views on the specific question of how the crisis is to be resolved. In any case, India's cool and reserved statements on the issue have been publicly appreciated as "sober" and "realistic" by the Soviets, who are undoubtedly pleased to have at least one large non-Communist country abstain from the noisy condemnation of their Afghan adventure.

SOVIET–INDIAN DISAGREEMENTS

On some other occasions, when the Indians have adopted positions or taken actions in support of Soviet objectives, they have done so in a context that has lessened some of the potential satisfaction that such support might have given to their Soviet friends. For example, in 1970, after much apparent urging from members of the socialist bloc, India took actions that constituted recognition of regimes whose legitimacy Moscow was hard-pressed to establish. Within a two-week period, the government of India announced the impending official visit to New Delhi of Madame Binh, foreign minister of the Vietcong government, and the establishment of consular-level relations with the German Democratic Republic. These actions were taken in the wake of the dismissal by Mrs. Gandhi of her pro-Soviet foreign minister, Dinesh Singh, almost as if their chief purpose were to soften the blow for Moscow of this important cabinet change.[31]

In similar fashion, India's recognition in July 1980 of the regime of Heng Samrin, Vietnam's puppet in Kampuchea, took place some 16 months after Premier Kosygin had, during a visit to New Delhi, urged that the action be taken. It was not coincidental that Mrs. Gandhi's decision to extend recognition was taken in the wake of the announcement that Chinese

Foreign Minister Huang Hua would visit India at the end of 1980. By this timing, the Indians accomplished the dual purpose of giving a nod to the Soviets at a time when their concern would be aroused, while taking a slap at the Chinese at a time when they might have interpreted India's invitation as a concession and a sign of weakness.

India's gestures toward the Soviet Union thus have not brought unalloyed happiness in Moscow; often, they have seemed less than the gifts of a "reliable friend." And yet it is a sign of Moscow's sense of need that it has seemed to seize upon India's actions as a sort of victory for the forces of peace and progress. A press commentary on Soviet-Indian relations published in Moscow in October 1980 said:

> Its sober approach to the Afghan events and recent official recognition of the People's Republic of Kampuchea are but two instances of the peaceableness, common sense, and realism distinguishing the policy followed by Indira Gandhi's government.[32]

A later comment suggested that Moscow's appreciation of the Indian actions might well have been enhanced by the grief that these acts had brought to Washington and Beijing: "U.S. imperialist circles and the Beijing hegemonists are enraged by Delhi's sensible, realistic stand on the question of Afghanistan and its official recognition of Kampuchea and its government headed by Heng Samrin."[33]

While there have been occasions on which Soviet actions in the subcontinent have occasioned shock or disappointment in New Delhi, these have been relatively few in recent years, in part because of the willingness of both sides to mask their disagreements. Certainly there has not since been a year as difficult for Indo-Soviet relations as 1968 was. India's disquiet over the Soviet invasion of Czechoslovakia pales in significance next to its alarm over the Soviet sale of military hardware to Pakistan. Coming on the heels of Pakistan's decision to close down the U.S. intelligence facility in Peshawar, the Soviet sale of armored personnel carriers, tanks, and artillery to Pakistan was part of an effort to wean Islamabad from its close ties to Washington and Beijing. The resulting protests from India were accompanied by riots at the Soviet embassy in New Delhi. The widespread disillusionment over India's alleged "special relationship" with the USSR included the introduction by a parliamentary opposition group of a motion calling for the censure of the government for its friendly policy toward the Soviet Union.

The Soviets hastened to reassure India that they had no intention of altering the military balance in the region. Characteristically, Mrs. Gandhi's response in Parliament was to express profound concern and misgivings about the Soviet deal while refusing to question the motives or good faith of the Soviet government. Her answer revealed a great deal about her expectations concerning "friendship" while indirectly revealing almost as much about India's own standards of behavior. Warning against complacency or a lack of realism, she noted that one could not reasonably expect a friendly country to "give up everything, even its own interest, for the sake of our friendship. . . . We must accept friendship as it is; it may be more, it may be less. I for one cannot understand the argument that trusting a country or believing in its friendship has done us harm."[34]

During the same year the Indians had reason to be disappointed by a Soviet action in the sphere of commercial relations. During a January 1968 visit, Premier Kosygin had promised that the Soviet Union would purchase all the rails and freight cars that India could produce over the next five years—though in fact Soviet railroads were built on a different scale. This pledge raised Indian hopes of boosting the production of some of their public-sector industries to a level closer to full capacity. A protocol was signed that called for 2,000 cars to be delivered in 1969, and up to 10,000 per year by 1973, with a total over the period of 26,000.

But the deal fell through after prolonged haggling between the two sides. The Soviets offered a price amounting to roughly half of India's production costs, and then stipulated in the specifications for the wheel assemblies the use of lead and zinc alloys available only from the USSR at a high price. The Russians reportedly even attempted to make their purchase of Indian freight cars conditional on India's purchase of Soviet commercial aircraft. After the deal collapsed, the Indians tried to convince Soviet negotiators of their obligation to buy other manufactured goods equivalent in price to the rejected freight cars. This argument, however, was apparently spurned by the Soviets.[35] The entire incident, especially when viewed in the context of the Pakistani arms deal, hardly enhanced the Soviet Union's reputation for reliability. It is worth noting, however, that although there have been subsequent Indo-Soviet disagreements in the commercial field, there apparently has been nothing in recent years to rival in scale this particular breach of promise.

Indeed, since the late 1970s the Indians have proved to be far more reluctant customers, and the Soviets far more ardent salesmen, than their relative economic standings might have suggested. Clearly, political attitudes play a role in this realm, and India's reluctance to conclude certain deals with the USSR stems at least in part from its calculation that overreliance on a single supplier or market can bring undue political dependence. One of the most pointed demonstrations of Indian dissatisfaction came in 1977, when the Indian government refused the offer of Soviet participation in construction of the second stage of the giant Bokaro steel complex, the first stage of which was built under Soviet auspices. The decision, announced a few days before Gromyko's arrival in April 1977, was officially couched by both New Delhi and Moscow in terms of India's achievement of a self-reliant position in steel production—until then the primary sector of Soviet-Indian economic collaboration. The main purpose of the 250 million-ruble credit announced during Gromyko's visit was thereby obviated, though the Russians offered it on terms more generous than previous credits and hastily agreed that it could be used for any other projects mutually agreed upon.

Subsequent press reports indicated that the Indians were actually seeking a better grade of technology than the Russians could supply. A Steel Ministry spokesman confirmed in August that the Soviets lacked the sophisticated technology necessary for completion of the Bokaro plant, and that two American firms had been approached for help on the project.[36] The Bokaro case could thus be seen as an instance of a more general Indian shift from Soviet to Western industrial technology. Other examples of this phenomenon include the replacement of Soviet designs for 200-megawatt power generators with West German designs (for generators with 1,000-megawatt capacity), the gradual displacement of Russian antibiotics by drugs based on Italian technology, and the replacement of Russian and Romanian oil-exploration experts and of Soviet oil rigs with Western ones. The share of the Indian market for machinery and equipment accounted for by Soviet imports fell from about three-fourths in 1968 to under one-fourth in 1977. The coming of age of Indian industry had necessitated a search for the best technology, which Moscow was only rarely able to supply. India was thereby becoming a far less reliable customer of Soviet export firms.[37]

Even in the sphere of arms merchandising, the Soviets have been unable to use their political sway to persuade the Indians not to deal with the competition. Just one example of India's greater disposition to shop for military supplies in the West came in 1977, when a press report indicated that it had decided to purchase the French Magic air combat missile for its air force rather than one offered by the Soviet Union. According to this report, India "will go in for the best equipment regardless of political considerations and the rupee trade account."[38]

A year later, it was announced that India would accept an Anglo-French offer to supply the Jaguar deep-penetration strike aircraft in preference to a competing offer from Moscow of an improved version of the MiG-23. At the same time that he announced this decision, the Indian defense minister revealed that India was negotiating with European manufacturers of submarines for the establishment of a submarine plant in India.[39]

What is illustrated by these examples is not merely the failure of Soviet influence in the critical realm of arms supply, but also the dogged Indian determination to avoid a relationship of dependence on the USSR and to achieve a position of military self-reliance. As Prime Minister Desai put it in an interview, in the context of a discussion of India's technological borrowing, "we must learn and then be independent again, not remain perpetually dependent on someone else."[40]

The Soviets used the occasion of Brezhnev's December 1980 visit to try to recapture some of the Indian market and reestablish the close economic and military relationship that had existed prior to Mrs. Gandhi's defeat. In addition to new Soviet commitments to the development of key public-sector industries, Indo-Soviet collaboration was announced in the manufacture of transport aircraft, and it was revealed that a contract was under discussion for the purchase and manufacture of advanced MiG-23s. As one Western account put it,

> [Brezhnev] . . . showered India with gifts and promises . . . as part of an obvious attempt to win back the country to the close relationship that existed until four years ago . . . [and to] check a drift toward economic collaboration with the West, not only on new projects but in the expansion of existing plants, some of which had been the exclusive preserve of the Soviet Union.[41]

In the spring of 1981, India found new impetus for its arms shopping after the Reagan administration announced its intention to sell a substantial quantity of modern weapons, including the F-16 fighter-bomber, to Pakistan. Although India had only recently made major arms purchases, it viewed the American arms agreement with Pakistan as provocative and destabilizing. Announcing that "a few" MiG-25 aircraft had been acquired, India visibly stepped up the pace of talks with both Soviet and Western arms merchants.[42]

The Soviets could scarcely contain their glee at this deterioration of Indian-American relations. The American arms deal with Pakistan, together with the Reagan administration's decision to consider arms sales to China, effectively removed the Indian spotlight from the Soviet military presence in Afghanistan and again seemingly underscored for New Delhi the value of its alliance with the USSR. On the tenth anniversary of the Soviet-Indian treaty, Foreign Minister Gromyko accused the United States of trying to destabilize Asia by selling arms to Pakistan and China, and he pointedly warned that the Soviet Union would "take all measures" needed to defend itself and its allies.[43]

Once again, however, Mrs. Gandhi took pains to emphasize India's independent stance. She coolly declined an invitation to appear in Moscow on the treaty anniversary, and seemed again to play down its significance in her own statements. Subsequently, she journeyed to Paris for talks that included plans for enlarging Franco-Indian military cooperation. In February 1982, India and France signed a preliminary agreement for Indian purchase of 40 of the new Mirage-2000 fighter-bombers.

Only a month later, an extraordinary delegation of Soviet military personnel descended on New Delhi in a last-minute effort to prevent the loss to Western competition of a major arms contract. The delegation of 16 senior Soviet officers, including Air Chief Marshal Kulakhov and Admiral of the Fleet Gorshakov, was led by Defense Minister Dimitri Ustinov, making his first visit to a non-Communist country. Despite reaffirmations of Soviet-Indian friendship from both sides, the Soviets failed to steer India away from its purchase agreement with France. Significantly, a major issue in the negotiations was the two prospective suppliers' willingness to agree to transfer production rights and facilities to India, thus aiding in its effort to become self-reliant in arms manufacturing.[44]

Far more serious than India's reluctance as a Soviet customer in the commercial and arms spheres have been the occasions on which it has refused to endorse major Soviet political initiatives, especially when the Soviets have ardently sought India's support. The best example of this is found in India's persistent refusal to endorse Brezhnev's 1969 proposal for creation of "a system of collective security in Asia." When various attempts in the early 1970s to enlist Indian spokesmen in support of the proposal met with failure, Brezhnev took on the role of salesman. During his November 1973 visit to India, he expounded at length before Parliament on the merits of collective security in Asia. Again, no explicit Indian endorsement of the concept was forthcoming—an obvious personal rebuff to Brezhnev. Another attempt was made during Mrs. Gandhi's June 1976 visit to Moscow, but again the joint declaration failed to endorse the concept. In fact, Mrs. Gandhi appeared to throw more cold water on the Soviet proposal by means of her skillful evasiveness at a Moscow press conference:

> A correspondent asked about holding an Asian conference on security similar to the Helsinki conference. The Prime Minister said the problems of Asia are exceedingly complex. Everything should be done to see that there is greater stability. . . . She pointed out that security depends on many factors. To us, the most important factor now is stability with economic strength. Bilateral and multilateral economic cooperation is the best way to ensure stability.[45]

Other examples of India's unwillingness to endorse Soviet diplomatic initiatives or to change its stance in response to Soviet requests include New Delhi's long-standing refusal to sign the Non-Proliferation Treaty, despite Soviet urgings that it do so; the persistent differences between the two countries on the issue of declaring the Indian Ocean a "zone of peace" free of superpower naval rivalry; and the cool Indian reaction in the mid-1970s whenever Soviet leaders sought endorsement of Soviet-American détente.

On the latter subject, Mrs. Gandhi occasionally infuriated the Soviet leaders by her equal application of the term "big powers" to Moscow and Washington. For example, during a trip to Canada in 1973, she implied that the Soviet-American summits might amount to a big-power conspiracy to carve out spheres of influence, and she declared that the only safeguard against such big-power hegemony was for smaller nations to stand together. Communist Party leader Bhupesh Gupta made a scathing attack on Mrs. Gandhi's statement, and the Soviets reportedly were ready to call upon their Indian friends to mount a letter-writing campaign in criticism.

The striking feature of these occasional Indo-Soviet disagreements is the care that both sides have taken to confine their frankest exchanges to private meetings and in other ways to limit the damage that such conflicts inevitably impose on the relationship. It is this quality, rather than the unrealistic expectation of totally convergent interests, that is the true hallmark of the "reliable friendship" between India and the Soviet Union.

Thus India, in making its overtures for a reopening of relations with China, was always careful to emphasize in public that its actions were not intended to detract from its relations with Moscow. Typical was the statement of Foreign Minister Vajpayee in November 1977: "In seeking new friends we have no desire to abandon tried and proven friends with whom we have shared ideals and common interests."[46] More recently, in the context of Soviet-Indian disagreements over Afghanistan, Mrs. Gandhi referred publicly to attempts that were being made in the press to misrepresent Indo-Soviet relations or to create misunderstandings between the two. "But we have withstood all such attempts and have constantly striven to strengthen mutual trust."[47] Addressing the same theme, the lead editorial in an issue of *New Times*, a widely circulated Soviet foreign affairs periodical, explained that what was important was not agreement on every detail, but closeness in basic positions:

> The social systems of the USSR and India differ from each other. It is not surprising then that at times differences of nuance are to be observed in their assessments of some international problems. But in vain do the opponents of rapprochement between the two countries count on capitalizing on this. The important thing is the identity of their basic positions of principle, their awareness of the sameness of their fundamental historical interests. . . .[48]

CONCLUSION

A major element that is present in Moscow's approach to South Asia, and utterly lacking in the American policy, is a sense of a need to seek influence in the region that stems from a policy framework that sets a relatively high priority on the region. We have seen in detail how this Soviet dependence on India has produced a greater willingness to devote a steady flow of resources and diplomatic energy toward preserving Moscow's rather large investment in the Indo-Soviet friendship. To lose its standing as the "reliable friend" of the strongest regional power in South Asia would cost Moscow heavily. It would entail some risk to its security in a bordering region that has both offensive and defensive value in the Soviet conflict with its primary rival, China. Moscow's substantial stake in the existing order in South Asia thus gives it an interest in helping to stabilize the region by playing the role of "reliable friend" to India.

The United States, by contrast, has developed very little stake in South Asia. Its interest in the region has been sporadic at best, and is usually occasioned by a threat or challenge to its interests that arises in an adjacent region (Southeast Asia or the Persian Gulf region). American attention to India and Pakistan has, like the American military aid program in the region, been turned on and off periodically, in response to specific crises or provocations. Having not needed India (or Pakistan, for the most part) in the pursuit of any of its more vital objectives, the United States has had no particular incentive to establish its presence or develop its influence in the subcontinent.

Understanding this point should help us to avoid being surprised by the substantial Soviet interest and presence in South Asia and by the relatively high esteem with which Moscow is regarded by the states of the region. It might also help us to avoid being alarmed at the Soviet presence in South Asia, having seen that Moscow's considerable investment has by no means won it inordinate influence or turned India into a puppet state, and that much of the Soviet "victory" over the United States in the superpower competition in this region has in effect been won by default.

NOTES

1. "Mission of Peace and Friendship," *New Times* (1980), no. 50: 5.

2. R. K. Jain, *Soviet-South Asian Relations 1947–1978* (Atlantic Highlands, N.J.: Humanities Press, 1979), I, p. 455.

3. Foreign Broadcast Information Service, *Daily Report: Soviet Union* (hereafter FBIS *Soviet Union*), April 12, 1978, p. J1.

4. For an extended analysis of this point, see Robert H. Donaldson, *The Soviet-Indian Alignment: Quest for Influence* (Denver: University of Denver, 1979).

5. *New York Times*, March 29, 1977, p. 2.

6. *New York Times*, March 30, 1977, p. 27.

7. *New York Times*, August 2, 1977, p. 7.

8. Peter Sager, *Moscow's Hand in India: An Analysis of Soviet Propaganda* (Bombay: 1967).

9. Stephen Clarkson, "Non-Impact of Soviet Writing on Indian Thinking and Policy," *Economic and Political Weekly* (Bombay) 8, no. 15 (April 14, 1973): 715–24.

10. Indian Institute of Public Opinion, *Monthly Public Opinion Surveys* 12 (September 1977): special supplement.

11. FBIS, *Soviet Union*, June 14, 1976, p. J2.

12. *Far Eastern Economic Review*, October 7, 1977, pp. 32–34.

13. Mohan Ram, "Soviets Wary of Indian-Chinese Ties," *Christian Science Monitor*, March 1, 1978, p. 5.

14. Mohan Ram, "Flowers for the Congress," *Economic and Political Weekly* 8, no. 49 (December 5, 1973): 2160.

15. FBIS, *Soviet Union*, March 12, 1977, p. J1.

16. *Pravda*, April 26, 1977, p. 4.

17. V. Shurygin, "India: Thirty Years of Independence," *International Affairs* (Moscow) (1977), no. 9: 74.

18. See, for example, *Izvestiia*, March 23, 1978, p. 4.

19. *New York Times,* November 30, 1971, p. 2.

20. *New York Times*, February 17, 1972.

21. *U.S. News and World Report*, June 19, 1979, p. 30.

22. *The Statesman* (New Delhi), December 29, 1976.

23. *New York Times*, December 14, 1980.

24. For a discussion of the case, see Gloria Duffy, "Soviet Nuclear Exports," *International Security* 3, no. 1 (1978). However, Duffy's conclusion that India was "ultimately forced to accept the Soviet position" appears to be in error.

25. "The Czech Crisis," *Indian and Foreign Review*, no. 5, September 1, 1968.

26. *New York Times*, January 4, 1980.

27. *New York Times*, January 13, 1980, p. 25.

28. Barry Kramer, "Sanjay Gandhi Death Hobbles India," *Wall Street Journal*, September 18, 1980.

29. *Pravda*, June 8, 1980, p. 4; *Pravda*, October 8, 1980, pp. 1, 8.

30. *Pravda*, December 12, 1980, p. 2.

31. R. H. Donaldson, *Soviet Policy Toward India: Ideology and Strategy* (Cambridge, Mass.: Harvard University Press, 1974), pp. 215–16.

32. A. Usvatov, "Together for Peace," *New Times* (1980), no. 41: 5.

33. Sergei Irodov, "The Fruits of Friendship," *New Times* (1980), no. 49: 9.

34. Jain, op. cit., p. 366.

35. *The Statesman* (New Delhi), November 18, 1969.

36. Kasturi Rangan, "India Drops Soviet for U.S. Aid in Steel," *New York Times*, August 25, 1977, pp. A-1, D-9.

37. "Why not the Best?" *The Economist* 266, no. 7014 (February 4, 1978): 94.

38. "India's Choice up in the Air," *Far Eastern Economic Review* 98, no. 28, (July 22, 1977): 5.

39. *Washington Post*, October 8, 1978, p. A-32.

40. *U.S. News and World Report*, June 19, 1978, p. 30.

41. Kasturei Rangan, "India Is Showered by Largess by the Soviet Union," *New York Times*, December 14, 1980.

42. Michael T. Kaufman, "Diplomacy Swirls Around Pakistan," *New York Times*, August 25, 1981, p. 2.

43. *Pravda*, August 8, 1981.

44. Michael T. Kaufman, "Soviet Generals Descend on New Delhi," *New York Times*, March 16, 1982, p. A-3; and "Soviet Says It Is Eager to Help India Produce Arms," *New York Times*, March 20, 1982, p. 11; Paul Lewis, "India Chooses French Jet over a Soviet Plane," *New York Times*, April 18, 1982, p. 6.

45. FBIS, *Soviet Union*, June 14, 1976, p. J2

46. Jain, op. cit., p. 511.

47. Rangan, "India Is Showered by Largess by the Soviet Union."

48. *New Times* (1980), no. 51: 6.

FOUR

Soviet Influence in Contemporary Iran
MURIEL ATKIN

The Soviet Union has had a greater opportunity to evolve a strategy for influencing affairs in Iran than in most of the countries of Asia. By the time the Bolsheviks took power, Russia had been actively involved in Iran's affairs for more than a century. Thus, for Lenin and his colleagues, Iran was not a remote and obscure place of undemonstrated importance, as it was for the United States before World War II. For Russian politicians of various ideologies, Iran was important as the object of a heated struggle for dominance between Russia and Britain. That perception has endured throughout the Soviet era, with the modification that the United States became an additional rival when it sent a small force to join in the Allied occupation of Iran in 1943 and then supplanted Britain as the chief adversary in the period between 1945 and 1953.

Not only did the Soviet leadership inherit a concept of the significance of Iran to its interests, but it also had the benefit of learning from the example of tsarist techniques for manipulating Iranian affairs. A wide assortment of techniques, including military intervention, economic deals, intimidation, inducement through formal diplomatic channels, and the encouragement of forces hostile to the central government produced occasional impressive gains as well as some setbacks. They were all part of the tsarist legacy that the Soviet Union has drawn upon and adopted in dealing with Iran.

As the Soviets experimented with various techniques aimed at producing a cooperative, perhaps even friendly, government in Teheran, they encountered several major setbacks and, until recently, made at best modest gains. The most recent such failures occurred in 1952 and 1953, when Moscow and the Iranian Communists linked closely to it missed the opportunity to turn to their advantage the extremely volatile political situation touched off by the oil nationalization crisis and the conflict between nationalists and the monarchy. For the next decade, relations between the restored monarchy and the Kremlin were coolly correct, with

Moscow reverting to the style of policy it had followed in the 1920s, emphasizing criticism of the Teheran government, demands, and intimidation, while Teheran banned the Communist party (the Tudeh) and was more closely tied than ever to the West, especially the United States.

The turning point in relations between the two countries came in the early 1960s, when both deemed it in their interests to revert to the older tactic of using Russian involvement in Iran to balance that of the West. The shift in Soviet policy, from confrontation to conciliation, netted substantial advantages. While Iran hardly became the USSR's ally, it did downplay diplomatic confrontations, increase greatly the economic relations between the two countries (including welcome exports of natural gas to Transcaucasia and the establishment of a host of Soviet-sponsored development projects), and allow some exchanges of personnel, with Soviets going to Iran as experts associated with the development projects and a small number of Iranians going to the Soviet Union for technical training.

The Soviets have had experience, ever since they decided to make a costly peace with Germany soon after the Bolsheviks seized power, with differentiating between the ideal and the pragmatically acceptable in their foreign relations. Thus, while never abandoning the principle that Marxist socialism would ultimately come to Iran, the Soviets were reconciled to what they came to view for the foreseeable future as the enlightened, progressive rule of Mohammed Reza Shah. This attitude persisted until the spring of 1978, when Moscow began to consider the possibility that the shah could not suppress his opponents as he had in the past. When Moscow realized that the revolutionaries were likely to win, and were virulently anti-American, it declared its support for them, although it was a bit confused at first about which was the dominant faction, and had to overcome a certain distaste when it realized that the most powerful element was the Islamic clergy.

The creation of a revolutionary regime in Iran has brought the Soviet Union the greatest opportunity since the early 1950s to expand its influence there. However, it has also brought an end to the quite satisfactory modus vivendi that the Soviets had developed with Mohammed Reza Shah. The Soviets traditionally have preferred to deal with rulers who fit into certain familiar categories, such as the modernizing-nationalist-anti-Communist strongman, to which the shah (as well as Gamal Abdel Nasser and Muamar al-Qaddafi) belonged, than with people who are unfamiliar and unpredictable, and whose ability to retain power in the context of a heated rivalry remains unclear.

Thus, while the Soviets are aware that Iran's post-1979 political turmoil raises at least the possibility that a pro-Soviet government might be installed at some time in the future, the more immediate concern is to secure an accommodation similar to the one that existed with the shah. Toward that end, the Kremlin is using the latest version of the tactics Russia began to use in Iran in the nineteenth century. These fall into two broad categories. The first is official contacts between states, including diplomacy, economic agreements, cultural exchanges, and other formal contacts between the two countries. The second category comprises unofficial contacts, such as propaganda, the activities of the Tudeh Party, relations with other parties, attempts to build a following among minorities at odds with the central government, and clandestine activities.

OFFICIAL CONTACTS

Diplomatic Relations

The Soviet Union has repeatedly declared its support for the revolutionary regime in Iran even though it criticizes individuals and political groups associated with the government. The two terms most frequently used in Soviet sources to characterize the revolution, "anti-imperialist" and "democratic," provide a key to the basis for this policy. The term "anti-imperialist" means that Iran's foreign policy parallels some of the Soviet Union's likes and dislikes. The animosity toward the United States is the most important element, from Moscow's (and Teheran's) perspective, but Iran also has broken relations with Israel and South Africa and withdrawn from the moribund CENTO. At the same time, the new regime has improved relations with Syria, Libya, South Yemen, North Korea, and Cuba, and has joined the nonaligned movement (currently led by Cuba). Teheran maintains diplomatic relations with the Soviet bloc states of Eastern Europe, but this is a continuation of the shah's policy, not a recent innovation.

"Democratic" is used to mean three things: that the revolution and Ayatollah Khomeini have broad public support, that the revolutionaries favor extensive social and economic reforms designed to expand the public sector of the economy and improve the standard of living of workers and peasants, and that the new rulers have allowed the Tudeh Party to operate legally, in sharp contrast with the vigorous repression directed against it by the shah.

The most important way in which the Soviet Union has tried to use diplomacy to influence the new regime in Iran is its backing of the revolutionaries in their confrontations with the United States. This began with a declaration by Brezhnev on November 19, 1978, that any foreign intervention in Iran would be intolerable to the Soviet Union because it would pose a threat to Soviet security.[1] This stance was elaborated as the United States sought ways to respond to the disastrous change in relations with Iran and to the Soviet invasion of Afghanistan. The expanded formula was dubbed the Brezhnev Doctrine in December 1980. The Soviet leader argued that there should be no intervention in the affairs of Persian Gulf states by countries outside the region, that such extraregional powers should have no military facilities in the Persian Gulf, and that there should be no interference with the navigation of the Persian Gulf or the regional powers' disposition of their natural resources.[2] The Soviets have asserted that it is Brezhnev's strong stand against foreign interference in Iran's affairs that has deterred the United States from launching its allegedly numerous counterrevolutionary plans against the new regime.[3]

The Soviets demonstrated their diplomatic support for the revolutionary government in Teheran by endorsing the seizure of the U.S. embassy and the holding of some of its staff as hostages. From the start, the Soviets argued that these actions did not violate international law and that the guilty party was the United States, which was alleged to be engaged in many anti-Iranian activities. When the United States brought the matter before the United Nations, the Soviets rejected the American arguments and refused to endorse a trade boycott of Iran.

While Moscow openly welcomed the embassy seizure because it undercut the possibility of repairing U.S.-Iranian relations[4] in the foreseeable future, there are some hints of concern at first that the affair might backfire. The Soviets expressed concern that this issue was distracting the Teheran government from what should have been the highest priorities of the revolution (including resolution of the dispute with the Kurds).[5] However, the Soviets eventually put aside their qualms. They still saw their best option as support for the Khomeini line, and he had endorsed the takeover of the embassy. The risk of an escalation of the confrontation was reduced by the nature of the American response. Thus, the Soviets had little choice but to support the embassy occupation unequivocally, unless they were willing to risk losing influence in Iran and had reason to expect that the cost of such a policy would not be dangerously high.

Moscow continues to try to use the Babrak Karmal government, which it is keeping in power in Afghanistan, to increase the diplomatic ties between Iran and the Soviet bloc. The Soviets have repeatedly urged Teheran to accept Karmal's offer of good neighborly relations and anti-imperialist cooperation[6] but Teheran remains scathingly critical of the Communist regime in Afghanistan and the Soviet military presence there.

The war between Iran and Iraq, which began in September 1980, has been a source of acute embarrassment to the Kremlin, which wants good relations with both countries. The official Soviet position is that this war is "fratricidal" and serves the interest of imperialism, not the two combatants.[7] Moscow has declared itself neutral in the conflict and has tried to balance friendly gestures to the two countries. Press coverage contains reports from Iraqi and Iranian sources. When dealing with Arabs, the Soviets refer to the Arab Gulf; when dealing with Iranians, they call it the Persian Gulf. Moscow notes its years of cooperation with Iraq while wooing the Iranian ambassador.

The USSR is presumed to have given military aid to Iraq, though it denies this to the Iranians. Western reports indicate that Moscow also has sent military equipment to Iran. Though Teheran has denied this indignantly, President Mohammed 'Ali Khamene' i came close to confirming it when he said that Iran would never accept Soviet military aid because that would involve the presence of Soviet military personnel in Iran, but that in time of war, Iran could not deny itself the option of buying matériel from the Soviets.[8] The Soviets argue that the only appropriate way to resolve the dispute between Iran and Iraq is by negotiating, and have voiced regret that Iran's demands are so far-reaching and unyielding. Nonetheless, Moscow has been unwilling to risk the deterioration of its relations with Teheran that would likely result from any indication of preference for the Iraqi side. The reverses suffered by Iraq in the spring of 1982 make such a move by the Soviets even less likely.

The only time when the Soviet Union was willing to show less than full support for the revolutionary government in Teheran was in the second half of 1979, up to the seizure of the American embassy in November. The problem, from the Soviet point of view, was that the provisional government, led by Mehdi Bazargan, was comparatively moderate on domestic issues and not particularly anti-American. By these criteria, the Islamic Republican Party (IRP), which was anti-Bazargan, and some members of his cabinet, had links to the political tradition of Mohammed Mosaddeq, prime minister during the oil nationalization crisis of the early 1950s.

At that time, the Soviet Union was cool to Mosaddeq for being too willing to deal with the United States. After Mosaddeq's fall, Moscow decided this was a critical mistake, and during the current political turmoil indignantly rejected the charge, leveled by Abolhasan Bani Sadr and others, that it had failed to support Mosaddeq.[9] In addition, when the Soviets realized that the revolutionary movement constituted a serious threat to the shah, they assumed, until comparatively late, that it was led by the secular nationalists of the Mosaddeq tradition, not the politicized mullahs.[10] The most important way Soviet coolness towards the Bazargan government was displayed was in increased support for the Kurds' grievances against the central government.[11] Yet the Soviets did not burn their bridges to Bazargan until he had been forced from office as a consequence of the takeover of the American embassy. From the Soviet point of view, Bazargan's fall was yet another beneficial result of the seizure of the embassy.[12]

The existence of Soviet-Iranian diplomatic relations permits the Soviet Union to maintain embassy and consular personnel in Iran. Iranian officials expressed some suspicion of the activities of consular staff in the Caspian Sea city of Rasht. They ordered the consulate closed in retaliation for the Soviets' refusal to allow Iran to open a consulate in the capital of the predominantly Muslim Tadzhik SSR. (The Soviets still have a consulate in Isfahan.) In reaction to the invasion of Afghanistan, Teheran required the Soviets to reduce the size of its embassy staff in Teheran.[13]

The Soviet Union's diplomatic tactics in Iran have brought very modest gains. Anti-Americanism is certainly a powerful force, but this was internally generated, not the product of Soviet efforts. After all, the Soviet Union had maintained good relations with the shah as late as the first half of 1978 despite his close diplomatic, economic, and military ties with the United States. Nonetheless, this is the brightest diplomatic development from the Soviet perspective, and is important enough to outweigh the Soviets' grounds for displeasure over other aspects of Iran's foreign policy.

The political leadership of revolutionary Iran is not a homogeneous body. Those who have held government office belong to a variety of factions, many of them mutually hostile, as the careers of Bani Sadr, Bazargan, and Sadeq Qotbzadeh show. Even within the Islamic Republican Party and the Islamic clergy there are different orientations. In light of this, it is not surprising that the attitude toward the Soviet Union also varies. If anything, Bani Sadr and Qotbzadeh were more overtly critical of the Soviets than were some of the powerful mullahs, especially in late 1979 and early 1980, while other mullahs regard everyone left of center as a Communist and are very anti-Soviet. Still, if one considers the people at the apex of power in the central government, certain overall trends are discernible.

While most Americans and Soviets may see the central issue in international relations as the rivalry between their two countries, this is not the central issue for many Iranian politicians. For them, the central issue is to promote the interests of Iran (or their own party, or themselves). The American-Soviet rivalry may be useful toward that end, but any benefit derived by either superpower is secondary to the benefit derived by Iran. Thus, many Iranian politicians believe that the Soviet Union owed Iran support because of its anti-Americanism, and therefore deserves no special gratitude. Even Mohammed Mokre, the new regime's ambassador to Moscow and a leading proponent of close Iranian-Soviet relations, has said, "We are engaged in a struggle against the U.S. government, and the Soviet Union has no alternative but to support our struggle. . . ."[14]

Bani Sadr, though not particularly well disposed toward the Soviet Union, shared this attitude.[15] The view of Khomeini, the Islamic Republicans, and others is that the revolution has made Iran a strong, independent state not subject to the domination of any foreign power. They insist that the elimination of American influence in Iran does not mean that the Soviet Union can take the United States' place.[16]

The high point for Soviet prestige in Iran came in late 1979 and early 1980 because of Soviet diplomatic support for Iran on the hostage crisis.[17] Yet this situation deteriorated rapidly from the end of December 1979 because of the Soviet invasion of Afghanistan, which has consistently been denounced in scathing terms by Iran's leaders.[18] The outbreak of war with Iraq increased Iran's dissatisfaction with Soviet policy. Soviet neutrality was deemed inadequate; the Soviet arms deliveries to Iraq, particularly offensive.[19] Even though Iran may well have obtained weapons from the Soviet Union, this does not of itself betoken a qualitative change in relations between the two. The shah bought some military hardware from the Soviet Union without being pro-Soviet. The emergency created by the war with Iraq has forced Iran to buy arms wherever it can. It has had arms dealers in Western Europe looking for deals, and has obtained some U.S.-made spare parts from the Israelis while supporting the PLO diplomatically against Israel.[20]

Iranian diplomatic rhetoric contains many references to the "superpowers," meaning the United States and the Soviet Union, a pairing the Soviets find invidious. The superpowers are accused of having a common ambition that outweighs their differences: the desire to dominate the world by dividing it into two shares. Thus Teheran argues that the Soviet Union endorses America's anti-Iranian activities.[21]

One telling indication of Iranian mistrust of Soviet intentions is Teheran's unilateral abrogation in November 1979 of two articles of the 1921 treaty between the two governments. These provisions allowed Soviet military intervention in Iran when a third party based there posed a threat to Soviet security that the Iranians could not eliminate. This was the basis on which the Soviet Union justified military intervention in Iran during World War II and threatened it on other occasions, including, by implication, the Brezhnev pronouncement on Iran in November 1978.

Iran's new leaders objected to these provisions not only because the treaty was associated with "the debased regime of the past" but also because, as they accurately observed, the provisions were intended to have narrow applications, referring only to White forces that had fled to Iran as the tide of the Russian civil war turned against them. Although the decision to repudiate these provisions was made by the Bazargan government, its successors have stood by that decision.[22] (Moscow does not recognize this action.)

Although revolutionary Iran has improved or established relations with a number of countries that are close to the Soviets, it has also improved its relations with Turkey and Pakistan, with which the Soviets are on poor terms. The Iran-Pakistan rapprochement is a dramatic reversal stimulated by the Soviet invasion of Afghanistan. Relations with China remain correct, as under the shah, despite Moscow's open displeasure.

Economic Agreements

Since tsarist times, Russia's rulers have regarded economic relations with Iran as the continuation of diplomacy by other means. This principle was recognized by Lenin, and has remained an element of the Soviet approach. Both countries are now quite willing to pursue economic arrangements with each other regardless of the problems in their diplomatic relations. Most of this involves the completion or expansion of agreements that were made in the shah's time for dams, power plants, machinery, silos, and, most prominently, the Isfahan steel mill. There are also commercial agreements with most of the East European countries, as there had been under the shah.

Soviet-Iranian trade was not insignificant before the revolution, and has increased rapidly since, exceeding a value of $1 billion by 1981.[23] In 1980, the two countries signed a transit trade agreement modeled on one concluded during the monarchy in 1957. This trade also has increased since the revolution. The electrification of the railway linking Iran's principal northwestern city, Tabriz, and the Soviet Transcaucasian border was completed at the start of 1982, with Moscow promising to send Iran ten locomotives to use on that line.[24] This route certainly has the potential to be of major aid to increased Soviet-Iranian communications, especially since Iran's port facilities on the Caspian (and elsewhere) are quite limited.

Whether the extensive economic links between the two countries have in fact increased Soviet influence in Iran remains questionable. Qualitatively, very little has changed since the days of the monarchy. An opportunity exists for the Soviets to increase Iran's need for their cooperation, especially since some of Pahlavi Iran's important economic partners, particularly the United States and France, are now politically unacceptable and some other countries, notably Japan, seem reluctant to invest in an economy where inflation and labor unrest are so high and productivity so low. In the 1920s, when northern Iran traded extensively with the Soviet Union, the Soviets occasionally stopped trade between the two countries as a way of applying political pressure on the Teheran government. Yet this probably did the Soviets more harm than good, encouraging Iranian efforts to promote economic self-reliance and in general intensifying anti-Soviet feeling.

The Soviets now contend that their trade and passage for Iran's imports have been essential in helping Iran minimize the damage done by the American boycott initiated in response to the embassy seizure. Some Iranian officials agree, but put more emphasis on Iran's ability to defy a superpower than on gratitude toward the Soviet Union.[25] Iran trades with a variety of other countries, including West Germany, Turkey, China, and many other Asian and African states. While Iran's trade via the Soviet Union with other countries (including West Germany and Japan) has increased since the revolution (300 percent, according to Soviet figures), as of the spring of 1981, more of Iran's foreign trade still went through its southern ports.[26] Given the poor state of the Iranian economy, including an estimated drop of one-third or more in industrial production, it is possible that some Soviet-backed enterprises in Iran are not functioning.[27]

The economic and trade agreements provide for a number of Soviet (and East European) citizens to work in Iran as technical experts and cargo expediters. As a very tentative estimate, there may be somewhat more than 2,000 such people there.[28] They have the opportunity to influence Iranians with whom they come in contact and to engage in activities not related to their public mission in Iran. There are some hints that they may have had some success at this in the northern port city of Rasht, but in the central city of Isfahan, where the largest number is concentrated, their efforts do not seem to have produced any spectacular results, though there is probably a certain amount of support among workers in the Soviet-backed plants. As under the shah, Iran has agreements to send people to the Soviet Union for technical training. The Soviets claim that more than 1,000 Iranians have already received technical training in the Soviet Union.[29] The overwhelming majority did so before the revolution.

In one economic area, the Soviet Union has suffered a major setback since the fall of the shah. Under the monarchy, Iran exported natural gas to the Soviet Union through a pipeline connecting the source of the gas in southwestern Iran with the Soviet Transcaucasian border, and there was a project to construct a second pipeline. The new regime soon canceled that construction project and demanded a higher price for the gas being delivered. The Iranians argued that the existing price was far below the world market level, and began negotiations for a price increase of roughly 500 percent. By March 1980, with the Soviets' best offer still about one-third below the Iranians' demand. Iran canceled all gas sales via the pipeline.[30] (However, it does sell oil to the Soviets and East Europeans.)

The end of gas sales and the talk of building a pipeline through Iran and Turkey, announced in the spring of 1982, are at least as important politically as they are economically, a gesture of Iran's independence of the Soviets. While the Soviets would have preferred that Iran follow a different natural gas policy, this setback has not upset them to the point that they have ceased to pursue other economic agreements with Iran or have broken off existing ones. (The Iranians also have shut down a number of Soviet economic operations within their country, including a bank, an insurance company, and the Iranian branch of the Soviet transportation agency.)[31]

Cultural Exchanges

Moscow has tried to continue the practice, begun under the monarchy, of cultural exchanges and visits of specialized delegations between Iran and the Soviet Union as a way of encouraging a favorable attitude toward the Soviet Union. Some of these exchanges, such as concert tours by the Moscow State Symphony in 1978, are now impossible because of the mullahs' hostility toward Western culture. The Islamic Republic has also signaled its lack of enthusiasm for cultural exchanges with its northern neighbor by abolishing in 1982 the Iranian Society for Cultural Links with the USSR, founded during the Soviet occupation of northern Iran during World War II.[32] Soviet Muslim clerics have invited their Iranian counterparts to visit them, and have sought to visit Iran, although since the Soviet invasion of Afghanistan, Iran's response has been negative and the Soviet attitude toward Islam condemned.[33] Secular Iranian government officials have visited the Soviet Union to get information about areas of Soviet technical expertise and meet Soviet Muslims. However, in at least one case in 1981, such a visitor brought back a very negative report on the status of Soviet Muslims that was broadcast in Iran.[34] A small number of Iranian students have attended Soviet schools.[35]

UNOFFICIAL CONTACTS

Propaganda

The Soviet Union maintains a vigorous propaganda campaign directed at Iran, primarily by means of broadcasts by regular Soviet radio stations in Moscow and Baku (the capital of Soviet Azerbaijan). The former broadcasts to Iran in Persian; the latter, in Azeri Turkish, spoken by millions of inhabitants of northern Iran. Much of the propaganda is devoted to lauding Soviet policy toward Iran since the days of Lenin. The Soviet Union portrays itself as a consistent friend of Iranian national interests and the best friend of the Iranian revolution. In the process, it does some interesting revising of history. For example, the Soviet occupation of northern Iran during World War II is explained as saving Iran from the fascist menace, including Germany's plans to make northern Iran its colony. The Soviets also claim to have been stalwart supporters of Mosaddeq, and seek to give the impression that they were on poor terms with Mohammed Reza Shah. The Soviet invasion of Afghanistan is justified as an internal Afghan matter, the legitimate government of the country having asked for Soviet aid in dealing with a counterrevolution backed by the United States and other imperialists and reactionaries. The Karmal regime there is depicted as popular, anti-imperialistic, and respectful of Islam, thus giving it much in common with Iran.

Next to the exaltation of Soviet benevolence toward Iran, the most important theme of Soviet propaganda is the ceaseless American threat to the survival of the Iranian revolution. There is a steady stream of stories about American military preparations for an attack on Iran and other efforts to foment counterrevolution. An analogy is often drawn between alleged American activities in the early 1980s and at the time of Mosaddeq's overthrow in 1953. Every American move during the hostage crisis was interpreted in this light. As the end of the crisis neared, the Soviets tried to discredit Washington's terms for a settlement. According to Soviet broadcasts, the crisis was merely used as a rationale for America's existing intervention plans. Therefore, the hostages' release had not reduced the American menace. Israel and China are also subject to denunciation as part of the American-led imperialist conspiracy against Iran.[36]

This extensive propaganda campaign does not seem to have produced any significant change of attitude among Iran's current leaders, who became extremely anti-United States and anti-Israel for reasons having to do with their variety of Iranian nationalism, not Soviet broadcasts. For all the Soviets' efforts, Iran's leaders remain hostile to the Karmal regime and the Soviet presence in Afghanistan while refusing to become hostile toward China. Soviet radio propaganda also contains criticism of various secular revolutionary figures, especially those who are not sufficiently anti-western or who have fallen afoul of the Islamic Republican Party, as well as competing leftist groups. However, the heated power struggle within Iran reflects internal political traditions, not the influence of Soviet propaganda. While the Soviet attitude toward Bani Sadr has been sometimes critical, sometimes positive, by the time the Islamic Republicans drove him from power, Moscow considered him the lesser evil but had to reconcile itself to a change it could not control.[37]

Ayatollah Khomeini is never criticized in Soviet propaganda broadcasts. To do otherwise would be counterproductive, since the Soviets consider him to be the overwhelmingly prestigious figure in post-Pahlavi Iran.[38] Some of those close to Khomeini and in the Islamic Republican Party are occasionally criticized, usually not by name but in general terms as people who are not really following Khomeini's intentions.[39] Yet that is really a way of criticizing elements of current Iranian policy that Khomeini endorses without attacking him or appearing hostile to the current government in Teheran. Therefore, it is unlikely to have much influence with the regime or its supporters.

The Tudeh Party

The Tudeh Party is Iran's pro-Soviet Communist Party. (There are other, small Communist parties in Iran, with a Trotskyist, Maoist, or other non-Soviet orientation.) As the Tudeh itself says, it "has the most close and fraternal ties with the Communist Party of the Soviet Union. . . ."[40] That is one of Tudeh's biggest problems, since most non-Tudeh members in Iran see it as a tool of the Soviets, not as a party that puts Iran's interests first. The last time the Tudeh was a powerful force in Iranian politics was in the Mosaddeq era, when it was by far the largest and best-organized party. Between that time and the revolution, it was in eclipse, with the shah's government waging a fierce campaign of repression against it, the party leaders in exile in Eastern Europe, and many members of its traditional constituency (intellectuals, students, and workers) no longer interested in its message.

The active opposition to the shah in 1978 did not include extensive or influential participation by the Tudeh, although the party did join the revolution once it was well under way. Given the demonstrable strength of the religious-political movement, and the determination, particularly on Moscow's part, not to repeat the mistakes of the Mosaddeq era, the Tudeh declared its support for Ayatollah Khomeini as the monarchy neared collapse. This has been the keystone of the Tudeh's public policy ever since. Khomeini is never criticized, and is often cited in the Tudeh's clandestine radio broadcasts to justify its own demands.[41]

The Tudeh also supports the Islamic Republican Party, formed after the revolution, although it is frequently critical of it. Thus, in the 1980 presidential election, the party did not even attempt to run a candidate of its own, nor did it support Bani Sadr, a secular reformer who has been influenced by socialist thought. Instead, it supported Hasan Habibi, who was close to some prominent clerics and finished a distant third in the elections. The Tudeh sided with the IRP against Bani Sadr in the power struggle that drove the president from office in 1981.[42]

Yet the Tudeh's relations with Khomeini and the IRP remain uneasy. As a Tudeh spokesman conceded, expressions of goodwill have been fairly one-sided in this arrangement.[43] The Islamic Republicans have allowed the Tudeh to exist as a legal party and have not tried to destroy it, as they have tried to do to various guerrilla organizations. However, the elements that dominate the IRP are not allowing the Tudeh to do more than exist, not allowing it to contest for a share of political power.

The Tudeh has been subject to various forms of harassment by IRP members and Islamic fundamentalists (the Hezbolahis): government officials have not come to the aid of the Tudeh when it has been attacked. Its offices have occasionally been ransacked and occupied, the main party paper (*Mardom*) banned, party members abused, and some of its candidates barred from running for office.[44] The Tudeh's frequent complaints about the IRP's desire for a monopoly of political power, the "fanaticism" of some of its members, and its belief that the difference between religious and nonreligious political elements is more important than their shared support for the Iranian revolution all reflect the Tudeh's sense of weakness and frustration.[45] Yet the Tudeh has not broken with the IRP, and has little alternative but to support it because it is the one party with power.

As part of the strategy of bolstering its position by cooperating with larger political parties, the Tudeh has sought alliances with other leftist groups. Many of these have a low opinion of the Tudeh because its leaders spent a generation in exile, far from Iranian realities; because it was critical of the guerrilla methods of its rivals on the left and generally opposed violent confrontation with the monarchy in the 1970s; because it is seen as a Soviet puppet; and because its support of Khomeini and the IRP appear to be hypocritical and ideologically unsound.[46]

Initially, the Tudeh wooed the Mojahedin-e-Khalq, which offered the attraction of being comparatively large and combining elements of Islamic thought with socialist influence. However, the Mojahedin were not interested, and remained hostile to the IRP and the central government, which put it in conflict with the key element of Tudeh strategy. Having failed to reach an accommodation with the Mojahedin, the Tudeh sought alliance with the Fedayan-e-Khalq, a secular, avowedly Marxist-Leninist guerrilla organization whose members were formerly called "infantile leftists" by the Tudeh.[47] A coalition has been achieved with the self-styled "majority" faction of the Fedayan. As this name implies, the Fedayan are split. They have been further weakened by declining popularity and government harassment. Thus, it is unlikely that the Tudeh's success in finding an ally has materially strengthened its position.

The main themes of the Tudeh's platform since the revolution have the common purpose of eliminating the party's political rivals. Thus it frequently calls for a purge of the administration, Revolutionary Committee, and the military, in order to eliminate holdovers from the days of the monarchy and counterrevolutionary agents.[48] These terms are used to mean anyone the party does not like; the significance of removing such people from such powerful institutions is obvious. The fact that the Tudeh continues to advocate purges and to complain that they have not been made reflects the strength of anti-Tudeh personnel in positions of power. The other main area of reform endorsed by the Tudeh involves economic measures designed to better the lot of the workers and peasants while breaking the power of their exploiters: large landowners, big businessmen, and wealthy bazaar merchants. All these groups are identified by the Tudeh as enemies of the revolution whose power must be broken in order to end political subversion.[49]

The Tudeh generally credits the IRP with having good intentions in these matters but faults it for failing to take sufficient action. A land reform law has been on the books since the spring of 1980 but has not been put into effect. Some businesses have been nationalized, which meets with Tudeh approval, but often it is mullahs who are appointed to manage them, not pro-Tudeh technocrats, as the party had hoped. In any case, many businesses, public or private, are doing very poorly in the generally beleaguered Iranian economy. The party's hostility toward the leading bazaar merchants reflects the IRP's attempt to use them as the scapegoats for Iran's high inflation rate (estimated to run 60–70 percent annually). This may be a politically dangerous move, in that the wealthier bazaaris, and some others, who apparently are antagonized by this policy, have been particularly important supporters of the mullahs in political as well as religious matters.[50]

Tudeh is engaged in extensive propaganda efforts through a wide variety of serial publications in Persian and Azeri Turkish, tape recordings, and radio broadcasts in both languages on the clandestine station National Voice of Iran, which transmits from Soviet Azerbaijan. The National Voice of Iran does not acknowledge any link to the Tudeh or the Soviet Union, but portrays itself as representing Iranian patriots who are loyal to the revolution, Islam, and Khomeini. The message Tudeh seeks to communicate includes lengthy defense of all Soviet actions, advocacy of the same arguments the Soviets make to Iran, including the American menace, and advocacy of the Tudeh's domestic program.[51]

The Tudeh also serves as a means of encouraging a pro-Soviet attitude among the two largest minorities, the Azerbaijanis and the Kurds. While the party has some supporters among both groups, in neither case is its position strong. Despite the many rumors circulating about extensive Tudeh penetration of Iran's ruling circles, its current position is in fact quite weak. Many of these stories come from anti-leftist religious-political figures within Iran and from antigovernment émigré groups who are engaged in a furious power struggle in which polemics are more important than factual reporting. Many of the charges are put in general terms, which makes them hard to verify. There are often problems with specific charges. For example, one of the people accused by his enemies of being subject to Tudeh influence is Bahzad Nabavi, the minister of economic affairs. Yet Nabavi has criticized the Soviet Union, using the standard rhetoric about the "superpowers," for which he has been attacked by the Soviets.[52]

The Tudeh was probably most influential in late 1979 and early 1980. Its statements were reported at length and without editorializing by newspapers not affiliated with it, including government-controlled papers, as well as by the state radio.[53] One small indication of the influence of Tudeh propaganda in this period is the way Teheran Radio, which ordinarily gives little attention to Latin American affairs, discussed the overthrow of Chile's Salvador Allende in connection with American attempts to destabilize anti-imperialist regimes two days after the National Voice of Iran raised the same issue in one of its broadcasts.[54] The Tudeh claimed to have influence among some of the people close to Khomeini, and some state officials acknowledged being Tudeh members.[55] Whether these reports were exaggerated or the Tudeh's fortunes declined because of later developments, the party appears to be in an unenviable position. If it has many supporters in the state radio, as alleged, they have not been able to prevent blistering criticism of the Soviet Union over the invasion of Afghanistan as well as other issues.

The Tudeh did badly in the Majlis (parliament) elections of 1980. If the elections were rigged, this failure nevertheless shows that the party did not have enough friends in ruling circles to enable it to share in the benefits of the rigging. In the spring of 1982, the government launched a purge of the state administration and the educational system, moves that the Tudeh found threatening. Well before this, the government shut down the universities, depriving the Tudeh of one of its most important areas for recruiting. The party complains about how misguided young people and workers are (that is, not subject to its influence) and about the extent to which the masses continue to follow the leadership of the mullahs.[56] The alliance with the IRP has put the Tudeh in an awkward position. It has little to offer the secular nationalists who are dissatisfied with the IRP but, with its reputation as atheist and Communist, has little to offer those to whom Islam is important. The only line on which it does not face strong competition from other parties is complete support for the Soviet Union, including over the invasion of Afghanistan. There is a small audience for such an appeal.

Minorities

The Soviets (and the British) have in the past used some of Iran's ethnic minorities to pressure the central government and establish local enclaves of influence. Since 1979, Moscow has been actively pursuing influence among the two largest ethnic minorities, the Kurds (perhaps 5 million in Iran) and the Azerbaijani Turks (perhaps 10 million in Iran). However, this time its policy is more ambivalent than it was in 1945 and 1946, when Moscow openly supported autonomy movements among both peoples. The main complication now is that Moscow is also pursuing good relations with the central government and feels it has made some progress. In the past, the minorities were used because Moscow's relations with the central government were poor. The general Soviet position on Iran's minorities since the revolution is that they have legitimate rights to their own cultural expression and to a share in the benefits of the new order.

However, this line is not directed against the central government.[57] Rather, it is argued that the minorities' problems were caused by the shah's repression. Therefore, the installation of the new regime in Teheran marks an end to the oppressive policies. Khomeini is portrayed as sensitive to the minorities' grievances and desirous of resolving them. The Soviets fault the central government for not doing enough for the minorities, but continue to express the hope that it will see the wisdom of conciliation. The crux of the Soviet argument is that whatever hurts the central government aids the cause of the counterrevolution and imperialism, and that is against the interests of all Iran's inhabitants, whether Persian or minority.[58]

The Soviets seem to have little influence among some strategically located minorities, including the Turkomans in the northeast, the Baluchis in the southeast, and the Arabs in the southwest. Members of these groups have engaged in clashes with central authorities, but the Soviet characterizations of these incidents is extremely negative. The leaders of these groups are described as the local reactionary elite, agents of imperialism, and, in the case of the Baluchis, Afghan drug smugglers.[59] It is unlikely that this rhetoric is intended to conceal Soviet involvement with these peoples, since the tone is so very hostile and since the Soviets did not use such language to describe the Kurds and the Azerbaijanis it has wooed.

The Soviets made a genuine effort to reach an accommodation with the Kurdish Democratic Party (KDP) of Iran. The prospects seemed promising, especially given the contacts between the two before the revolution and the years its leader, Abdorrahman Qassemlu, spent in exile in Eastern Europe. However, relations between Moscow and the KDP broke down because of the Kurds' hostility toward the central government and Moscow's continuing support for the new regime in Teheran, which has refused to make concessions to the Kurds and has tried to subdue them by force. A minority of the KDP leadership broke away and maintains ties to the Soviets and Tudeh, but Moscow's relations with the Qassemlu faction are now bad.[60] Kurds engaged in fighting Teheran's forces are believed to have not only Soviet and Czech, but also American and Israeli, weapons.

Soviet relations with Iranian Azerbaijanis constitute a special case. There are no particular targets of Soviet wrath among this group. In fact, the Soviets, including Soviet Azerbaijanis, have expressed enthusiasm for the resurgence of Azerbaijan since the revolution. A host of Azeri-language publications have been established, and there are Azeri-language theaters in Tabriz, and metropolis of Azerbaijan, and in Teheran. The Tudeh's Azerbaijani affiliate, the Azerbaijan Democratic Party, is actively involved in such ventures. Soviet Azerbaijanis seek contacts with their Iranian counterparts both within Iran and abroad. Publications from Soviet Azerbaijan are sent to Iran.[61] The link between the Azerbaijanis on both sides of the border is stressed in Soviet statements, in which Iranian Azerbaijan is invariably called Southern Azerbaijan.

Yet all this may be less significant than it seems. The Soviet message to the Iranian Azerbaijanis has been that their interests are linked to the survival of the revolutionary regime in Teheran. Azerbaijanis were not alone, it is pointed out, in suffering under the shah; Persians suffered, too, and have broken with the past by means of the revolution. There are references to Mosaddeq, but never in the sense that he was regarded as sympathetic to Azerbaijani autonomist demands, and only in the sense that the paramount issue is to save a central government opposed to foreign domination from the dangers of counterrevolution.[62]

There would certainly be problems with encouraging an Azerbaijani autonomist movement analogous to the one in 1945–46, even apart from the possible international ramifications. The Iranian Azerbaijani population is more dispersed now than it was then, with many Azerbaijanis having moved to Teheran in search of better economic opportunities. Moreover, Moscow is concerned about unwholesome "chauvinism" among Soviet Azerbaijanis.

Encouraging nationalism among Iranian Azerbaijanis and their sense of kinship with their Soviet cousins could be a very dangerous move, especially since there are perhaps 10 million Iranian Azerbaijanis, while the total population of Soviet Azerbaijan, including Russians and members of other ethnic groups, is only a little over 6 million. Finally, there are indications that for all their efforts, the Soviets and the Azerbaijan Democratic Party (ADP) have not garnered much support among Azerbaijani nationalists, who seem much more interested in Ayatollah Kazem Shariat-Madari's People's Muslim Republican Party.[63] Whether the ADP can pick up support in the wake of the IRP's crackdown on Shariat-Madari and his followers remains to be seen.

Clandestine Activities

Reports have surfaced in the West of clandestine Soviet activities in Iran. The very fact that they are clandestine makes their existence difficult to verify or categorically disprove. Rumors of KGB involvement in SAVAMA, the new regime's secret police, or the establishment of a Soviet listening post in Zahedan, the main city of Baluchistan, are countered by rumors that insist such events have not taken place. There are also stories of Soviet infiltration of Iran across that country's northwestern border, but these too are unconfirmed.

A report from West Germany indicated that the Soviets in Teheran facilitated the seizure of the American embassy there. This account gives no specifics, but simply argues that the people who took over the embassy must have had Soviet help because there is no other way they could have known the embassy's layout and the location of its staff.[64] While this cannot be disproved outright, one can at least speculate that since the people who took over the embassy had the wherewithal to piece together hundreds of documents put through the U.S. embassy shredder, they might very well be able to find out whatever they wanted to know about the embassy's layout without necessarily being handed the information by the Soviets.

There are also rumors that Tudeh members were involved in the occupation of the embassy. During the 14 months the embassy was held, there seem to have been different groups that entered the embassy compound, acting without much coordination among themselves. Thus, the possibility of Tudeh involvement cannot be automatically ruled out. Still, there is strong evidence that the takeover was conceived by young followers of Khomeini and directed by a close associate of his, Hojatolislam Mohammed Kho'ini, without any prompting from the Tudeh.[65] Moreover, immediately after the takeover, the Tudeh, even more emphatically than the Soviet Union, expressed concern that the matter would go too far—that a demonstration at the embassy had produced good results, but to continue the matter further could do more harm than good.[66] Whatever the Soviets and the Tudeh may have done covertly in Iran, it so far has brought them no discernible benefits.

MILITARY INTERVENTION

One of the traditional tactics of Russian and Soviet involvement in Iran, military intervention, has not been used since the fall of the monarchy, although occasional references to the 1921 treaty between the two countries, and to Soviet occupation of the north during World War II, raise this possibility. Nonetheless, there are reasons for doubting that such a move is likely for the foreseeable future. The Soviets indicate that they believe they have gained as a result of the revolution. The costs of invading a country led by people with whom the Soviets still feel they can deal would seem prohibitively high. Iran's situation is very different from Afghanistan's. By the time of the Soviet invasion, Afghanistan had a pro-Soviet, Communist government that had lost control of most of the country to anti-Communist insurgents. In addition, the United States had made it known during Eisenhower's first term that it considered American defense of Afghanistan unfeasible.

As interested as the Soviets are in Iran, they have higher priorities in other countries. When Vietnam was embroiled in a war with Cambodia and China in 1979, that seems to have been considered more important than developments in Iran, judging by the amount of coverage given both subjects in *Pravda*. Since 1980, antigovernment sentiment in Poland has been a source of particular concern to Moscow. The Soviet Union certainly has the means to invade Iran. However, it has the means to do many things it has not done.

CONCLUSIONS

Soviet efforts to promote the USSR's interests in Iran since 1979 have produced mixed results. While the style is different, the overall substance of relations between the two countries has not changed much since the late years of the monarchy. Moscow was satisfied with its relations with Iran then, and is satisfied now. Soviet writings on Iran in the principal newspapers and the journals in which the expert advisers on Iran publish continue to take a positive tone toward the revolution and the new regime. The economic relations between the two countries and Teheran's "anti-imperialism" are considered particularly gratifying.[67] In theoretical terms, the revolution has been progressive even though it is not Marxist, champions Islamic values, and is led by mullahs.[68] In practical terms, the Islamic Republicans' hold on power is deemed stable and is expected to endure.[69] Yet Soviet observers also see analogies between recent events in Iran and earlier revolutions there and in Russia, even the Russia of 1917.[70] Under such circumstances, further changes might occur, but the Soviets have not revealed any expectations of what those changes might be or when they would occur.

NOTES

1. *Pravda*, November 19, 1978, p. 1.

2. *Washington Post*, December 11, 1980, p. A34.

3. *Pravda*, March 9, 1982, p. 4. Moscow Radio in Persian, January 16, 1980 Foreign Broadcast Information Service (FBIS), *Daily Report: Soviet Union*, January 18, 1980, p. H4; December 7, 1981, FBIS, *Soviet Union*, December 8, 1981, pp. H7-8; January 11, 1982, FBIS, *Soviet Union*, January 12, 1982, pp H1-2. (All citations of FBIS publications refer to the *Daily Reports*.)

4. Moscow Radio in Persian, November 5, 1979, FBIS, *Soviet Union*, November 7, 1979, p. H1; November 6, 1979, FBIS, *Soviet Union*, November 7, 1979, pp. H2-3; November 9, 1979, FBIS, *Soviet Union*, November 13, 1979, pp. H1-2; January 6, 1981, FBIS, *Soviet Union*, January 16, 1981, pp. H1-2; January 20, 1981, FBIS, *Soviet Union*, January 23, 1981, p. H1.

5. Moscow Television, November 18, 1979; FBIS, *Soviet Union*, December 11, 1979, p. H2; Moscow Radio in Persian, January 11, 1980, FBIS, *Soviet Union*, January 14, 1980, p. H1.

6. Moscow Radio in Persian, June 19, 1981, FBIS, *Soviet Union*, June 22, 1981, p. H4; January 1, 1982, *Soviet Union,* January 5, 1982, p. D1.

7. Moscow Radio in Persian, October 1, 1980, FBIS, *Soviet Union*, October 2, 1980, p. H3; October 10, 1980, FBIS, *Soviet Union*, October 14, 1980, p. H1; January 9, 1982, FBIS, *Soviet Union*, January 12, 1982, p. H5; Moscow Radio in Arabic, October 22, 1980, FBIS, *Soviet Union*, October 23, pp. H1-2; *Pravda*, January 19, 1981, p. 6.

8. *Yanki* (Ankara), February 22–28, 1982, FBIS, *Daily Report: South Asia*, March 4, 1982, p. I1.

9. Moscow Radio in Persian, June 1, 1981, FBIS, *Soviet Union*, June 3, 1981, p. H4.

10 *Pravda*, September 13, 1978, p. 5; November 3, 1978, p. 5; December 19, 1978, p. 5; December 26, 1978, p. 5.

11. A. Sella, "Soviet-Iranian Relations from the Fall of the Shah to the Iran-Iraq War," *The Soviet Union and the Middle East* supp. 2 (1980): 2.

12. Moscow Radio in Persian, November 9, 1979, FBIS, *Soviet Union*, November 13, 1979, pp. H1–2.

13. Teheran Domestic Radio, August 20, 1980, FBIS, *South Asia*, August 21, 1980, p. I1; *Ettela'at* (Teheran), September 6, 1980, FBIS, *South Asia*, September 6, 1980, pp. I6–7; *Keyhan* (Teheran), September 16, 1980, FBIS, *South Asia*, September 20, 1980, pp. I6–7, and September 25, 1980, pp. I24–25.

14. Teheran Domestic Radio, November 20, 1979, FBIS, *Middle East and North Africa* (*MENA*), November 21, 1979, p. R5.

15. *Le Monde*, November 24, 1979; FBIS, *MENA*, November 28, 1979, p. R42.

16. Teheran Domestic Radio, June 29, 1979, FBIS, *MENA*, July 2, 1979, pp. R3–4; January 14, 1980, FBIS, *MENA*, supp., January 15, 1979, p. 9; May 1, 1982, FBIS, *South Asia*, May 5, 1982, p. I4; January 13, 1980, BBC, *Summary of World Broadcasts*, pt. 4, *Middle East,* January 15, 1980, p. A/3.

17. Teheran International Radio in English, November 11, 1979, FBIS, *MENA*, November 13, 1979, p. R29; Teheran Domestic Radio, November 12, 1979, FBIS, *MENA*, November 13, 1979, p. R33; November 27, 1979, FBIS, *MENA*, November 28, 1979, p. R4.

18. Teheran Domestic Radio, December 29, 1979, FBIS, *MENA*, supp., December 31, 1979, pp. 19–20; April 7, 1980, FBIS, *South Asia*, April 8, 1980, p. I30; October 7, 1980, FBIS, *South Asia*, October 8, 1980, p. I8; June 5, 1981, FBIS, *South Asia*, June 9, 1981, p. I9; January 11, 1982, FBIS, *South Asia*, January 12, 1982, p. I1; February 3, 1982, FBIS, *South Asia*, February 4, 1982, p. I3; Agence France Presse in English, December 29, 1980, FBIS, *South Asia*, December 29, 1980, p. I21.

19. *Le Monde*, October 9, 1980, FBIS, *South Asia*, October 10, 1980, p. I12; *Ettela'at*, December 2, 1980, FBIS, *South Asia*, December 10, 1980, pp. I3–4.

20. *Kurier* (Vienna), October 22, 1981, Joint Publications Research Service (JPRS), no. 79358, pp. 31–32; *Washington Post*, May 28, 1982, pp. 15.

21. Teheran International Radio in Arabic, November 6, 1981, FBIS, *South Asia*, November 10, 1981, p. I10; December 22, 1979, FBIS, *MENA*, supp., December 24, 1979, p. 21; Teheran Domestic Radio, February 4, 1980, FBIS, *MENA*, February 5, 1980, pp. 9–10; February 13, 1980, FBIS, *MENA*, February 14, 1980, p. 1; August 14, 1980, FBIS, *South Asia*, August 15, 1980, p. I7; December 11, 1980, FBIS, *South Asia*, December 12, 1980, pp. I4–5; June 10, 1981, FBIS, *South Asia*, June 11, 1981, p. I8; June 14, 1981, FBIS, *South Asia*, June 15, 1981, pp. I5–7; January 7, 1982 FBIS, *South Asia*, January 8, 1982, p. I3; January 12, 1982, FBIS, *South Asia* January 13, 1982, pp. I2–3; February 10, 1982, FBIS, *South Asia*, February 11, 1982, p. I3.

22. Teheran Domestic Radio, November 14, 1979, FBIS, *MENA*, November 15, 1979, p. R16; November 5, 1979, FBIS, *MENA*, November 6, 1979, p. R17; November 20, 1979, FBIS, *MENA*, November 21, 1979, p. R5.

23. *Economist*, March 20, 1982, p. 60.

24. TASS in English, January 16, 1982, FBIS, *Soviet Union*, January 7, 1982, p. H5.

25. *Pravda*, March 9, 1982, p. 4; Moscow Radio in Persian, December 11, 1980, BBC, *Summary of World Broadcasts*, pt. 4, *Middle East,* December 15, 1980, p. A4/4.

26. *Izvestiia*, February 11, 1982, p. 4; *Burs* (Teheran), September 9, 1981, JPRS, no. 79439, pp. 39–40.

27. A Faroughy, "L'effondrement de l'économie iranienne," *Le monde diplomatique*, December 1981, p. 9.

28. AFP in English, August 23, 1980, FBIS, *South Asia*, August 25, 1980, p. I3; *Economist*, March 20, 1982, p. 60.

29. Moscow Radio in Persian, March 15, 1982, FBIS, *Soviet Union*, March 22, 1982, p. H9.

30. Teheran Domestic Radio, February 2, 1980, FBIS, *MENA*, supp., February 4, 1980, p. 29; March 14, 1980, FBIS, *MENA*, March 14, 1980, p. 12; April 6, 1980, FBIS, *South Asia*, April 7, 1980, p. I28.

31. *Pravda*, March 9, 1982, p. 4.

32. TASS in English, February 10, 1982, FBIS, *Soviet Union*, February 11, 1982, p. H1.

33. Teheran Domestic Radio, November 18, 1979, FBIS, *MENA*, November 19, 1979, p. R37; October 7, 1980, FBIS, *South Asia*, October 8, 1980, p. I7; *Keyhan* in English, February 14, 1980, FBIS, *MENA*, supp., February 27, 1980, pp. 16–17; TASS in English, June 17, 1981, FBIS, *Soviet Union*, June 18, 1981, p. H1.

34. Teheran Domestic Radio, October 21, 1981, FBIS, *South Asia*, October 23, 1981, pp. I7–11; February 16, 1982, FBIS, *South Asia,* February 17, 1982, p. I1; Moscow Domestic Radio, October 24, 1981, FBIS, *Soviet Union*, October 27, 1981, p. H9; TASS in English, October 19, 1981, FBIS, *Soviet Union*, October 20, 1981, p. H2.

35. Teheran Domestic Radio, June 17, 1979, FBIS, *MENA*, June 18, 1979, p. R14; National Voice of Iran (NVOI) in Persian, May 6, 1982, FBIS, *South Asia*, May 6, 1982, p. I7.

36. Moscow Radio in Persian, October 30, 1979, FBIS, *Soviet Union*, November 1, 1979, p. H1; January 25, 1980, FBIS, *Soviet Union*, January 28, 1980, pp. H4–5; April 29, 1980, FBIS, *Soviet Union*, April 30, 1980, pp. H4–5; May 28 and 29, 1981, FBIS, *Soviet Union*, June 2, 1981, pp. H7–19; January 11, 1982, FBIS, *Soviet Union*, January 12, 1982, p. H1.

37. Moscow Domestic Radio, June 13, 1981, FBIS, *Soviet Union*, June 15, 1981, p. H1.

38. *Pravda*, March 9, 1982, p. 4.

39. Ibid.

40. Central Committee of the Tudeh Party, "Thirty-Fifth Anniversary of the People's Party of Iran," *Information Bulletin* (of the *World Marxist Review*) (1978), nos. 15–16: 30.

41. NVOI in Persian, April 18, 1979, FBIS,*MENA*, April 26, 1979, p. R17; May 15, 1981, FBIS, *South Asia*, May 18, 1981, p. I11; January 21, 1982, FBIS, *South Asia*, January 25, 1982, p. I16; *Pravda*, April 17, 1979, p. 5.

42. *Keyhan* December 29, 1979, FBIS, *MENA*, supp., January 3, 1980, p. 11; NVOI in Persian, January 21, 1980, FBIS, *MENA*, January 23, 1980, p. 10.

43. *Elevtherotioia* (Athens), November 28, 1979, FBIS, *MENA*, November 29, 1979, p. R7; *Le Monde*, April 18, 1980, FBIS, *South Asia*, April 25, 1980, p. I25.

44. *Horizont* (East Berlin) no. 7 (1980), FBIS, *MENA*, supp., February 22, 1980, pp. 6–7; MTI (Budapest) in English, March 16, 1980, FBIS, *MENA*, March 26, 1980, pp. 22–23; PARS (Teheran) in English, August 1, 1980, FBIS, *South Asia*, August 4, 1980, p. I25; *Le Monde*, November 4, 1980, *South Asia*, November 6, 1980, p. I20; AFP in English, May 4, 1981, FBIS, *South Asia*, May 5, 1981, p. I1; Teheran Domestic Radio, June 7, 1981, FBIS, *South Asia*, June 8, 1981, p. 16; July 19, 1981, FBIS, *South Asia*, July 20, 1981, p. I1; NVOI in Persian, March 16, 1982, FBIS, *South Asia*, March 18, 1982, pp. I7–8; *Mardom* (Teheran), March 3, 1981, JPRS, no 77874, pp. 4–6.

45. NVOI in Persian, September 10, 1980, FBIS, *South Asia*, September 17, 1980, p. I24; December 29, 1980, FBIS, *South Asia*, January 2, 1981, pp. I23–24; August 31, 1981, FBIS, *South Asia*, September 2, 1981, p. I12; January 21, 1982, FBIS, *South Asia*, January 25, 1982, pp. I15–16; N. Kianuri, "Iran: For Unity Among Patriotic Forces," *World Marxist Review* 24, no. 7 (July 1981): 19; and "The Iranian Revolution: Its Friends and Its Enemies," ibid. 24, no. 11 (November 1981): 34.

46. *Le Monde*, November 18–19, 1979, FBIS, *MENA*, November 20, 1979, p. R22; *Dagens Nyheter* (Stockholm), December 2, 1979, FBIS, *MENA*, supp., December 12, 1979, pp. 39–40.

47. *Le Matin*, November 27, 1979, FBIS, *MENA*, supp., December 4, 1979, p. R27.

48. NVOI in Azeri, April 13, 1979, FBIS, *MENA*, April 17, 1979, p. R18; NVOI in Persian, November 19, 1979, FBIS, *MENA*, November 23, 1979, p. R32; August 1, 1980, FBIS, *South Asia*, August 6, 1980, p. I12; June 3, 1981, FBIS, *South Asia*, June 4, 1981, p. I6; *Pravda*, May 6, 1979, p. 5.

49. NVOI in Persian, September 13, 1981, FBIS, *South Asia*, September 16, 1981, p. I12; January 29, 1982, FBIS, *South Asia*, February 3, 1982, p. I5; February 27, 1982, FBIS, *South Asia*, March 3, 1982, pp. I16–17; *Mardom*, January 3, 1981, JPRS, no. 77516, pp. 17–18.

50. NVOI in Persian, September 13, 1981, FBIS, *South Asia*, September 16, 1981, p. I12; April 17, 1982, FBIS, *South Asia*, April 21, 1982, p. I9; *Economist*, March 14, 1981, p. 37.

51. NVOI in Persian, November 5, 1979, FBIS, *MENA*, November 7, 1979, pp. 20–21; December 28, 1979, FBIS, *MENA*, supp., December 31, 1979, pp. 25–26; January 11, 1980, FBIS, *MENA*, supp., January 14, 1980, p. 13; April 9, 1980, FBIS, *South Asia*, April 10, 1980, pp. I27–29; December 7, 1980, FBIS, *South Asia*, December 11, 1980, p. I22; September 1, 1981, FBIS, *South Asia*, September 2, 1981, pp. I12–13; January 2, 1982, FBIS, *South Asia*, January 5, 1982, p. I5.

52. Moscow Radio in Persian, December 25, 1980, BBC, *Summary of World Broadcasts* pt. 4, *Middle East*, January 1, 1981, p. A4/4.

53. *Bamdad* (Teheran), October 25, 1979, FBIS, *MENA*, November 2, 1979, pp. R6–7; *Ettela'at*, November 7, 1979, FBIS, *MENA*, November 16, 1979, p. R16; November 25, 1979, FBIS, *MENA*, November 30, 1979, pp. R22–23; Teheran Domestic Radio, December 1, 1979, FBIS, *MENA*, December 4, 1979, pp. R7–8.

54. Teheran Domestic Radio, November 17, 1979, FBIS, *MENA*, November 19, 1979, pp. R19–20; NVOI in Persian, November 12, 1979, FBIS, *MENA*, November 15, 1979, p. R28.

55. *Le Monde*, November 23, 1979, FBIS, *MENA*, November 26, 1979, p. R15; *Le Matin*, November 27, 1979, FBIS, *MENA*, December 4, 1979, pp. R26–28; *L'Humanité*, January 31, 1980, FBIS, *MENA*, supp., February 11, 1980, p. 23.

56. NVOI in Persian, April 16, 1982, FBIS, *South Asia*, April 20, 1982, p. I11.

57. *Le Matin*, November 27, 1979, FBIS, *MENA*, December 4, 1979, p. R27; NVOI in Persian, February 12, 1980, FBIS, *MENA*, supp., February 15, 1980, p. 38; May 19, 1981, FBIS, *South Asia*, May 21, 1981, p. I9; N. Kianuri, "The Iranian Revolution: Its Friends and Its Enemies," p. 32.

58. Moscow Domestic Radio, March 28, 1979, FBIS, *Soviet Union*, March 29, 1979, p. H7; Moscow Radio in Persian, May 31, 1979, FBIS, *Soviet Union*, June 1, 1979, p. H4; NVOI in Persian, April 3, 1979, FBIS, *MENA*, April 13, 1979, p. R7; December 7, 1979, FBIS, *MENA*, supp., December 10, 1979, p. 50; February 13, 1980, FBIS, *MENA*, February 14, 1980, p. 38; NVOI in Azeri, December 9, 1979, FBIS, *MENA*, supp., December 11, 1979, p. 31; April 19, 1980, FBIS, *South Asia*, April 25, 1980, pp. I34–35.

59. *Pravda*, April 8, 1979, p. 5; Moscow Radio in Persian, April 3, 1979, FBIS, *Soviet Union*, April 5, 1979, p. H8; TASS, April 16, 1979, FBIS, *Soviet Union*, April 17, 1979, p. H9; NVOI in Persian, December 19, 1980, FBIS, *South Asia*, December 22, 1980, p. I26; May 10, 1981, FBIS, *South Asia*, May 12, 1981, p. I14; May 28, 1982, FBIS, *South Asia*, May 29, 1981, p. I9; January 2, 1982, FBIS, *South Asia*, January 6, 1982, pp. I7–8; *Mardom*, February 1, 1981, JPRS, no. 77717, p. 25; April 19, 1981, JPRS, no. 77953, p. 8.

60. *Le Monde*, September 7–8, 1980, FBIS, *South Asia*, September 17, 1980, p. I11; December 13, 1980, JPRS, no. 77291, pp. 5–6; E. Shevernadze, "The CPSU's Nationalities Policy in the Period of Developed Socialism," *World Marxist Review* 23, no. 1 (January 1980): 11; NVOI in Persian, February 4, 1981, FBIS, *South Asia*, February 5, 1981, pp. I15–16; *Mardom*, January 27, 1981, JPRS, no. 77667, pp. 41–43; May 26, 1981, FBIS, *South Asia*, June 5, 1981, p. I8; Moscow Radio in Persian, November 27, 1979, FBIS, *Soviet Union*, November 28, 1979, p. H3; C. Kutschera, "La poudrière kurde," *Le monde diplomatique*, September 1980, pp. 7, 8.

61. *Adabiyat va iniasanat* (Baku), February 15, 1980, JPRS, no. 76542, p. 32; March 7, 1980, JPRS, no. 76309, pp. 55–59; September 5, 1980, JPRS, no. 77230, pp. 61–63; May 1, 1981, JPRS, no. 78786, pp. 43–44; September 18, 1981, JPRS, no. 79847, p. 49; *Azerbaijan* (Baku) in Azeri (1981), no. 5, JPRS, no. 79497, p. 33; Baku International Radio in Azeria, October 17, 1980, BBC, *Summary of World Broadcasts*, pt. 1, *Soviet Union*, October 27, 1980, p. B/1.

62. NVOI in Azeri, March 4, 1980, FBIS, *MENA*, supp., March 12, 1980, pp. 27–28; NVOI in Persian, December 12, 1980, FBIS, *South Asia*, December 17, 1980,

pp. 122-23; *Adabiyat va injasanat*, March 7, 1980, JPRS, no. 76309, pp. 56-57; Baku International Radio in Azeri, February 15, 1982, FBIS, *Soviet Union*, February 16, 1982, pp. H4-5; April 3, 1982, FBIS, *Soviet Union*, April 6, 1982, pp. H1-2.

63. A. Faroughy, "Le pouvoir islamique face aux aspirations autonomistes en Iran," *Le monde diplomatique*, February 1980, p. 9.

64. DPA (Hamburg), November 29, 1979, FBIS, *MENA*, November 30, 1979, p. R5.

65. *Washington Post*, January 28, 1981, p. A28.

66. NVOI in Persian, November 5, 1979, FBIS, *MENA*, November 7, 1979, pp. R20-21; November 12, 1979, FBIS, *MENA*, November 15, 1979, p. R28; November 20, 1979, FBIS, *MENA*, November 21, 1979, p. R17; November 21, 1979, FBIS, *MENA*, November 23, 1979, pp. R33-34; December 5, 1979, FBIS, *MENA*, December 6, 1979, pp. R13-14.

67. Moscow Radio in Persian, March 5, 1982, FBIS, *Soviet Union*, March 9, 1982, p. H4; *Pravda*, April 14, 1979, p. 1; *Pravda*, March 9, 1982, p. 4; "XXVI s"ezd KPSS i problemy natsional'no-osvoboditel'nogo dvizneniia," *Narody Azii i Afriki* (1981), no 3: 3, 6.

68. A. V. Gordon, "Sovetskaia Vostokovedy i Afrikanisti o protsessakh formirovaniia natsional'nogo i klasovogo soznaniia v osvobodivshchikhsia stranakh (1976-1980)," *Narody Azii i Afriki* (1981), no. 1:186-187; S. Aliev, "Islam i politika," *Aziia i Afrika segodnia,* December 1981, pp. 5-9; G. Kim, "Sotsial'noe razvitie i ideologicheskaia bor'ba v razvivaiushchiknsia stranakh" *Mezhdunarodnaia zhizn* (1980), no. 3: 70-82.

69. Moscow Radio in Persian, March 3, 1982, FBIS, *Soviet Union*, March 9, 1982, p. H4.

70. *Pravda*, May 2, 1979, p. 4; *Bakinskii rapochii*, January 8, 1982, p. 4; E. M. Aimakov, "Zakon neravnomernosti rasuitiia i istoricheskie sud'by osvobodivshikhsia stran," *Mirovaia ekonimika i mezhdunarodnye otnosheniia* (1980), no. 12: 31, 35-37, 39-40, 45, 46.

FIVE

Libya and the Soviet Union: Alliance at Arm's Length
ELLEN LAIPSON

INTRODUCTION

The relationship between the Soviet Union and Libya under the leadership of Colonel Mu'amar al-Qaddafi has been enigmatic; its financial and military dimensions are impressive, and have expanded rapidly since the late 1970s, but the ties are clearly less than a formal alliance or a conventional client/sponsor relationship. In fact, while there are obvious convergent objectives in particular areas, there is a noticeable dissociation on general ideological attitudes and long-range goals.

On one level, the Soviet Union finds in Libya a strongly anti-Western state with an activist leadership willing to use its own resources to encourage weaker regional states to limit their ties to the West. But at the same time, Libya has proved to be a reliable trading partner of major Western industrial states, declares itself nonaligned, and has refused to consider a Soviet base on its soil. The relationship defies easy explanations from the Soviet perspective as well; the Soviets see only limited opportunities in Libya, place restrictions on the depth and scope of the ties, and may see Libya more as a wealthy trading partner than as a reliable political ally. There are indications, however, that changing regional dynamics since 1980 may be tipping the balance in the Soviets' favor, and by responding to Libyan concerns, the Soviets may strengthen their military position in the area.

The Soviet connection to Libya cannot be seen as a model for its Third World relations because it is unusual in several respects. Libya is simultaneously an extremely wealthy and a very underdeveloped nation. Its wealth affords it greater flexibility than more dependent states; it can purchase the development services it seeks on the open market. But at the same time, its internal weaknesses make it dependent on outside help, and for security and practical reasons, this help often comes from Soviet or Eastern bloc states.

The views expressed here are those of the author and do not reflect those of CRS or the Library of Congress.

133

It is also unusual because the Soviets rely almost exclusively on the military dimension to define their role in Libya. There are both strategic and economic aspects to the military component, but more significant is the general absence of other conventional tools and techniques of Soviet power and presence. The sparse population and lack of major urban centers greatly inhibit the kind of Soviet behavior common elsewhere in the Third World.

The relationship is nonetheless important to watch. Both nations have particular strengths and special needs. There is reason to believe that since 1981, each party has been more willing to respond to the other's concerns, although there is not perfect symmetry; Qaddafi seems to seek greater Soviet military protection but is hard pressed to provide the Soviets with the hard cash they want.

For the West, the relationship is an intriguing one and merits special attention. Neither Libya nor the Soviet Union has found in the other a panacea for all its problems, and some observers argue that the achievements of this bilateral bond are indeed modest, although others credit the Soviet-Libyan connection with numerous instances of African instability. One cannot question that the degree of Soviet military penetration of Libya, the prospects for Qaddafi's radical transformation of Libya into a new form of Islamic Arab society, and the future of Soviet-Libyan energy and economic cooperation are critical concerns for Western policy in the Mediterranean, and in the Arab and African arenas.

THE LIBYAN CONTEXT

At independence in 1951, Libya was described in U.N. documents as the poorest nation in the world. The circumstances of its achieving independence, long before many other colonized states with more advanced infrastructure and more abundant resources, including its North African neighbors, were part of the nascent East-West rivalry of the immediate postwar period. From most accounts, U.S. strategic interest in establishing a major Mediterranean base converged with British political interests. Those two nations worked for the independence option over the Soviet-backed alternative of placing Libya under a U.N. trusteeship.[1] The Soviets were also interested in developing a Mediterranean presence, and saw in the well-located, sparsely populated Libyan coast an ideal site. When spurned, they concentrated their efforts on Egypt, which was politically more valuable but required considerably more effort.

Upon independence, the pro-Western Sanusi monarchy was installed, artifically uniting the country's east-west divisions of Tripoli and Cyrenaica. In September 1969, a 27-year-old captain named Qaddafi and 70 young officers, following in the footsteps of their spiritual father, Gamal Abdel Nasser, seized power in a bloodless coup. The well-organized takeover had been planned over a period of years, as these officers grew disillusioned with King Idris' ineffective reforms. The coup was received calmly and without resistance in Libya and abroad. By the end of the first week, Qaddafi emerged as the de facto head of state, defining his task of restructuring Libyan society in terms that recall the attempts to create a Libyan republic in 1916-20.

Since 1969, Qaddafi has experimented with three different political forms. The initial ruling apparatus was modeled on Algeria's Revolutionary Command Council (RCC), designed in theory for informal, collegial decision making among military peers, with no dominant personalities. In addition, he organized the Arab Socialist Union, modeled on Egypt's mass party-cum-social organization. In 1973, dissatisfied with both, Qaddafi abolished the RCC and organized the country into 450 people's committees, establishing the base for his theory that is outlined in the *Green Book* of 1976. He called for the transformation of Libya into the original *jamahiriya*, a coined term roughly translated as "direct democracy." The *Green Book* describes a new society that straddles capitalism and Communism, with little institutional structure. For Qaddafi, the ideal goal is a kind of pure popular sovereignty, where "fraudulent forms of democracy" like parliaments are not necessary. On the foreign policy front, he advocates positive neutralism as the solution for all underdeveloped states, and is beginning to formulate his goal of a united Arab Islamic republic, post-Nasser pan-Arabism.

Some sociologists have seen parallels between the Soviet system and the institutional forms of Qaddafi's *jamahiriya*, comparing the General Popular Committee with the Soviet cabinet, the General Secretariat with the organism of the same name in the Soviet system, and the Permanent Secretariat with the Politburo.[2] Part Two of the *Green Book* outlines "the solution to the economic problem" in terms borrowing heavily from Marxist socialism. Other have seen in the *Green Book* the contribution of such Western thinkers as Rousseau.[3]

Two points should be noted. First, Qaddafi's political theories, for all practical purposes, remain theories, and have not been implemented or realized to a point where valid comparisons with the Soviet system are possible. Second, Qaddafi himself gives no credit to outside influences, and presents his theory as indigenous, as emanating from his spiritual experiences in the Libyan desert. Therefore, whether the current structures of the Libyan political system are akin to Soviet political values and institutions may have little bearing on Soviet influence on or access to the Libyan polity.

In practice, as a foreign policy "positive neutralism" has meant considerable contact between Libya and the West. After the takeover of

1969 and the abolition of the monarchy, Qaddafi closed the American and British bases, but continued to seek and receive military help from the West. The United States provided military aid until 1974. While Qaddafi began purchasing Soviet weapons in 1970, he considered France a more important arms provider than the Soviets until the mid-1970s. A diversified arms supply strategy was more than just practical for Qaddafi; it was a reflection of his independence of any bloc, and therefore was a matter of national security policy.

Over time, Qaddafi has lost some of that maneuverability, and has grown increasingly oriented to the East for arms, training, and economic cooperation agreements, although he has sought diversity within the Eastern bloc, presumably to prevent Soviet domination. The United States began placing restrictions on high-technology sales to Libya in the early 1970s because of Qaddafi's support for terrorism and other foreign policies considered contrary to American interests. France, in the context of its Africa policy, has limited its arms trade with Libya, although the Mitterrand government is inclined to use arms sales as a positive inducement in political relations, and has not ruled out future contracts with the Qaddafi government.

The reluctance of the West to trade with Qaddafi has gone a step further under the Reagan administration, and the confrontational tone of Libyan-American relations not only has reinforced the trend toward Libyan reliance on the East as an exclusive arms source, but also may have induced Qaddafi to redefine his security needs and his attitude toward great power alliances. In a significant speech on the anniversary of the September 1 Revolution in 1981, Qaddafi proclaimed his willingness to sacrifice his neutralism for a protecting alliance. "We desperately need to be in military alliance with any ally who will stand by us against the United States"[4]

Other aspects of Qaddafi's foreign policy activities may directly or indirectly enhance Soviet interests in the region. Qaddafi has been rebuffed in his search for political unions with Egypt, Syria, Tunisia, and Chad. But he succeeded, in late 1981, in forming an alliance with Ethiopia and the People's Democratic Republic of (South) Yemen that could be significant in the context of his relations with the Soviet Union. Both of these states are more clearly Soviet clients than Libya, and the prospects of coordinating shipments and transfer of arms within the alliance, which forms an arc around pro-Western Sudan and Egypt, could facilitate Soviet regional planning and give the Soviets indirect access to Libya via these more compliant states.[5] The presumed Libyan financing of its pact partners also provides considerable benefit for the Soviet Union.[5]

Libyan involvement in international terrorism, through financial support and through training provided in Libya to a broad spectrum of terrorist groups, is another Libyan activity of special interest to the Soviet

Union. Experts generally concur that while the Soviets may not be responsible for the growth of political terrorism that has plagued most Western societies since the early 1970s, they have benefited from its destabilizing effects and must at least passively support it. Qaddafi's reputedly unmatched activity in this field is, at a minimum, an unspoken dimension of the Soviet interest in Libya.

The situation in Libya in 1983 is one of considerable uncertainty. Many believe that Qaddafi's radical internal measures have alienated groups that were once among his supporters. Those who continue to back him are the have-nots of Libya, those who did not have a stake in the dismantling of the existing order. Some believe that the severe economic dislocations caused by Qaddafi's rulings on banks, private ownership, and income distribution will have serious repercussions on the future stability of the country, even after Qaddafi. Two military-organized coup attempts have occurred between mid-1981 and mid-1982. The second, in late April 1982, has been cited as the reason for Qaddafi's last-minute cancellation of a state visit to Greece. The oil glut and U.S. boycott of high-priced Libyan oil have created cash flow problems for Libya in 1982, and this has increased the scarcity within the country of the consumer goods and manufactured imports on which the population depends, although the situation stabilized somewhat by year's end. The Soviet Union must consider this state of flux when dealing with the present Libyan government and predicting the long-term stability of that regime.

SOVIET OBJECTIVES

Given the unusual personality of the Libyan state and its leader, the Soviet Union has opted for a limited relationship with the country, and has not sought a high degree of association or involvement in its day-to-day affairs. The Soviets appear reconciled to the sometimes strident stance of nonalignment espoused by Libya, and have been willing to agree to disagree on philosophical questions when more tangible interests are at stake.

Libya holds a number of attractions for the Soviets. Its 1,100-mile Mediterranean coast, with a natural port at Tripoli, has considerable strategic importance. Its proximity to Egypt, the heart of the Arab world, is significant, as is its location on the Soviets' north-south axis to Black Africa. Libya has also been a cash-paying buyer of Soviet goods of considerable importance, and has certain political affinities with the Soviet Union.

Western analysts differ dramatically on how to assess Soviet priorities in Libya; some see them as overwhelmingly strategic in nature, while those inclined to take a nonalarmist view of Soviet intentions see the economic aspect of the relationship as equally important. The differences also reflect diverging time perspectives. The economic-interests group tends to look at the short run, and to point to the already realized Soviet-Libyan trade as more important than the elusive and continuing military alliance talks. But the strategic camp takes a longer-term view and ascribes considerable patience to the Soviets, who cannot overlook the advantages of close military ties with Libya. For those who see the Soviets as reactive and opportunistic in the Third World, Libya has provoked responses and provided opportunities in a pattern that suggests its increasing importance to the Soviets.

Strategic Objectives

The Soviets cannot overlook Libya's location on the southern flank of the Mediterranean. A Soviet presence there could cause considerable alarm in NATO circles. In addition, Libya is located between two pro-Western states. Both Tunisia and Egypt have expanding military cooperation arrangements with the United States, permit port-of-call visits, and have conducted joint operations. The Soviet desire to monitor or counterbalance that presence is evident.

Libya is also strategically located, from the Soviet perspective, along a north-south axis, in that its airfields could provide en route refueling access for Soviet actions (interventions, airlifts) in sub-Saharan states.[6]

Libya's strategic attractiveness to the Soviets has grown principally since Anwar Sadat expelled the Soviets from Egypt in 1972. They had virtually unlimited access there, with tens of thousands of military personnel in residence and almost total control of parts of Alexandria harbor. Libya cannot compensate for the loss of Egypt, which was devastating militarily and humiliating politically for the Soviets. According to some accounts, Libya was initially seen as a place to store weapons for use by Egypt, should Cairo have decided to return to the Soviet-backed rejectionist camp. But with Egypt deeply committed to the American camp, Libya by the late 1970s became an alternative, albeit an inferior one, and a place from which to pressure Egypt.[7]

The Soviets have reportedly pressed the Libyans for naval and air base rights, but to date have been more successful in negotiating interim, more modest steps, such as landing rights and port-of-call visits. The Soviets have technical advisers in residence (about 1,000), but for financial and political reasons, the Libyans have balanced their numbers with non-Soviet Eastern bloc advisers. A considerable number are presumed to be from Yugoslavia and Romania, suggesting even less control from Moscow than is the case with the East German security and intelligence personnel. Coproduction of weapons with Libya and joint exercises with Soviet and Libyan troops do not seem to be high-priority goals for the Soviets, as they have become in U.S.-Egyptian military relations.

There has been considerable controversy over whether the Soviets have an understanding with Libya about the use of the Soviet-provided weapons stockpiled in the Libyan desert. Some have seen the estimated $12 billion spent on arms by Libya since 1969, so greatly in excess of what Qaddafi can use, as a Soviet cache.[8] But many dispute the usefulness of these weapons because of deterioration under desert conditions, and the likelihood that Qaddafi would have accepted Soviet restrictions on use of the arms by Libya.

On the other hand, it is not beyond the imagination to contemplate circumstances under which Soviet-Libyan military cooperation could occur, involving the use of the Soviet-supplied equipment beyond Libya's borders. Soviets were reported alongside Libyans during their Chad intervention (December 1980–November 1981), although only to repair and maintain equipment operated by Libyans. But other scenarios for this kind of complementary use of the Soviet-supplied arms are plausible, particularly if the current signs of Qaddafi's altering his ideological position to permit closer identification with the Soviet Union prove accurate. In sum, the use of the Libyan-purchased weaponry can be arranged on an ad hoc basis, and written agreements about such use may not prove necessary.

Political Objectives

Soviet political objectives in Libya are based on a vague ideological affinity that underscores the anti-imperialist, anti-Zionist, anticapitalist rhetoric of Colonel Qaddafi. They do not appear to be aimed at forging a closer political alliance,[9] or at portraying Libya as a close protégé or client of Moscow. This was demonstrated in the Soviet leader's remarks on the occasion of Qaddafi's state visit to Moscow in April 1981: ". . . Our states differ largely from each other. There are also certain differences of ideological nature between us. . . ."[10]

Moscow's reluctance to deepen the political association with Libya may reflect concern about Qaddafi's mixed reputation in the Third World, anxieties about his Islamic ideas arousing interest among the Soviet Muslim population, and a demonstrated willingness to accord nonaligned countries a degree of rhetorical independence. In the same speech, Brezhnev outlined the code of behavior observed by the Soviet Union in its dealings with "the young states of the three continents," which included "respect for the status of non-alignment chosen by the majority of African, Asian and Latin American states. Renunciation of the attempts to draw them into military political blocs of big powers."[11] Some analysts think that this attitude best serves the Soviets' political objectives by permitting them to draw a stark comparison between the entangling alliances of the Western states with their Third World friends and the Soviet approach.

The dissociation between the Soviets and Libya, however, seems to betray past strains and problems in the relationship. The Soviets may have felt thwarted in past attempts to move closer to Libya, and are opting for a more distant posture. Another source of strain has been Libyan criticism of the Soviet intervention in Afghanistan. After abstaining on early U.N. votes condemning the Soviets, Libya has become more outspoken in support of the struggle of the Afghan people, and in Moscow, Qaddafi referred to the need to ensure the independence and neutrality of Afghanistan. The Soviets, in contrast, were supportive of the Libyan intervention in Chad, and have called the Libyan action "a decisive factor in the restoration of peace in Chad,"[12]

On a day-to-day basis, there is ample room for vague statements of ideological affinity (opposition to Camp David, support for liberation movements) that do not entail close coordination or sophisticated joint policy formulation. On a large number of issues debated in the United Nations and in regional forums, the Soviet Union can be reasonably certain that the Libyans will work for positions and decisions compatible with Soviet interests.

It is not clear whether the Soviets have the leverage to alter Libyan positions on questions that may have long-term implications for the Soviet Union and on which Libyan and Soviet political objectives may not coincide. An interesting example of this is the question of the western Sahara and Libyan support for the Polisario. The Soviets have been noticeably quiet on the war, presumably trying to avoid jeopardizing important economic ties with Morocco, and viewing the conflict as a localized problem. Prospects for a negotiated solution to the problem are now bogged down in Organization of African Unity (OAU) infighting, in no small measure created by Libya and Qaddafi's scheduled chairmanship of that organization. At this point, and at other watersheds in the war and its resolution efforts, one can easily imagine diverging Soviet and Libyan perspectives. The Libyans have been strongly identified with the Polisario, and may consider the political price of making concessions for peace too dear, whereas the Soviets, looking at other regional dynamics, may make a different calculation. What remains for further analysis is how much the Soviets, in the context of their political relationship with Libya, could influence Libyan policy on this or other issues.

Libyan support for terrorism is another murky area in which Soviet interests may be served, but where the Soviets may be more passive beneficiaries than active agents of influence with decision-making power. Some observers however, believe that over time, the Libyans and Soviets have learned to cooperate well in the training of disparate groups of terrorists whose targets include major European states as well as Israel and conservative Arab governments.[13] Soviet-Libyan cooperation also includes the seemingly more benign activity of setting up seminars and political conferences to bring together leftists of various nationalities to discuss the common struggle.[14]

Economic Objectives

For many who see the Soviet connection to Libya as plagued with a number of problems, only the economic relationship can be explained in clear terms. The Soviets have found in Libya, perhaps more than in any other Third World state, a highly valuable trading partner. The arms-for-dollars trade has provided the Soviets with important foreign exchange to meet their balance-of-payments needs.

Libya has not been an important source of oil for the Soviets, but those who predict that the Soviet Union may be a net importer of oil in the 1990s see Libya as a logical and likely outside source. The prospect of an arms-for-oil barter arrangement seems more plausible now than in the mid-1970s, because Libyan cash reserves reportedly are dangerously low; its oil output has been reduced by 60 percent since 1981, and its reserves are down from $14 billion to $9 billion. The Soviets might be interested in pursuing such a barter deal for their East European clients, which would be of indirect economic benefit to them, although presumably less desirable than cash payments.

Libya has over 30,000 Soviet and Eastern bloc economic technicians, who serve in both training and advisory capacities.[15] Many of the Soviets fill the need for cadres in the civil service. Soviet technicians are paid more than their East European counterparts, and the Libyans have consequently lowered the ratio of Soviet to non-Soviet economic personnel.

MEASURING SOVIET SUCCESS

Assessing the Soviets' achievements and setbacks in Libya since 1970 is best done according to one's particular perception of their objectives. Nevertheless, there is ample evidence to document in a neutral fashion the real and recent growth of Soviet exposure to Libya. In the military field, the ties have grown qualitatively and quantitatively, and are likely to expand in the near future. In political terms, the relationship remains more or less constant within its specific limitations. In economic terms, some deterioration of the Soviet objective has occurred with the dramatic decline of Libyan oil sales, but may be restored with new adjustments in the world oil market.

Strategic Achievements

A major breakthrough for the Soviets occurred in July 1981, when Libya granted port visiting rights for the first time since the 1969 revolution. It has been reported that several such calls have taken place, and thus the Soviets have quietly normalized an important aspect of their naval presence in the Mediterranean. Similar rights to Libya's airfields have not been granted, according to information available on the public record.

There has also been progress toward the achievement of a Soviet-Libyan friendship and cooperation treaty along the lines of the Soviet-Syrian treaty. Although no date has been suggested, many analysts believe the treaty could be realized in 1983, and speculation soared following the March 1983 visit to Moscow by Major Jallud. Such an event may be contingent upon Qaddafi's perception of the threat from the West, notably the United States. One measure of this positive trend is Qaddafi's remarks to a German journalist: ". . . in its present situation facing the enemy, Syria had the right to establish such an alliance and conclude such a treaty. Syria is not the only country to do so. . . . We too might find it necessary for us to conclude such a treaty."[16]

Developing Libya's conventional military capabilities for its own national defense and as a deterrent against Egypt and other regional rivals has met with considerable success since 1970, in terms both of accumulating advanced weaponry and of training personnel. The intervention and airlift into Chad, while not providing combat experience, proved considerably more effective than Libya's past adventures beyond its borders, and led many analysts to the conclusion that Libyan military capabilities have improved. The short border confrontation between Egypt and Libya in 1977 is the other major measure of enhanced conventional capabilities of the Libyan state.

A few essential features of the current scope of Libyan military capabilities, which in large measure can be considered a Soviet contribution, include the following:

- The armed forces, numbering 55,000, have one of the highest ratios of military equipment to manpower in the world.[17]
- It is estimated that Libya has spent $12 billion on defense since 1969.
- The air force consists of four squadrons of MiG-23s, MiG-25s, and Mirages. Libya has been among the first non-Warsaw Pact countries to receive the most advanced of the MiG line.
- Libya's arsenal of missiles is diverse, including British, French, and Soviet equipment. Reports that Libya contracted with a West German firm for medium-range missiles capable of carrying nuclear warheads were denied by the company, OSTRAG, in late 1981.
- Libya has over 2,500 tanks, including the Soviet T-55s, T-62s, and T-72s.

- Several thousand Libyan officers have been sent to the Soviet Union for training.
- The air force remains dependent on foreign pilots, including Pakistanis, Palestinians, and Soviets.[18] North Korea withdrew a group of its pilots in early 1980.
- There are reports that the Soviets are helping Libya construct a major naval facility in the eastern part of the country.
- Libya's domestic manufacturing capability remains limited; it exported an estimated $35 million in defense goods during 1974–78.[19]
- There have been reports of Libyan interest in setting up coproduction facilities with Turkey, as well as a MiG assembly plant in the country.
- There are an estimated 1,800 Soviet and Eastern bloc military advisers living in Libya.[20]

The trends clearly demonstrate that the military component has proved to be an effective instrument of Soviet influence in Libya, and has succeeded in achieving one strategic objective by making Qaddafi's nation a force that Egypt, Sudan, Tunisia, and other states of the region must reckon with in their defense planning. But French and Italian sales, as well as Qaddafi's wariness, have prevented the Soviets from achieving total domination of the Libyan market. There also is no clear indication of what understanding the Soviets have with Libya about the cooperative use of the Libyan arsenal.

Economic Achievements

The Soviets have found Libya to be an important trading partner, and have benefited enormously from an ironic triangular relationship: major Western powers, including the United States, have been paying in dollars for high-grade Libyan oil. Libya has purchased Soviet arms, and paid for them in dollars, which the Soviets have used for balance-of-payments purposes. The Soviets may have received as much as $10 billion in this way since 1969, approximately the level of U.S. arms agreements with Iran in 1973–77, and roughly one-fourth the total value of U.S. arms agreements with Saudi Arabia since 1975.

In addition, the Soviets are paid for providing technical and advisory services to Libya, both military and nonmilitary, and for other high-technology items. In the nuclear field, the Soviets offered Libya a research facility in 1975, and power plants in 1978 and 1981. Of these, only the research facility is presumed to be under construction, and the financial details of the project are not available on the public record.[21] Its small population (under 3 million) makes Libya an unlikely market of significant proportions for Soviet manufactured goods.

At present, it appears that there is not significant room for growth in the Soviet-Libyan economic relationship. With current world oil market conditions and the state of Libya's liquidity, transactions on a cash basis are less likely than before, and may inhibit Soviet military and commercial trade plans. After the summit meeting of Libyan and Soviet leaders in April 1981, a cooperation agreement pertaining to oil, gas, nonferrous metals, and irrigation was signed. Again, its financial dimensions were not disclosed.[22]

Political Achievements

If one accepts the premise that Soviet political objectives in Libya are modest and are not aimed at creating a Libyan society modeled on that of the Soviet Union, then the achievements should be measured by examining the coincidence of Soviet and Libyan views on major world issues. There is a general identity of the positions of the two states on foreign policy questions in the short run: U.S. policies in the Middle East, continued resistance to negotiated peace with Israel, Egyptian-American joint military exercises. But many consider the political "affinity" unnatural and not based on any profoundly held convictions. To John Campbell, Soviet policy in Libya "is a pure gamble, for any resemblance between Soviet aims and the consequences of Qaddafi's foreign policy is coincidental."[23]

Qaddafi's scheduled chairmanship of the OAU in 1982–83 may provide the Soviets with certain political benefits in Africa, as compared with a more Western-oriented head of state in the chair. But the question of the western Sahara has split that organization into moderate and radical camps, and Qaddafi's ability to polarize regional groups may limit the political gains for the Soviet Union in having one of its closer African partners directing the debates.

There is no indication that the Soviets have succeeded in altering Qaddafi's political thinking on Islam and Arabism as bases of a future unified Arab Islamic state, or that they consider his stated goal desirable. But while considerable ideological distance remains on long-term political objectives, the two nations' ability to agree to disagree on important issues has improved. Ironically, a case can be made that the main political achievement of the Soviet Union in Libya since 1977 has been to become reconciled to the likelihood that no greater political affinity can be achieved with the present Libyan regime. The record indicates that in the early years of Soviet approaches to Libya, the political expectations were higher and the disappointments greater. The Qaddafi visit to Moscow in 1981 suggests a political dissociation that can also be viewed as a maturing of the political relationship into something more realistic.

CONSTRAINTS ON SOVIET POLICY

There are three major constraints on the Soviets' finding in Libya a receptive partner in the economic, military, and political arenas, as well as an effective agent in promoting pro-Soviet policies and practices in the Arab and African worlds.

Ideology, both political and religious, is a major obstacle. Libya and the Soviet Union do not view the world in the same way. Qaddafi finds the Communist model as abhorrent as the capitalist, although socialism and collectivism are integral parts of his social ideal. His 1981 decision to ban free enterprise from the ideas contained in part two of the *Green Book* indicates considerable sympathy for and attachment to Marxist economic theory, but the Soviet experience does not seem to provide models for his restructuring of Libyan society, and its atheism is abhorrent to him.

Islam is a central aspect of Qaddafi's experience, and he has mobilized religion into his political thinking in a more dynamic and fundamental way than have other Arab revolutionaries, who have used Islam more as a slogan than as an operational set of principles and values. For Qaddafi, Islam provides some important answers to how society and state should function, and he has even attempted to spread Islam in Africa through conversions of African leaders.[24] For the Soviets, this is anathema. It runs contrary to the profoundly secular nature of their system, and touches a sensitive nerve because of the large number of Soviet citizens who are Muslim. This divergence between the Soviet and Libyan perspectives cannot be resolved.

The second major constraint is Qaddafi's reputation. The Soviets have to assess whether identification with one of the most controversial figures on the world political scene is too costly for them. This would be a major consideration if a heavy commitment through a long-term friendship treaty were consummated. Qaddafi's image as a maverick might cause the Soviets some loss of prestige among countries that are nonaligned and that might be prospective Soviet treaty partners.

Because of what some consider Qaddafi's penchant for unpredictability, the Soviets run the risk of losing control over their investment in Libya. Their experience in Egypt under Sadat—being abruptly expelled from a country in which their presence was extensive, by a strongly independent nationalist leader—may give them pause. Qaddafi could turn his back on the Soviets, causing economic and strategic dislocations for them, and could conceivably use Soviet-supplied arms in situations where other Soviet interests could be jeopardized. While to date there is nothing to lend credence to the notion that Qaddafi might cut ties with the Soviets, his past behavior may make Soviet planners cautious about the degree of involvement.

The third major constraint is the nature and size of the Libyan polity. This constraint is operational for the more conventional kind of Soviet penetration strategy. Libya does not provide the standard vehicles for the Soviets to subvert the political views and attitudes of its population: the small press establishment is strictly censored and functions as a government agency, there is no trade union movement in the traditional sense, and the current government structure of people's committees and congresses cannot be compared in a useful way with classic political party organization. There has never been a Communist party in Libya, and the ground on which it might have taken root has been preempted by Qaddafi's efforts to radically transform the state.[25]

SOVIET-LIBYAN RELATIONS IN A POST-QADDAFI ERA

Predictions about the prospects for a change in Libyan leadership in the not-too-distant future have grown more frequent and more fervent since 1981. Colonel Qaddafi's abrupt cancellation of a planned trip to Greece in late April 1982 fueled these fires. Some analysts have concluded from the increasing number of dissident groups abroad, and from the presumed feelings of grievance and disillusionment among Libyans subjected to extreme economic disruptions, that Qaddafi's demise may be imminent. Yet others point out that his East German security apparatus has served him well in the past, and his concerns for his personal safety may prevent him from exposing himself to risks. Some analysts also believe that when a change occurs, it may be a more random event, more like Sadat's assassination than a well-organized uprising. The considerable speculation about the survivability of Qaddafi's regime warrants taking a look at such an event's consequences for the Soviet Union.

At present, the Soviet Union is presumed to be firmly supporting Qaddafi and not actively involved with any of the organized dissident groups. The large Libyan communities in Italy, in England, and in other Western nations are composed of many who left Libya when King Idris was deposed. They are persons whose economic fortunes were adversely affected by the colonel's coup and, because of their background, presumably would favor restoration of a free market economy.

Another major opposition figure is Dr. Mohammed Yusuf Maqaryif, whose remarks to a Saudi newspaper in March 1982 show that some opponents of Qaddafi strongly believe that Libya's future will be in the forefront of Arab and Islamic solidarity. Organized into the Libyan National Front and based in other Arab countries, these opponents criticize Qaddafi for having been a divisive rather than a unifying factor in the struggle for the Palestinian cause. A post-Qaddafi Libya, for them, could heal the wounds Qaddafi has caused in the Arab, African, and Islamic worlds.[26]

If Libya enters a period of turmoil, with different factions jockeying for leadership, the Soviets may well find the second group relatively more attractive, although there may not be any greater ideological affinity than with the present regime. The Soviets may become convinced that Qaddafi is no longer a viable figure, and may try to affect the outcome of such a power struggle in its early stages. It does not appear that any current group of dissidents would present the Soviets with a radically improved position in Libya; more likely would be a continuation of current conditions, if not a slight deterioration.

The prospects of a very active Soviet response to Libyan instability, comparable with that in Afghanistan, seem unlikely. The Soviets have not demonstrated to date that they consider Libya to have a comparable degree of strategic value, and the chances for European and American opposition are great. While the United States is no longer critically involved in the Libyan economy, Libya's proximity to Egypt, a close ally of the United States, NATO considerations, and the prospects of a strong European reaction should inhibit such a Soviet approach.

CONCLUSION

Soviet-Libyan ties continue, on balance, to be of mutual benefit. Until recently, one could argue that the Libyans were able to use the Soviet Union without compromising their political or ideological integrity, while the Soviets were receiving somewhat less than they sought. The balance may be shifting, with greater Libyan dependence on the Soviet Union militarily, as European states restrict arms trade, and psychologically, with American-Egyptian military cooperation and current U.S. policy toward Libya causing considerable alarm in Tripoli. One can imagine the two states growing closer militarily, with expanded Soviet access to Libyan facilities and a possible long-term friendship treaty.

At the same time, the political association between the two states remains limited, sometimes strained, and unlikely to change. Qaddafi has moderately altered his stance on alignment in order to rationalize Soviet protection, but has acquired new confidence and independence through his role in Chad, his scheduled OAU chairmanship, the treaty with Ethiopia and South Yemen, his support for Iran, and his continued leadership of the anti-Camp David radical Arab states. While any or all of these positions may coincide with current Soviet objectives, they involve regional and Islamic dynamics that may not always be of use to Soviet policy interests.

The economic state of affairs, over time of great benefit to the Soviet Union and its need for foreign exchange, appears to be in a state of decline. Whether Libya will continue to buy Soviet products on a significant scale will be determined by its pricing decisions and conditions in the world oil market. Opportunities in the nuclear technology field, potentially lucrative for the Soviets, have not been pursued actively in Libya. The long-term Soviet economic interests in Libya may not exceed their current dimensions.

Ultimately, the assessment of what the Soviets have achieved, what they have sought to achieve, and what they will seek in the future is a subjective judgment. The Soviet position, as measured in concrete terms and physical manifestations, has improved remarkably since Qaddafi came to power. The relationship with Libya, however lucrative, is not an adequate strategic substitute for Egypt, and clearly contains many pitfalls.

If one believes that Soviet policy in the Third World is reactive and opportunistic, then the Soviets are currently in a phase when they should be responding actively to new Libyan needs for security and protection. A Libya threatened by the West and leading the progressive nations of Africa may provide some excellent opportunities in the near future.

The Soviets should remain interested in Libya regardless of its government, and may not choose to get involved in the succession question. They have a foothold in a critically located state that at least in part fills their needs vis-à-vis NATO and Egypt. The current state of affairs could be the foundation of an expanded Soviet presence, essentially military in character, if circumstances permit and if the powers in Moscow deem it desirable.

NOTES

1. Ruth First, *Libya: The Elusive Revolution* (New York: Africana Publishing Co., 1975), ch. 4.

2. Omar Fathaly and Monte Palmer, *Political Development and Social Change in Libya* (Lexington, Mass.: Lexington Books, 1980), p. 142.

3. Sami Hajjar, "The Jamahiriya Experiment in Libya: Qaddafi and Rousseau," *Journal of Modern African Studies* 18, no. 2 (1980): 182.

4. Tripoli Domestic Service, September 1, 1981, FBIS, *Middle East and Africa (MEA)*, 2 September 1981, p. Q12.

5. Arnold Hottinger, "Arab Communism at a Low Ebb," *Problems of Communism*, July–August 1981, p. 30.

6. This can be compared with the east-west en route access the United States is negotiating with Morocco for its Persian Gulf contingencies.

7. Amnon Sella, *Soviet Political and Military Conduct in the Middle East* (New York: St. Martin's Press, 1981), p. 141.

8. See, for example, Drew Middleton, *New York Times*, March 14, 1980, p. A-11; Roger Pajak, "Arms and Oil: The Soviet-Libyan Arms Supply Relationship," *Middle East Review*, Winter 1980–81, p. 53.

9. Arnold Hottinger, "Three-way Pact: A Gain for the Kremlin?" *Swiss Review of World Affairs*, October 1981, p. 27.

10. TASS, April 27, 1981, FBIS, *Daily Report: Soviet Union* 3, 28 April 1981, p. H2.

11. Ibid., p. H4.

12. Pavel Fyodorov, "Situation in Chad," *Asia and Africa Today* (September–October 1981), no. 5: 21.

13. Claire Sterling, *The Terror Network* (New York: Holt, Rinehart and Winston, 1981), p. 263.

14. Ibid., p. 270.

15. U.S. Congress, House Committee on Foreign Relations, Subcommittee on Africa, *Hearings and Mark-up, Foreign Assistance Legislation for Fiscal Year 1982*, pt. 8, 97th Cong., 1st sess. (Washington, D.C.: U.S. Government Printing Office, 1981, pp. 238–39.

16. Report on Deutsche Welle radio interview, Tripoli, Voice of the Arab Homeland, February 15, 1981, FBIS, MEA.

17. Ronald Bruce St. John, "The Soviet Penetration of Libya," *The World Today*, April 1982, p. 137.

18. International Institute for Strategic Studies, *The Military Balance, 1981–82*. (London: IISS 1981), p. 43.

19. *DMS Market Intelligence Report* (Greenwich, Conn.: 1981), Summary, p. 5.

20. U.S. Congress, op. cit., p. 238.

21. U.S. Congress, Senate Committee on Foreign Relations, *Analysis of Six Issues About Nuclear Capabilities of India, Iraq, Libya, and Pakistan,* 97th Cong. 1st sess. (Washington, D.C.: U.S. Government Printing Office, 1981), p. 9.

22. *Middle East Economic Digest* 25, no. 19 (May 8, 1981): 32.

23. John Campbell, "Communist Strategies in the Mediterranean," *Problems of Communism,* May–June 1979, p. 7.

24. See, for example, *Jeune Afrique*, March 4, 1981, pp. 16-18.

25. Hottinger, "Arab Communism at a Low Ebb," p. 29.

26. *Al-Madinah*, March 4, 1982, Joint Publication Research Service.

SIX

Getting a Grip on the Horn: The Emergence of the Soviet Presence and Future Prospects
PAUL B. HENZE

HISTORICAL ROOTS

Russian strategic concern about the Horn of Africa has much deeper roots than that of the United States, which is almost entirely a post-World War II development. Russia was curious about Ethiopia as far back as the 17th century.[1] Curiosity was whetted by the appeal of an exotic, distant land inhabited by Orthodox Christians. In the mid-19th century, a dedicated Russian monk, Porfiry Uspensky, who cultivated friendships with Ethiopian clerics during several years of service in Jerusalem, wrote enthusiastically and at length about the possibilities that the ancient Christian kingdom offered the tsarist empire as a base for expanding influence throughout Africa. The Imperial Russian Geographical Society had already sent the Kovalevsky expedition to Ethiopia in 1847, to look for the sources of the Nile.[2]

Some Ethiopians were aware of Russia. In the 1850s, Emperor Tewodros sought support from the tsar for a project to liberate Jerusalem from the Turks. The Russians demurred, but in the last quarter of the 19th century, they became more adventuresome. After the Suez Canal was opened, they felt the need to secure their sea route through the Indian Ocean to the Far East. Rivalry with the British in Central Asia stimulated Russian ambitions for a foothold in the Horn of Africa.

There were numerous initiatives in the 1880s and 1890s. An attempt to set up a Russian colony on the Bay of Tajura (in what is now the Djibouti Republic) ended in failure, but subsequent Russian missions to Ethiopia established close relations with Emperor Menelik's court.[3] This great emperor, then in his prime, was feeling Italian pressure and was uncertain about the British. He was eager to find European allies, and warmly welcomed the Mashkov delegation in 1889 as "military representatives of my brother, the Negus of Muscovy." Other Russians followed: military men, church representatives, and diplomats. Military aid and technical assistance were provided. These activities have never been fully studied, but one of the most recent scholars to investigate them concludes that the role of Russian advice in the great Ethiopian victory over the Italians at Adowa in 1896 may have been much greater than was realized at the time.[4]

Russians continued to be prominent among Menelik's advisers into the early 20th century. Russian officers helped his armies consolidate control over the country's southwestern region. Russians led the Ethiopian expedition to the Nile that preceded the Fashoda crisis of 1895.[5] The Russians built and staffed a hospital in Addis Ababa that operated for several years. Church links were cultivated but came to little.

After the 1905 revolution the tsarist government was beset by mounting problems at home, and interest in the Horn of Africa waned. Several dozen tsarist officers found refuge in Ethiopia after the 1917 revolution, but the country attracted no attention from the Soviet government until the 1930s, when it became the center of international diplomatic concern as the Italians prepared to invade. The Soviets, characteristically, played an equivocal role during this period—actually supplying Italy with a good share of the grain and oil it needed to pursue the war against Ethiopia, but in the end refusing, like the United States, to recognize the Italian conquest. This put the Russians in a position to claim to be special friends of Ethiopia after it was liberated and Haile Selassie restored to power in 1941, though the war in East Africa was over for several weeks before the USSR was brought into it by Nazi attack.[6]

History had not been forgotten. The groundwork for resumption of Russian involvement in the Horn was laid with the establishment of a Soviet embassy at Addis Ababa in 1943. The USSR's first post-World War II foreign aid project, in 1946, was a "reopened" Russian hospital, declared to be a continuation of the one established in Menelik's time. This was a remarkable example of humanitarianism on the part of a country that itself lay devastated by the German invasion and five years of fighting. Like its predecessor at the turn of the century, the new Russian hospital in Addis Ababa did not acquire much status as a medical establishment, but came to be regarded as primarily of political significance.

The Soviets saw clearly the advantages of getting a grip on the Horn in the period immediately following World War II, but opportunities were limited, and so were their resources. One long shot was to try to get some degree of hold over Eritrea when the former Italian colony, under British administration since 1941, came onto the U.N. agenda. Haile Selassie wanted Eritrea rejoined to Ethiopia. Western strategic interests made that highly desirable. The Soviets played a part in the U.N. effort to dispose of former Italian colonies, but their first priority was Libya. The story of the diplomatic maneuvers that led to independence for Libya, an Italian trusteeship for Somalia with firm commitment to early independence, and

and federation of Eritrea with Ethiopia is too complicated to recount here, but it is worthwhile reflecting on the fact that as we look back over the subsequent history of each of these colonies, we find that the Soviets have played (or still play) a major role in all of them. This demonstrates how persistent the Soviets' interest in this part of the world has been and how they have persevered in seizing opportunities to expand influence.

Since the early 1970s, Libya has been a major Soviet ally and, moreover, financially profitable for the Russians, unlike most of the allies they have acquired. Long a major channel for destabilization of Ethiopia through support of the Eritrean insurgency, Libya after 1976 became an enthusiastic supporter of the Soviet-leaning Ethiopian revolutionary government. It appears to be easing the Soviet economic burden by providing some financial aid to Ethiopia.

For nearly a decade and a half, when they could not do better, the Russians tacitly encouraged Somali irredentism by pouring arms into the country and thereby building a position of military strength for themselves in the region. Open Somali attack on Ethiopia in 1977 put the Russians in a no-lose situation. If the attack had succeeded, the Russians would have dominated both countries, and thus played a decisive role in restructuring a truncated Ethiopia shorn of the territories claimed by Somalia and, perhaps, of Eritrea as well.[7] If the Somali assault on Ethiopia failed, the Russians had the option of changing sides and gaining the greater prize they had long sought—Ethiopia—in the framework of a rescue operation. It is difficult to imagine that the Kremlin leadership envisioned such a disorderly process, and a price so high, as was the case.

Some observers have seen events in the Horn during the latter half of the 1970s as the crowning phase of a Soviet master plan that had been devised in the final days of World War II and systematically implemented ever since. Others see them as the outcome of deeper processes in Russian history that can be traced back to the 1890s, or perhaps even the 1850s. History *is* relevant, but as much as they talk about historical inevitability, Communists are taught not to rely on history to produce the results they desire.

The only master plan that can be discerned in the Soviet approach to the Horn since the early 1950s is persistent, aggressive opportunism: a steady recognition of the strategic importance of the region and a determination to expand influence in it by whatever action is likely to be effective when openings develop. The Soviet approach involves a preparedness to act; a predisposition to advance its power interests without ideological restraint; and a steadiness of ultimate purpose. But at the same time caution has always played an important role, as became evident in the period following the advent of the revolutionary government to power in Ethiopia.[8]

Successes in the Horn have not come cheap for the Russians, and expansion of influence has brought broadened responsibilities and greatly increased demands on resources. It remains to be seen how severe the strains that these generate will be for the Soviet system. How the Soviets will respond to increasing costs and strains in the Horn cannot be determined by judgments that apply only to this region. All these power equations have many variables. Future Russian decisions about the Horn will be made in the context of competing demands and strains in other areas where the USSR is heavily committed: Cuba, Poland and elsewhere in Eastern Europe, and Afghanistan. Just as in the late 19th century, what happens in the Horn has a relationship to the "great game" in Asia. Before we examine looming challenges and choices that the Soviets must face in the Horn, let us examine in greater detail how they operated in the 1960s and 1970s.

MAKING THE MOST OF THE LEAST

The Soviets had to content themselves with a lean situation in the Horn during the 1950s. Only Ethiopia was independent. The 25-year U.S.-Ethiopian mutual defense agreement of 1953 formalized the movement Ethiopia had already made toward the Free World defense system. Haile Selassie had demonstrated his commitment to the concept of collective security by significant contributions to U.N. forces in Korea.

The Soviets maintained an embassy and built a large cultural center in Addis Ababa, cultivated relations with the Ethiopian Orthodox Church, and did some scholarly research on Ethiopia, but there was no opportunity for any major initiative. Until Sudan (1956), Somalia (1960), and Kenya (1962) became independent, there was no basis for Soviet presence in those countries. Only Sudan had a native Communist movement, the Sudan Communist Party (SCP), founded among Sudanese students in Cairo in 1945. Illegal both before and after independence, it offered little scope for Soviet initiative. Essentially, the 1950s were a time of modest but steady investment for the future, and the Russians had to bide their time.

Things began to change in 1959, when the Russians realized the advantages of economic aid. Haile Selassie was invited to Moscow, and came back with a $100 million credit. Economic assistance became an important instrument of Soviet policy in the Horn in the 1960s, though the amounts publicized always exceeded the services or goods delivered. A Russian vocational training institute was opened in the Ethiopian town of Bahr Dar in 1962, and work got under way on a petroleum refinery. An obsolescent facility that had been taken out of Romania in 1944 and set up at Baku was generously donated to Ethiopia, and went into operation at the southern Eritrean port of Assab in 1967.

The Soviets lost no time in getting economic aid programs under way in Somalia and Kenya, undertaking a port expansion survey of Berbera, Somalia, in 1962. Soviet aid to Kenya included a political training institute that opened in late 1964 but was closed six months later, when an anti-Kenyatta plot was discovered among the students. Only slightly less blatantly political was another Soviet project, a hospital that was not completed until 1973. Meanwhile, Kenyans had become alarmed by Soviet arming of Somalia and the Russians wasted no further economic aid on Kenya, whose free-market approach to economic development had attracted a steady flow of investment from America and Europe.

Somalia needed economic development more urgently than any other Horn country, and both the Soviets and the West vied to develop projects.[9] Few developed very promisingly. Politically, Somalis were obsessed with gaining their "lost" territories—Djibouti, the Ethiopian Ogaden, and the North Frontier Province of Kenya. They developed plans for a strong military establishment that no Western nation was willing to support. This gave the Russians a welcome opportunity to move into the Horn militarily. They acted quickly, providing Somalia with arms worth $30 million in 1964 and 1965, a level that even then exceeded average annual American military aid to Ethiopia.

A democratic parliamentary system produced pro-Western elected governments in Somalia until the fall of 1969, when a coup by Mohammed Siad Barre, then chief of the armed forces, brought a pro-Soviet revolutionary socialist regime to power.[10] The Russians were pleased, and showed their pleasure by launching a massive buildup of both military and security forces. Competition with the Chinese Communists gave them additional incentive.

Soviet military aid, which had been at modest levels in the late 1960s, increased rapidly in the 1970s. Somalia's armed forces had already expanded from 4,000 men in 1961 to 20,000 by 1970. On a per capita basis, Somalia already had nearly five times as many men under arms as Ethiopia did, and in absolute terms, its army was four times as large as Kenya's.[11] Since Somalia was threatened by none of its neighbors and had no serious internal security problems, expansion of its armed forces had to be a direct function of its irredentist ambitions. The Soviets could have had no illusions about this. Nevertheless, they poured more than $400 million worth of arms into Somalia during the eight years they were principal supporters of Siad Barre's regime.

During the final part of this period, the number of Soviet advisers in Somalia, both military and civilian, rose to 4,000. In addition, there were several hundred Cubans and East Europeans. Economic aid played a minor role in the Soviet buildup in Somalia, and pressure for large-scale Russian help did not develop because Somalia continued to attract Western and multilateral aid, and after 1973 began to receive Arab assistance.[12] Available statistics indicate that per capita GNP in Somalia declined in 1969–78 from $136 to $127.[13]

Somalia was not the only recipient of major Soviet investment in the Horn. There was a brief period of high adventure in Sudan that started when Colonel Jaafar al-Numeiry seized power in the spring of 1969. He looked like a classic Arab radical military man: anti-Western, talking socialism, and eager to be embraced by the East, he sought the cooperation of the Sudanese Communists. The Soviets responded quickly, rushing in advisers and large quantities of military aid. At a time when Arab/black African feelings were strained and the Russians had interests to protect with both groups, they opted for support of the northern Sudanese, who were Muslims and Arabs, in the war against the black Christian southerners. This war had taken on a semi-genocidal character even before the Soviets got into it. Their military support brutalized and broadened it. In the end, however, it was not the southern rebellion but the presence of a native Communist movement in Sudan that proved to be the Russians' undoing.[14]

In the summer of 1971, the Sudanese Communists came within a hair's breadth of ousting Numeiry. It still is not known whether the Soviets knew of or abetted this plot.[15] It proved enlightening to Numeiry, for he decided to disengage from the Soviet embrace. He sought Haile Selassie's help in mediating a settlement with the southerners. Ethiopian good offices were effective. By the summer of 1972, the reconciliation process was largely complete, and Numeiry reorganized his government to give the southerners real participation in Khartoum and autonomy in their own region. The Russians had delivered more than $60 million worth of military aid to Sudan during a two-year period. It was difficult for them to give up so promising an opening, and Numeiry could find no other arms source, so some deliveries continued after 1972. Following the 1973 Egyptian-Israeli war, Sudan's reorientation toward the West accelerated. Periodic Qaddafi plots against Numeiry, which the latter suspected of being Soviet-encouraged, and Egyptian influence, as Sadat broke with the Russians, encouraged the process.

The Russians had not forgotten that Ethiopia was the most important country in the Horn, but they lagged in competition with the West during the 1960s. This did not deter them from maintaining a large embassy and training a sizable group of young Soviet officers in Amharic. But Communism had little appeal for young Ethiopians, who took scholarships for study in the USSR only if they could not qualify for study in the United States. The Peace Corps had more volunteers in Ethiopia than in any other country, and most of them were teaching in secondary schools, far outdistancing any comparable influence the Russians might hope to exercise.

Haile Selassie had recovered rapidly from the coup attempt of December 1960, and consolidated his leadership of the country during the remainder of the decade.[16] A modest but steady level of U.S. military aid was a key factor in modernization of Ethiopia's 45,000-man armed forces, judged the best in Africa at the time. Russian economic aid was eclipsed by dozens of American, European, Israeli, and international projects. Ethiopia, in contrast to Somalia, made good use of economic aid. Modernization was advancing as rapidly as most thoughtful observers, Ethiopians and foreigners alike, considered desirable in view of the strains the process could (and occasionally did) cause in a country so steeped in tradition and exhibiting so many regional differences.

One of the most significant changes during the 1960s was the entry into government service and public life of thousands of young men and women with modern education. At the upper end of the spectrum these included several dozen men with advanced U.S. and European university degrees who rapidly rose to subministerial and ministerial rank in major government departments. At intermediate levels, thousands of new graduates of the Ethiopia university system staffed ministries, development projects, and the rapidly expanding school system. All these people provided the basis for more effective governmental performance during a period when expectations were rising rapidly, but they also represented a source of discontent and frustration when modernization did not proceed as rapidly as they expected.

While maintaining a solid facade of good formal relations with and respect for Haile Selassie, the Russians had their sights on a future period of ferment in Ethiopia that, from the vantage point of the 1960s, must have seemed, even to them, much farther away than it turned out to be.[17] But patience and persistence have always been the hallmarks of Russian foreign operations. They did their best to hasten the advent of basic change. The Soviet agenda for gaining greater influence in (and/or on) Ethiopia had three aspects:

1. First, and most expensive, support of Somalia as an eventual avenue of pressure on—or even dismemberment of—Ethiopia
2. Encouragement of Eritrean rebellion
3. Development of an internal radical movement, based primarily on students.

Eritrean separatism, which includes many disparate currents, originally had no leftist orientation, and seems to have been judged by Moscow as having low potential until the late 1960s.[18] There are, it is true, indications of some East European arms and money finding their way into Eritrean hands in the mid-1960s, but it was only in the wake of the wave of anti-Western feeling that engulfed the Arab world after the 1967 defeat of Egypt by Israel that Eritrean insurgency appears to have risen from a low position on Moscow's priority list. By this time the Chinese had become interested in Eritreans, had brought some to China for training, and had begun sending aid through South Yemen. During 1967–69, arms and money flowed in from Eastern Europe through radical Arab governments, and young Eritreans found opportunities to train in several countries with close ties to the Soviets: Syria, Iraq, North Korea, and Cuba. There is little evidence of training in the USSR. The Russians kept their distance until Qaddafi came to power in Libya and Numeiry in Sudan.

The presence of a pro-Soviet government in Khartoum opened up support possibilities for the Eritrean insurgents that had hitherto been inconceivable. During 1969, emphasis shifted from assassinations, raids, kidnappings, and aircraft hijackings to serious military operations, as weapons and supplies poured across the Sudanese border and the insurgents were able to use Sudan as a safe haven. The total amount of support that Eritreans received during this period is unknowable with any exactitude, and not all of it can be charged to the Soviet or Chinese account, since some Arabs (such as Qaddafi) had resources of their own. Sudan, however, did not, and neither did poverty-stricken South Yemen, which became a major funnel for both Soviet and Chinese assistance.

The Eritrean insurgency was not as immediately destabilizing for Ethiopia as those who underwrote it must have hoped and, curiously enough, it was not targeted directly against the U.S. presence in Eritrea, the complex that constituted Kagnew Station.[19] Nevertheless, by 1970 half of Ethiopia's military manpower was tied down in an effort to keep ports and communications lines open, and the central government's authority in several rural areas was seriously challenged.

Conditions favoring expansion of insurgency in Eritrea reversed again in 1971–72. Numeiry's shift from the Soviet embrace and enlistment of Ethiopia as mediator with the southern Sudanese brought a sharp reduction in Sudanese toleration of Eritrean support operations. At the same time, Haile Selassie was able to secure from Peking a commitment to abandon support of the Eritreans in return for recognition and acceptance of Chinese assistance for Ethiopia. With help from Israeli counterinsurgency experts, Ethiopia was able to bring insurgent advances to a standstill and regain ground in Eritrea during 1972. Qaddafi and the South Yemenis, as well as the Syrians and Iraqis, continued to support the Eritrean rebels, and served as channels for Soviet and East European assistance. Cuba continued its support as well, and of course was completely dependent upon the Russians for the weapons and funds that were required.[20]

An avowedly Marxist group, with more Christians than Muslims in its leadership, split off from the Eritrean Liberation Front in 1970, and since then various leftist currents have been an important aspect of Eritrean separatist politics. The net result of being linked to an international leftist ideology has been to encourage factionalism in an always divided movement.

The Eritrean rebellion, which continues to bedevil Ethiopia's revolutionary leadership, is a fascinating study in itself and a subject worthy of more objective historical research than it has received. For purposes of this discussion, let us put it aside and examine another aspect of the Soviet effort in Ethiopia in the 1960s and early 1970s: students. This was a period of student agitation throughout the non-Communist world, so it is not surprising that Ethiopian students, eager to imitate Western models, became engaged.

In reality, Ethiopian university students had few true grievances. Haile Selassie took a direct personal interest in the development of education, and with the aid of Western advisers and funds be expanded university education rapidly. Any reasonably able and conscientious high school graduate stood an excellent chance of being given a free college education either in Ethiopia or abroad, and had fair reason to assume that the government would provide employment after graduation. But a Cinderella syndrome set in. So paternalistic a system in a society where the broad horizons of modernization had only recently opened up was bound to genate expectations that could not be fulfilled. Since the first men who came back from education abroad soon became ministers and ambassadors, students assumed they would all advance as rapidly. Law and humanities courses were overflowing; engineering and science were less appealing. Teaching in the provinces was not a popular job. Strains and minor grievances became magnified in the permissive university atmosphere, and politicking became a habit.[21]

The Russians were quick to recognize this as a fertile field where modest input in the form of money, tactical encouragement, and help in preparing propaganda materials could produce impressive dividends. After the Ethiopians expelled several Soviet and East European embassy officers in the late 1960s, techniques were refined. Student unrest in Ethiopia was supported through Ethiopian student organizations in Europe and America, which blossomed at this time and became hotbeds of Marxism and channels for funneling money, propaganda, and organizational guidance into Ethiopia. Security authorities discovered, for instance, that money was coming into Ethiopia in the guise of contributions from student organizations in Berlin, Paris, London, and Washington to charitable groups in Ethiopia, the national literacy campaign, and other worthy causes.

During 1969–72, university and even secondary school instruction was frequently interrupted for long periods by student demonstrations and boycotts. Each outbreak of violence led to charges of police brutality and the accumulation of new grievances and charges. Security authorities were relatively lenient in dealing with students, for the old emperor would not permit severe punishments, and regularly forgave arrested student leaders. The dramatic effect of all this commotion was the virtual elimination of the U.S. Peace Corps from Ethiopian education. Peace Corps volunteers, who were located in all parts of the country, generally had been warmly accepted by students and the communities in which they lived, and they made a major contribution to Ethiopian secondary education. Some Peace Corps volunteers affected counterculture life-styles and strong anti-U.S. government attitudes and a few became involved in student agitation against the Ethiopian authorities, but most kept a lower profile. Within a surprisingly short period of time, in much of the country students turned on Peace Corps teachers, prevented them from teaching, and hounded them out of many provincial centers. In the course of 1970, most Peace Corps volunteers were withdrawn from the Ethiopian secondary school system.[22]

Student agitation had little effect on Ethiopian governmental processes or daily life, but the educational process was set back, and many families who could afford the expense sent their children abroad, where some of them were even more directly exposed to Marxist influences from the well-established ESUNA and ESUE[23] and their subgroups. These groups had funds available for travel from one university to another and subsidized production of propaganda that was mailed into Ethiopia in large quantities.

In the larger sense, student agitation both at home and abroad resulted in creation of a politicized younger generation, oriented exclusively to the left, that could help accelerate the destabilization process that Moscow envisioned—and aimed to encourage—in Ethiopia when Haile Selassie's long reign came to an end. It was a good investment. Funds and manpower invested by the Russians for encouragement of student political activity cannot have been very great, wherever and by whatever circuitous channels they were brought to bear upon the situation.

To summarize the Russian approach to getting a grip on the Horn until the eve of the Ethiopian revolution, in a situation that offered little promise of rapid gains in the region as a whole, it is remarkable that the Russians spent lavishly, in terms of matériel, money, and manpower, on Somalia. Possessing not much more than a fraction of Ethiopia's population and much poorer in resources, Somalia was rated sufficiently valuable by the Russians to merit an outlay in 15 years of well over half a billion dollars, the equivalent of everything the United States spent on Ethiopia in 30 years.

In comparison, even if all the pre-1977 support for the Eritrean insurgency had ultimately come from Soviet resources (unlikely), it would still have been a low-cost operation. Perhaps as much as $10 million per year of ultimately Soviet origin went into this insurgency during the brief period when support through Sudan was easy. At the outside, however, total Soviet investment in the Eritrean rebellion during the period up to 1977 is unlikely to have amounted to even a tenth of the investment in Somalia. It was a more productive investment, however, in the sense that the Eritrean problem contributed more to the destablization of Ethiopia during the transitional period after the revolution than Somalia did.

Encouragement of student and intellectual dissidence and radicalization of the educated younger class in Ethiopia can have required no more than one-tenth—at the very most—of the resources that went into encouragement of Eritrean insurgency—less than 1 percent of the cost of the relationship with Somalia. This was the most productive political investment, for the students and intellectuals, actively infused with Marxism or, at a minimum, incapable of thinking politically in categories other than socialist-idealist nationalism contributed enormously to the ferment of the Ethiopian revolution.

In terms of risk, the support of Somalia was overt and widely publicized, and caused periodic strain and embarrassment for the USSR. The support of Eritrean insurgency was extremely discreet, through surrogates, and was carried out in such a way as to minimize likelihood of friction with Haile Selassie's government as well as with the United States. Support of students was initially quite direct; later, less so. It resulted in expulsions and protests, and aroused Ethiopian distrust and anger.

A final glance at Sudan is necessary before we close discussion of the prerevolutionary period in Ethiopia. The Soviet investment in Sudan turned out to be unproductive except insofar as it made possible acceleration of the Eritrean insurgency. The net impact of involvement with the Soviets was negative not only on Numeiry but also on the great majority of Sudanese. No new pro-Russian party was created, and the existence of the Sudanese Communist Party both complicated, and was complicated by, the Soviet relationship. Sudan, like Egypt, serves today as a model of the disadvantages of a close relationship with the Russians. The Russians, in turn, have never been able to forgive Numeiry for being successful in disengaging from his short, intense Soviet love affair.

EMPIRE IN FERMENT

As 1973 drew to a close, there was a growing sense of impending change in Ethiopia but little outward fear of it. There was little basis for expectation that change would entail drastic shifts in the course of development that the country had long followed with considerable success, or that Ethiopia's foreign relationships would inevitably be affected. There was almost no assumption that change would result in revolution. Officially nonaligned and particularistic in spirit, as it had been throughout its long history, the country remained intellectually and psychologically oriented toward Western Europe and America and dependent on Free World economic and military relationships.

It would have been impossible to identify any overt pro-Soviet, pro-Communist, or even vaguely pro-socialist group among officials or any segment of the population except students and a few intellectuals within the country, and a few more abroad. There was no new or unusual tension among nationalities. Muslims and Christians lived side by side more amicably in Ethiopia than anywhere else in the region. Insurgency notwithstanding, large numbers of Eritreans continued to live and work in Addis Ababa, and to participate in government and business in all parts of the country. That Russia armed Somalia and underwrote its forceful transition to a Communist-type regime was well known and was regarded as a threat to Ethiopia. Two decades of Soviet cultural efforts in Addis Ababa and various aid projects had produced almost no Ethiopians who advocated the Russian approach to anything or any noteworthy intellectual interest in Russian culture or language. The Communist Chinese, who had set up an embassy in 1971 and embarked on a road-building project, had more appeal, but primarily because their approach to Ethiopia was so conventional and their conduct so gracious.

Only a year later, as 1974 drew to a close, Ethiopia's political system had been radically altered and a mysterious military committee—whose membership was unclear and whose workings no one understood—was leading the country helter-skelter toward "Ethiopian socialism" (proclaimed on December 20), making no secret of its desire to have a close relationship with the Soviet Union and Communist states allied with it. Haile Selassie had been deposed at the beginning of the Ethiopian new year in mid-September.[24] His successor as head of state, the Eritrean general Aman Andom, had been killed in a bloody shoot-out at the end of November, some said by Major Mengistu Haile Mariam, already reputed to be a key Derg mover and shaker. During 1975, as Ethiopian socialism was implemented, Ethiopians experienced nationalizations, confiscations, rural and urban land reform, mass mobilizations, and vast outpourings of leftist propaganda—a process as sudden and as sweeping as any comparable society has undergone in modern times.

What had happened? Where had all this Marxism come from? Why such a compulsion to emulate the Soviet Union? Leftist enthusiasts of the Ethiopian revolution are categorical in asserting that the Russians had absolutely nothing to do with it.[25] There has been little serious scholarly effort to examine the issue.

One need postulate no Russian hand to explain the effect of a series of developments during 1973 that contributed to a climate of uncertainty in Ethiopia. Fate seemed to have conspired to confront the country with several awkward problems simultaneously. The crown prince, crippled by a stroke at the beginning of the year, was flown to London for treatment, with Ras Asrate Kassa, president of the Crown Council and one of the most vigorous and prominent members of the traditional nobility, accompanying him.[26] This opened up the question of succession, settled formally only after Haile Selassie declared the crown prince's eldest son, 20-year-old Zara Yakob, next in succession to his father at Easter time—too late to stem the widespread worry about the future of the monarchy that had already developed.

Meanwhile, famine had become serious in the central and northern highlands. Inept handling of the problem undermined confidence in the government. Intellectuals and officials became outspokenly critical of governmental incapacity, as did the foreign press and foreign governments. The October Arab-Israeli war provoked questions about reliance on Israel, and the old emperor's subsequent break in relations with Tel Aviv under Arab and African pressure raised doubt about his ability to manipulate an increasingly complex international situation. Psychologically more subtle in its impact, but more profoundly unsettling, was the growing realization among the Ethiopian elite that the United States, to which Ethiopia was linked in so many ways that had come to be taken for granted over more than two decades, was in the throes of self-doubt provoked by Vietnam and Watergate.[27]

The most direct causes of the government crisis that developed early in 1974 were domestic price rises resulting from the OPEC price hike and restiveness among the military rank and file in the south and in Eritrea. Suddenly the government found itself confronted with civilian and military demands from all sides. On February 28, Haile Selassie dismissed his long time prime minister, Aklilu Habte Wold, who had held office since 1958. He appointed a progressive aristocrat, Endelkachew Makonnen, in his place, and on March 5 announced that the 1955 constitution would be amended to make the prime minister responsible to Parliament. In the whirlwind of events that followed, this change never took place.

As long-frozen political processes thawed and political debate opened up, Ethiopians rejoiced in the short-lived hope that perhaps the succession period many feared would go more smoothly than anyone had heretofore thought likely. There was a sense of a new birth of freedom, and rapid progress toward more modern political institutions was expected even without a change of monarch. Exiles began to return to the country. Labor unrest developed. Students demonstrated. But there was almost no serious violence, and the revolutionary process remained good-natured. Nevertheless, the government always seemed to make reforms and concessions too late, and new demands constantly welled up. Ferment in the armed forces grew, and led at the end of April to organization of an armed forces coordinating committee. This committee went through several quick transformations before its consolidation in June.[28] Mengistu seems to have appeared on the scene only after the committee was formed, but by late June he was already an influential figure. By July the Derg had become the dominant factor on the Addis Ababa political scene. Haile Selassie had completely lost control over events. The country's traditional leadership—both the established aristocracy and the young technocrats who had risen to positions of responsibility and influence in the imperial government—failed to pull itself together to challenge or serve as a counterweight to the junior and middle-level army officers who systematically took the reins of power into their hands and prepared to push Haile Selassie off his throne.

This was no casual, spur-of-the-moment action; it was carefully prepared. Opposition was neutralized, co-opted, or circumvented. The final action took place within the framework of carefully thought-out nationalist concepts under the simple slogan "Ethiopia Tikdem"—which can mean either "Ethiopia United" or "Ethiopia First," and otherwise has no political implications whatsoever.

A comprehensive study of events during Ethiopia's unexpected year of revolution remains to be written.[29] Outside influences on the revolutionary process are not readily apparent. The United States stood aside while Haile Selassie faltered and was pushed aside. Military Aid and Assistance Group officers seem to have known almost none of the Ethiopian military men who formed the Derg. The U.S. Agency for International Development went about business as usual. This was the summer when Watergate reached its culmination and President Nixon resigned. Henry Kissinger had other priorities, including Greek-Turkish confrontation over Cyprus. There was no concerted or serious U.S. effort to influence the course of events in Ethiopia, and no other Western country seems to have tried to do so either.

Where were the Russians? Less diverted by crises at home than the Americans, they were present, as usual, in Ethiopia, but very much in the background. If some of the junior military men who played a role in the formation of the Derg had been recruited by Soviet intelligence officers in preceding years and were acting on the basis of Soviet guidance as they forged this secretive military committee into an instrument of power and took charge of the revolution, the undertaking was accomplished with extreme care and discretion. Clandestine encouragement and guidance—if successful—can hardly be expected to produce evidence, especially when carried out by experienced Soviet or East European operators.[30]

EAGER DERG—RELUCTANT RUSSIANS

Like the violent thunderstorms that pursue each other across the Ethiopian highlands during the annual great rains, the revolutionary process, once begun, seemed to gather inexorable momentum. The great rains cease after three or four months. It took three to four years for the revolutionary storms to abate. Each new "reform" brought others in its wake and generated various kinds of controversy and resistance, not only among the "broad masses" but also within government and Derg. Violence became the hallmark of a revolution that until November 1974 had been almost without bloodshed. The workings of the Derg remained obscure. Even its exact size was unknown. During 1975–77 it was periodically wracked by internal upheavals that, more often than not, ended with the death of the losers. General Teferi Banti, who had become head of state when General Aman was killed, survived until February 1977, when he perished in palace violence that took the lives of several others, including at least one Mengistu loyalist. As soon as he emerged the winner of this imbroglio, Mengistu received congratulations from Fidel Castro and a personal visit from Soviet Ambassador Ratanov.

As with the elimination of Atnafu Abate[31] later in the year, the political ramifications of all these clashes remain the subject of speculation. The possibility of concessions in Eritrean policy had been an issue in the fall of General Aman. The Derg adopted an uncompromising position immediately afterward. It has never deviated from this hard nationalist approach to the Eritrean rebellion. A major offensive was mounted in 1976, but it was an embarrassing failure. The end of that year saw over twice as many Ethiopian troops committed in Eritrea as in Haile Selassie's time, and much less of the province under central government control. By the end of 1977, almost all of Eritrea had been lost to insurgents, who failed to capitalize on their gains because of factional rivalries. These rivalries have remained a constant in the Eritrean situation ever since. Eritrea was not the only region in revolt with which the Derg had to contend. Land reform provoked disorders in several parts of the country. Students sent out to revolutionize the peasantry generated ferment no one could control. Political commotion welled up in many areas as traditional leaders rebelled, fled, or were driven out.

In Addis Ababa, several rival political parties, or groups aspiring to political power, appeared on the scene. In political coloration they ranged from moderate left to extreme left. There was no center and no right—in spite of constant condemnation of it in the press and by Derg spokesmen. Returned exiles, several of them Marxists who had made a name for themselves in the student movement abroad in the 1960s or early 1970s, went to work organizing followers. During 1975, the Ethiopian People's

Revolutionary Party (EPRP) surfaced, claiming that it had been in existence before the revolution. The claim appears valid, for the party seems almost certainly to be the direct descendant of a Soviet-supported student organization, the Ethiopian People's Revolutionary Movement (EPRM), of the late 1960s. It rapidly developed into a major rival of the All Ethiopian Socialist Movement (better known by the initials of its Amharic name, MEISON, which enjoyed greater Derg favor.

Factionalism on the outside was reflected in the Derg itself—it may also have reflected Derg factionalism or indecision. In addition to continuing support during this period for individuals and groups they had assisted in prerevolutionary times, the Russians appear to have given assistance to new political movements as well. There was a clandestine air about most of these competing political factions, uncertainty about their leaders, no information on their sources of funds, and a good deal of mystery about how they operated internally. Provincial branches sometimes seemed to be at odds with central organizations in Addis Ababa. The official press came under tight Derg control through the Ministry of Information, and reflected little of this political controversy. But there was a great outpouring of leaflets, unofficial news sheets, and journals that both reflected and helped generate political debate.

At a relatively low level of investment, the Russians and perhaps some of their surrogates appear during this period to have been testing various factions and leaders, different political formulas. Part of their purpose may have been to keep pressure on those who were their favorites or instruments in the Derg and governmental structure. But there may also have been competing viewpoints among different elements in the Soviet operational structure in Ethiopia. Whatever all the causes were, so much political turmoil was generated that no one could control it.[32]

The standard Soviet prescription for socialist regimes is to build a Communist-type party as the prime instrument for advancing (and containing) the revolutionary process, "educating the masses," and controlling society. The Derg, apparently including Mengistu himself, reached a very different conclusion as a result of all this turmoil. They became frightened of *all* parties, and feared a classic Communist-type party because it might develop its own momentum and dilute their power; worse still, it could be manipulated by the Soviets against the Derg leaders. So Mengistu and his allies, who increased their power after each internal Derg clash, resisted Soviet urgings to form a party—and have continued to do so to this day.[33]

Soviet encouragement of extreme factionalism had the result of frustrating application of a standard prescription for consolidating domination of a country won to "socialism." There was a deeper problem, too. Long-time Soviet support of radical students and intellectuals had produced a hyperpoliticized class that had an almost unlimited capacity to debate and theorize, but little sense of organizational management and discipline.

Nevertheless, the problem may not have been as frustrating for key Soviets concerned with Ethiopia as some analysts have assumed. Through 1976, the Russian approach to Ethiopia was still essentially a spoiling policy. It was a continuation of the prerevolutionary approach, now greatly accelerated—but the aim was still destabilization of Ethiopian society. Destabilization has been the goal since the 1960s, when decisions were made to support Eritrean insurgency, encourage student dissidence, and permit the Somalis to harass Ethiopia by arming guerrillas in the Ogaden and Bale. Gaining control of the Ethiopian revolution was a long-sought aim—but how could the Russians be sure that this aim had really been achieved? They were not deceived by the flood of adulatory Communist propaganda with which they helped to fill Ethiopian media. They knew that at heart most educated Ethiopians were profoundly Western-oriented, and the rest of the population deeply anchored in traditional modes of thought. Even the Marxists who debated theory and constantly increased the tempo of factional political infighting were suspected of being contaminated by exposure to Western ways in Paris, Rome, and Washington.

But worst of all, the country remained dependent on the Americans for military support and received large amounts of U.S. and other Free World economic aid. Military force was more important than ever for holding the country together, and economic aid could not be readily dispensed with. The United States made no coherent effort to influence the course of events in Ethiopia during 1975 and 1976, other than to bemoan violence and timidly protest propaganda excesses, but it substantially increased military aid to the revolutionary regime. U.S. military assistance in 1974 was double the amount it had been in any previous year. It increased by another 55 percent in 1975 and there were plans for further increases. In addition, the United States facilitated purchase by Ethiopia of additional military supplies with its own funds, and the Derg spent $100 million in this fashion. A commitment to Haile Selassie to modernize the Ethiopian air force was honored. Ethiopia received its first F5-Es in April 1976.[34]

There had been another development that must have seemed sinister to the Russians: Ethiopia had quietly resumed informal relations with Israel in the summer of 1975. Israel was supplying specialized military equipment and helping with training. The internal turmoil that intensified steadily in Ethiopia during 1975 and 1976 had two major consequences for the future, neither of which is likely to have been regarded as undesirable by the Russians at the time: it undermined the basis for a continuing military relationship with the United States, and it whetted Somali desires to strike while Ethiopia was weak.

The Western press dramatized bloodshed in Ethiopia. An increasing flow of refugees told horror stories of cruelty and oppression. Pressure built up in the United States to cut off military supplies. Reports of the original genocidal intentions behind the great peasants' march into Eritrea in 1975 heightened American concern.[35] The U.S. Senate held extensive hearings in August 1976. The hearings were indecisive, but a great many different things were said, with the result that commentators ever since have drawn on the record of these hearings to demonstrate what U.S. policy either was or was not, and to make U.S. intentions seem much more definite than they were—in any direction—during these final months of the Ford administration. President Ford decided that in light of the continued violence in Ethiopia, the United States could neither deliver nor sell further ammunition to the Derg. Other delays that commonly occur in military aid arrangements were misread by some Derg members as efforts to pressure them. The Russians may have encouraged such suspicions with disinformation. But they were slow to move toward a program of their own.

Constraints on resources may have influenced the Soviets to go slowly, especially in the wake of their recent success in Angola. But they still had a case for biding their time in order to get the best possible arrangement in Ethiopia from a political viewpoint, and to be sure that the Ethiopian ruling team to which they eventually committed themselves had a capacity to maintain its hold on power. Americans felt weak and frustrated at the end of 1976, and the Ford administration was smarting from the rebuff Congress had dealt it on Angola. But the Russians could not be sure; the United States had responded unpredictably before. Angola had not been a primary U.S. responsibility and commitment. Ethiopia, on the other hand, had been, ever since the early 1950s. Too precipitate a Soviet move for military domination in Ethiopia could provoke a surge of American reaction that would undermine the steady Russian effort to gain a grip on the country that had been pursued for a quarter of a century—just when it was coming closest to realization. Patience and caution were still in order.

Mengistu is reported to have been challenged on U.S. military aid by a group of radical air force officers at Debre Zeit in June 1976. He replied, with an air of annoyance, that he preferred Soviet help and had asked for it, but the Russians were not responding. There was no alternative but to remain dependent on the Americans.

Professions of friendship, laudatory socialist rhetoric, and the to and fro of delegations and training groups notwithstanding, the USSR was still making its major investments in the Horn in Somalia. Ethiopia was costing very little. Promises of increased economic aid resulted in few deliveries. The $100 million credit given to Haile Selassie in 1959 had never been fully used. The Derg would have appreciated generous Russian aid offers and publicized them, but such aid was not urgently needed because in spite of nationalizations, aid continued to come from the United States and Europe, and international lending agencies and the country's sound financial condition enabled it to meet many of its own import requirements.[36]

The Soviets signed a friendship treaty with Somalia in 1974 and found Siad Barre eager to do what no one in the Derg wanted to risk: establish a classic Communist-style party. The Somali party was proclaimed in 1976 with enthusiastic Soviet endorsement. At the same time, the Somali security service was strengthened along standard Soviet lines. Siad was a model friend of the Russians, who lavished military aid on him to ensure that conservative Arab offers would be less attractive. The Russians sent more than $300 million in arms to Somalia in 1974–77—*after* the Ethiopian revolution was under way.[37] This was far in excess of total U.S. military aid and sales to Ethiopia during the same period—approximately $180 million—and, in fact, more than the entire amount of U.S. military aid to Ethiopia during the entire period of mutual security relationship (1953–77)—$287,300,000.[38] Meanwhile, the Russians continued to supply Somalia with only modest economic support, and the country's economy stagnated.[39]

Russian military advisers worked directly with the Somali armed forces down to the battalion level, and Russians, East Germans, Cubans, and others worked closely with the Somali security services. It is inconceivable that the Russians were not aware of Siad's preparations for a major assault on Ethiopia, for the Somalis had begun to expand guerrilla capabilities as early as 1975. Somali-supported insurgency in the Ogaden, Bale, and Sidamo would have aroused more Ethiopian concern in 1976 if the Derg had not been so preoccupied with Eritrea and growing resistance movements in more highly developed and populated parts of the country.

Since 1977 the Soviets have been encouraging the myth that they opposed the Somali invasion of Ethiopia.[40] Western writers inclined to be sympathetic to Soviet activities in the Horn, whether in Somalia or in Ethiopia, have built up a body of charitable speculation about the extent to which the Russians were allegedly unaware of Siad Barr's aggressive plans.[41] At the same time, they credit the United States with responsibility for the full-scale Somali invasion.[42] To say that such interpretations are mistaken is to be much too kind; they are an egregious whitewash of Soviet conduct.

One has to postulate a phenomenal degree of ignorance of political processes to argue that the Soviet Union could not have seen the implications of Somalia's irredentism when it began its military aid program in the mid-1960s. Military aid was increased after Siad Barre came to power. Finally, the Soviets decisively upgraded Somali military capabilities in the wake of the Ethiopian revolution. In view of this sustained effort to equip the Somalis so they could move to satisfy their irredentist ambitions, any advice to the Somalis in the summer of 1977 has to be taken lightly as a measure of real Soviet intentions. Why did they not take military measures against the Somalis in the summer of 1977? Or at least take the initiative to break relations or organize diplomatic pressure?

The most logical conclusion is that the Russians knew full well what they were about during 1975 and 1976. They were capable of generating strong desires and demands in the Derg for a comprehensive military relationship, and did so. But they were not sure. Political ferment in Ethiopia and the inexperience of many members of the Derg justified doubts about the wisdom of trying to get a firm grip on Ethiopia too soon. After all, memory of the disaster with Numeiry and the Sudanese Communist Party was still fresh. And it was important to get the United States out of Ethiopia as thoroughly as possible. The investment in Somalia was large, and it was desirable to try to preserve it. So the Russians played hard-to-get with the Ethiopian revolutionary leadership as long as they could be reasonably sure that they were improving their ultimate chances for hegemony over the whole region by doing so.

YEAR OF DECISION: 1977

Between November 1976 and November 1977, the Kremlin leadership had to take several major decisions in respect to the Horn. More than 30 years of Russian effort and between half a billion and a billion dollars of investment in the region had to be justified, defended, and capitalized upon—or lost. There must have been sharp differences of opinion on these issues in Moscow and among Russians in Horn capitals—factions favoring various tactics and aims must have formed. We know practically nothing about them.

All that we can say is that if there was hesitation to move and act, it did not last long. The aging Soviet leadership team, beset by mounting problems at home and in other parts of the Soviet empire, was able to meet the challenge. Additional manpower and resources were expended in the Horn on a prodigious scale, and risks were taken. And in the end, sizable gains were made.

The general outlines of the story are well known, but highlights are worth recapitulating. Angola was a necessary preliminary to high adventure in the Horn. Two important lessons were learned: the utility of Cubans as mercenaries and the extent to which détente had succeeded in inhibiting American ability to protect seemingly marginal interests. The U.S. election of November 1976 must have been an important milestone in the Soviet decision process. The Democrats' victory led Moscow to conclude that it was safe to move on Ethiopia. Mengistu was invited to Moscow in early

December and promised military aid, on condition that he cut the American military connection. This caused dissension in the Derg that led to bloodshed in early February, the death of Teferi Banti, and Mengistu's assumption of the position of head of state.

Carter administration criticism of the Ethiopian regime for human rights violations provided a convenient pretext for Mengistu to expel all U.S. military personnel and terminate the military aid program in April, but had nothing to do with precipitating these actions in any fundamental sense. Some other pretext would have served as well—such as failure to release ammunition or other "lethal"[43] military supplies or an issue relating to nationalized property. The human rights issue was more dramatic and divisive, and Carter has been criticized ever since, primarily by conservatives, for undermining American foreign policy by displaying excessive zeal on human rights. The fact remains that human rights were being grossly violated in Ethiopia at that time, and the Ford administration had already become deeply concerned about the violations. The human rights situation in Ethiopia worsened during the next year and a half. In the spring of 1977, the time was long past when the United States might have tried using military and economic aid as a lever for coercing the Derg into more moderate behavior.[44]

In March, while Mengistu was busy consolidating his hold over the Derg and preparing for military disengagement from the United States, the Soviets brought Fidel Castro onto the scene to try to reconcile all the contradictions that resulted from their decision to become Ethiopia's main military supplier. Castro's visit to Somalia, Ethiopia, and Aden may have been a hasty attempt to fend off impending disaster. It could also have been a more carefully conceived scheme for maintaining a grip on both Somalia and Ethiopia that had developed over some time. Castro proposed federating the whole Horn with autonomy for the Ogaden and Eritrea and the possibility that South Yemen would eventually join the federation.

A political construct of this sort, if it could have been brought into being, would have represented a formidable Soviet advance toward consolidation of control over the Red Sea approaches to the Indian Ocean. The Soviet investment in Somali facilities would have been preserved; a heavy new investment in Ethiopia would have been unnecessary. Djibouti, not yet independent, and the best port in the region, might also have been brought into this new political entity. Last, but not least, the arrangement would have subsumed the Ogaden and Eritrean conflicts—both to a substantial degree the consequence of Soviet support over a long period of time, though many other factors bore on them as well. It was an imaginative scheme, and one from which the clear net gainer would be the Soviets alone.

No one accepted Castro's proposition. All the Horn leaders saw more disadvantages than gains in it, and preferred to stick to courses they were already following. For the Soviets, the Castro proposition probably seemed to be a no-lose initiative—if the now looming Somali assault on Ethiopia quickly succeeded, the Russians could hope to dominate the entire area anyway. It should be remembered that the Soviets made no move at this time to reducing their comittments to Somalia or their personnel there. And Siad himself was patient. Castro, going home disappointed, denounced Siad as more of a nationalist than a socialist. But the same could have been said of Mengistu. There is no reason to believe that he committed himself to surrendering Ethiopian sovereignty over either Eritrea or the Ogaden.

At this stage all the participants in the great confrontation that was looming were holding firm and daring other parties to act. Mengistu flew to Moscow in May, as soon as American military installations had been closed, and returned with an agreement for full military support from the USSR. The Soviets had already made modest shipments of military equipment to Ethiopia, transferring some from Aden. Some Russian and Cuban military advisers arrived. But operations remained on a very small scale until fall.

Meanwhile, Siad's guerrillas stepped up operations. The vital railway from Addis Ababa to Djibouti was cut in early June. Ethiopians now knew the Somalis were playing for high stakes. Soon the distinction between guerrillas and Somali regulars blurred and disappeared. By August the Somalis were in control of large parts of southeastern and southern Ethiopia, and the country seemed to be on the verge of disintegration as other regional insurgencies expanded, the exile-based Ethiopian Democratic Union penetrated the country from Sudan, and factional political infighting raged in Addis Ababa and some provincial capitals. Siad had by this time convinced himself that the ancient empire, if toppled, would shatter like Humpty Dumpty, and could never be put together again.

The eastern stronghold of Jijiga, with a newly installed U.S.-supplied radar station, fell on the eve of the third anniversary of the revolution in September, and opened the road to Harar. As happened in Iran in 1981 in the face of the Iraqi attack, Ethiopia experienced an enormous surge of patriotic fervor, and psychologically the tide began to turn just when the country appeared to have suffered a crippling blow.[45]

The Derg appealed to the United States for resumption of a military relationship that at the very minimum would permit release of matériel that had been in the delivery pipeline when Ethiopia expelled the U.S. military mission in the spring. The Carter administration had made a very tentative tilt toward Somalia in June, but quickly realized that the Somalis were committing aggression with regular troops, and backtracked.[46] It then fell back upon what had always been U.S. policy in the area—recognition of the territorial integrity of all countries in the region, with the added proviso that the United States would supply no arms to any party in the conflict.[47]

During September 1977 both Soviet and U.S. official missions came to Addis Ababa to size up the situation. The U.S. mission reported that Ethiopia was not disintegrating and recommended no reversal of what was, in effect, a complete U.S. arms embargo on both Ethiopia and Somalia. The Russians delayed making a major commitment, perhaps wanting to be sure that Mengistu had the capacity to hold the Derg together and to rally Ethiopians to the defense of their country. Political infighting had reached a new high during this period, with the EPRP openly challenging the Derg for leadership. A group of Marxist intellectuals led by Haile Fida, who had initially been treated with favor by some Derg members and whose group may have appeared to the Soviets to be the best nucleus for setting up a Communist-style party, fell out with Mengistu, fled to the provinces, and were captured.[48] Mengistu was the target of several assassination attempts during the fall of 1977.

The Russians must also have wanted to feel sure that the United States would not start providing military aid again. It was bad enough to have Ethiopia dependent upon Israel for crucial specialized items and to have an unofficial Israeli political mission in Addis Ababa.

Siad Barre may have had as much impact as any other factor on Russian decisions which followed. The Russians took no steps to break with him, and though he had permitted Somali mobs to attack Cubans and Russians who were being withdrawn from Somalia (sometimes going directly to Ethiopia) in the late summer, he had not taken any preliminary measures toward a decisive break. Russian military aid appears to have continued to arrive in Somalia through August. Siad flew to Moscow late that month to try to persuade the Russians to abandon support of Ethiopia, which he pictured as being on the verge of collapse. The Russians continued to equivocate. Siad could not. He had to follow up on his initial successes against Ethiopia or risk fatal loss of momentum. Though by autumn he had captured most of the regions with Somali population, he pressed on into Oromo-inhabited territory along the edge of the highlands, besieged the ancient walled city of Harar, and came close to surrounding the modern railroad center of Diredawa, the only city in Ethiopia with a sizable Somali population.[49]

This was all that was needed to consolidate the great upwelling of national feeling that gripped Ethiopians throughout most of the country. The Derg was recognized as defending the national interest in a way it had not previously enjoyed. Like Stalin after the Nazi invasion in 1941, Mengistu made appropriate concessions to national feeling, quietly moderated some of the discriminatory measures that had affected the Orthodox Church, and eased the pace of implementation of revolutionary reforms. Nevertheless, while the Somali military advance had slowed during October, the initiative still lay with the invaders.

Mengistu flew to Cuba and Moscow at the end of October. Raul Castro flew to Moscow in early November, accompanied by the same Cuban generals who later figured prominently in the campaign in Ethiopia. Somewhere in this sequence of visits, the Soviet decision to commit massive numbers of Cubans, a greatly expanded Russian advisory group, and unprecedented quantities of Soviet arms and equipment to Ethiopia was made. Siad Barre got wind of it, and announced expulsion of the Russians and closure of all their installations in Somalia on November 13—but diplomatic relations were not broken. General Petrov, who became the senior Soviet commander in Ethiopia, arrived in Addis Ababa on November 17.

In the last week of November, the massive airlift of troops and supplies from the USSR to Ethiopia began. The decision to commit the forces needed to expel the Somalis from all Ethiopian territory had been taken. The high military cost of the operation was clearly recognized, for the airlifts and sealifts that followed during December and continued into early 1978, and the operations they enabled the Ethiopians to carry out, with direct Cuban combat participation and leadership and close Soviet advisory involvement, reveal no evidence of skimping or economizing. Everything that was needed to accomplish the task was provided, and a good deal of extra matériel and arms as well. By the close of 1977, $440 million worth of military assistance had been delivered. The Soviets brought in a further $1.1 billion in arms of all kinds in 1978 and another $210 million worth in 1979—$1,750,000,000 in military aid for Ethiopia in barely two and a half years to secure the long-sought position of preeminence there that represented the real prize in the Horn.[50]

Events in Ethiopia and elsewhere in the Horn made headlines in the world press during the winter of 1977-78 and well into the following summer. Cuban manpower, Russian advisers, and massive quantities of Soviet arms and supplies enabled the Ethiopians to regain control of all territory overrun by the Somalis. Siad Barre was unwilling, however, to give up the fight, and reverted to a sustained guerrilla harassment operation that made it impossible for the United States to provide military aid to Somalia until 1981. Developments in both Ethiopia and Somalia since 1978 have entailed many twists, turns, and contradictions. To review them is beyond the scope of this paper, which will now, in conclusion, be directed to consideration of two basic sets of questions:

1. What factors were most significant in Soviet advances in the Horn?
2. What have the Soviets gained? What problems must they overcome to consolidate their grip on the region? What are their prospects?

FLEXIBLE PERSISTENCE[51]

If we examine Soviet actions in the Horn only in the context of the late 1970s, they appear daring, provocative, and openly disdainful of the United States. But this is too narrow a view. If we start with the 1940s, we see a slow, deliberate effort to lay the groundwork for gaining influence based on a deeper historical awareness of the intrinsic strategic value of the region. There was not much movement until the end of the 1950s. In the 1960s a great burst of activity occurred, some of it naive and overly hasty. The Soviets did not do well in Sudan when opportunities opened up for them. In Somalia, on the other hand, they built steadily and came close to creating a model client state. They were patient and discreet in Ethiopia on the overt plane, clever and creative covertly.

Economic aid played no significant role in their success. They always gave sparingly, and reduced their commitments as time passed. They were not good at exploiting religion, even in Ethiopia, where old Orthodox Christian ties existed. Somalia, too, is a deeply religious country, but Islam was not a hindrance to the Russians there. Russian culture had no appeal to anyone in the Horn. Marxism in the abstract had little appeal either, but it provided slogans and a body of doctrine that was convenient as a rationalization for radical intellectuals and military men who aspired to get a handle on their societies and exercise power over them. The attractiveness of Marxist ideology as a basis for organizing a state-directed economy also appealed to these same groups, who were concerned about their own ability to compete in societies organized according to Western principles of free enterprise and the pluralistic interplay of political forces.

Two factors stand out above all others as the key to Soviet success in the Horn: willingness to supply large quantities of military aid with little worry about how it might eventually be used, and the capacity to develop and sustain subversive programs over long periods of time in order to promote political destabilization and build pressures that can be exploited to Soviet advantage.

Patience and persistence—even a fair degree of cautiousness—are the main characteristics of the Soviet effort to get a grip on the Horn when seen in long-term perspective. But when the pace of events quickened and threatened to get out of control, Russians demonstrated remarkable flexibility and readiness to take rapid and decisive action. Neither ideology nor moral commitments acted as a deterrent to action when it became necessary in 1977. The governmental decision-making machinery obviously functioned efficiently. Power considerations took priority—risks were taken and resources expended daringly to maximize opportunities for expanding power.

It is important not to idealize the Soviet performance, however. We must keep in mind that the Soviet advance into Ethiopia took place at a time when effective U.S. power there had almost evaporated. Some of the relative caution the Russians displayed during the first two years after the revolution can undoubtedly be ascribed to residual respect for the high degree of influence the United States and its Western allies had long exercised in the country. Even as it became apparent that the United States was no longer interested in—or perhaps even capable of—maintaining its influence, the Russians took no chances on provoking an unexpected American response. Instead, they concentrated on encouraging circumstances to develop in such a way that the United States was effectively blocked from acting in its own interest by self-imposed restrictions.

The prime feature of the U.S. predicament in respect to the Horn during 1977 was an extreme lack of flexibility, compounded by shallowness of political perspective. The roots of this problem go back to the period before the Carter administration took office. They lie in the deterioration of U.S. governmental processes and the tensions that arose between the legislative and executive branches in the early 1970s. They lie also in the illusions of détente. Détente as such, however, has little direct bearing on the situation as it developed in the Horn from 1977 on.

The Russians did not simply take advantage of openings created by détente to advance in this region. Détente created no new openings for them there. It was their own steady efforts that created them. Flexible persistence paid off. For the Americans, however, and for West Europeans with an interest in Ethiopia, détente inhibited not only the capacity to see the strategic significance of what was happening in the Horn, but also dulled the sense of moral commitment to people who had long placed their hope in the Free World.

When Mengistu, Derg members, and Ethiopian government officials berate the United States for having let their country down in its hour of need, and refer to the American refusal to supply spare parts and to release previous Ethiopian military purchases in the summer of 1977, after the Somali attack, they are being very selective, if not hypocritical, for it was they who—with some glee—had severed the American military relationship only a few months previously.[52] Some of them would clearly have been willing to cut it much earlier if the Russians had been ready to step in. In a larger sense, however, Ethiopians have justification for feeling let down by their American and European friends who, after providing so much economic aid, creating so many educational opportunities, and displaying so much sincere understanding and appreciation of the country and its problems, largely ignored it and let it drift into destabilization and revolution without making serious efforts to stem the process. Lack of Western will, nurtured by the illusions of détente, had a good deal to do with creating these circumstances.

CAN THE GRIP BE MAINTAINED?

The visitor to Ethiopia today is struck by the relative peace and order of the central part of the country, though there are many outlying regions to which travel is not permitted and insurgency still affects life in Tigre and Eritrea, though it has been much reduced in the latter province from the level of 1977-78.[53] And while on the surface—red flags, portraits of Marx, Engels, and Lenin, Communist sloganry everywhere—the country gives the appearance of greater loyalty to the Soviet system than the countries of Eastern Europe, where Russian hegemony has long been established, one does not have to penetrate very deep into the society to discover that Communism is far from consolidated. The visitor will also be surprised to find so little direct evidence of Soviet and Cuban presence, for at least 12,000 Cubans remain and there is a large group of Russian military and technical advisers.[54] The Cubans are mostly in camps in the countryside, training Ethiopian recruits, and the Russians are much less visible than the Americans were in their heyday. The Russians, particularly, seem uncomfortable in Ethiopia. No trend toward increasing Russian presence or influence is evident. Mengistu does not rely on Cubans or Russians for his personal security.

Cubans have stayed out of the fighting in Eritrea, and some Ethiopians are beginning to complain about having to keep paying local costs for them. At least 250,000 Ethiopians are under arms, more than half of them fighting intermittently in Tigre, Eritrea, and elsewhere in the north. Others are still on the alert in southern and eastern areas that had been overrun by the Somalis, where rehabilitation and resettlement are proceeding haltingly. Insurgency in these regions seems almost to have disappeared. Siad Barre no longer has the resources to sustain—or the political momentum to inspire—insurgency in the Ogaden and Bale. A large portion of the Somali population of this region—and some Oromos as well—are in refugee camps in Somalia. Siad's political dilemma is more acute than Mengistu's, for any return to an aggressive posture toward Ethiopia will undermine his chances of continuing to receive the modest military aid that has finally been provided to Somalia.[55]

The southwestern coffee-producing provinces, with their colorful and polyglot populations, have been one of the least disturbed parts of the country throughout the revolutionary period. They were among the last areas of modern Ethiopia to be brought under imperial control in the late 19th and early 20th centuries. Their loyalty to the Ethiopian state negates theories that disparage the viability of modern Ethiopia as an example of African imperialist colonialism, an artificial polity that lacks its own political dynamism.

Ethiopia is still governed by Ethiopians, as it always has been. There is still an obvious pride in being Ethiopian that manifests itself in dozens of ways. Old patterns have reasserted themselves. Mengistu's style of governing has a good deal in common with that of his imperial predecessors. The country is again, as it was in Haile Selassie's time, focusing on education and economic development. A sustained national campaign is said to have raised literacy markedly. Several languages are now used for elementary school instruction, newspapers, radio, and television, but the status of Amharic, the national language since medieval times, remains firm.

But there are also sharp contrasts with the imperial era. None is greater than among students, who are perhaps the most docile element in Ethiopian society today, studying and avoiding politics. Everyone in Ethiopia avoids politics now—memories are too sharp of the political turmoil of the immediate postrevolution years, culminating in the Red Terror that raged in 1978 as a deliberate Derg effort to bring it under control. Political life, such as it is, now revolves around marching and cheering and going to meetings to study the ideological pronouncements of COPWE, the substitute party that occupies the elegant former parliament building in the center of the capital. Ethiopia not only is without political parties, as it was under the emperor, but it lacks a parliament and a constitution (which it had then) as well. The government's title remains *Provisional* Military Government of Socialist Ethiopia. The workings of the Derg are as mysterious as ever. It does not appear to be evolving into either a parliament or a party. It may now consist of no more than 30 members.

Ethiopia's real problems remain: modernization, economic development, how to recognize ethnic and regional diversity and preserve national unity. Dealing with them requires money, organization, patience, and political and administrative skill. Nothing that has occurred since 1974 offers a basis for belief that the Russian-style "socialist" approach to these challenging tasks promises better results than the pragmatic "capitalist" approach that was taken, with considerable success, before 1974. Quite the contrary, for it is already becoming apparent that the Cubans and the Russians are much less relevant to most of these problems than Ethiopia's former friends were.

Ethiopia is already beginning to display many of the economic symptoms that are present, in much more advanced form, in countries that have experienced Soviet-style "socialism" for a much longer period of time: lagging agricultural deliveries, an expanding black market in basic commodities and key export crops (coffee, for instance), low productivity in state-run industry, skyrocketing costs in state-operated agricultural enterprises, inefficiency and corruption in government bureaucracies, and rising expectations on the part of the population that cannot be met. Far-reaching plans have been developed for collectivization of agriculture. None of them offers real promise of easing problems that are already apparent:

peasants find the rigidities of the present associations to which they belong uncomfortable, and are holding back on deliveries of produce because of low prices paid by state-operated purchasing agencies. The Russian prescription for such difficulties—more rules and regulations, more coercion, more bureaucrats devising more plans—compounds the problems. There has been no significant industrial development in Ethiopia since the revolution, little new construction. The country's limited resources are consumed in maintaining a military establishment that is at least six times the size of that in the time of Haile Selassie.

Unless Ethiopia can sharply reduce the proportion of revenue that goes to support this vast military apparatus, prospects for any economic development at all are poor—barring, of course, a major input of Soviet economic aid. The Soviets have been generous with military aid, but they have been parsimonious with economic help. Great plans for dams and irrigation schemes have been laid before groups of Russian technicians by eager Ethiopian bureaucrats. Nothing has happened. Modest Russian efforts to search for petroleum, capitalizing on earlier work done by Western companies, have brought no results. The Russians have been unwilling to offer Ethiopia a long-term petroleum supply guarantee. Detailed recent figures are not available, but it appears likely that Ethiopia is still receiving substantially more economic development assistance from European countries and international lending agencies than it does from the Russians and their friends. With Soviet economic prospects as poor as they now appear to be, how can Ethiopia expect to rank very high among competing demands: Poland, Cuba, Afghanistan, Vietnam?

Seen in a perspective stretching back to the 1950s, the Russian effort to get a grip on Ethiopia had few positive features, and these became less pronounced as the effort gained momentum. Religious and cultural relations and economic aid were maintained, but not expanded or increased, while priority went to efforts directed toward destabilizing Ethiopian society and putting greater strain on the established governmental apparatus. After a period of apparent doubt about the most efficacious way of gaining the upper hand in Ethiopia, the Russians in 1976–77 found themselves with no alternative to playing the role of Ethiopia's defender, sole source of military support, and direct sponsor of Cuban troop assistance to neutralize the Somali threat that the Russians themselves had created—in the sense that no matter what Somali irredentist ambitions might have been, they could never have taken concrete military form without massive Russian arms and training assistance. The Soviet Union was happy to serve as a model for socialism in Ethiopia through 1977 without paying a price. The events of 1977 forced the Russians to shift to a constructive posture. If they want to turn Ethiopia into a model of revolutionary success, Soviet style, they must pay for it. But how?

One expedient is now working itself out. The tripartite alliance that was created at Aden in August 1981 (Libya, Ethiopia, South Yemen) represents an interim effort to bring Qaddafi to the rescue. Reports of Libyan aid to Ethiopia have subsequently run as high as $900 million, but it is difficult to find even circumstantial evidence that resources approaching anything like this amount have been made available to Mengistu's government. Libya's available funds are contracting rapidly.

If Ethiopia is to have any hope of shifting its priorities to economic development and self-sustaining growth, it needs peace, both with its neighbors and internally. Peace has proved elusive, and the Soviets have little leverage on the situations that cause greatest strain: Eritrea and Tigre, for instance. This is particularly ironic, because both the Eritrean and the Tigrean rebel movements claim to be Marxist. Mentgistu continues to take an uncompromising position on Eritrea. The latest offensive intended to eliminate Eritrean insurgency—during the first months of 1982—fell short of its objective. Improved relations with Sudan could help reduce the insurgent threat in Eritrea, but the Russians have always been leery of close Ethiopia-Sudanese ties. They are also less than enthusiastic about too warm relations between Ethiopia and Kenya. From the Russians' viewpoint, strain between Ethiopia and its neighbors serves their advantage. But how long does it serve the Ethiopians' interest to let these strains persist?

Military and economic factors form the concrete issues around which the Ethiopian-Russian relationship now revolves. The likelihood that these issues can be worked out smoothly appears poor, and even those Ethiopians who are most eager to turn their country into a model junior partner of the Soviet Union are bound to be disappointed by the Russians' incapacity to meet Ethiopia's needs and expectations. But the problems are not going to be confined to the material dimension. Ethiopians' awareness of their history and traditions is deep. Religion is an important part of this awareness.

The Derg has been wary of offending religious feelings. In the early period of the revolution, Orthodox Christianity was subtly downgraded and Islam upgraded, but the process never went very far. While the Orthodox Church has been deprived of some of its traditional leadership, the hierarchical structure has remained intact. Among the population at large, the Orthodox Church has lost no significant influence. There appears, in fact, to be a marked resurgence of religion in Ethiopia. Government efforts to restrict evangelical church organizations do not appear to have had much effect. Churches of all denominations are well attended; so are mosques.

Among both Christians and Muslims, identification with Ethiopian national traditions remains strong, and may be increasing. The fact that the country's socialist leadership has felt compelled to communicate with the population in the old religious idiom is a measure of the extent to which religious habits of thinking remain embedded in the Ethiopian mind. But there is little reason to believe that writings such as the following poem do not strike the Ethiopian mind as ludicrous, as they strike us:

THE TRINITY
The myth of the old book reveals in the New Book
Three in Flesh but One in Soul.
Three in One and One in Three.
The Trinity in Unity for Man's Liberty!
Marx the Father, Engels the Son
And Lenin the Holy Ghost
Made the new Man free from Slavery![56]

The Russians have expended close to $3 billion on the Horn as a whole since the early 1950s: well over $500 million in Somalia and more than $2 billion on Ethiopia, less on Sudan. Their efforts have given them a grip on the heart of the Horn—Ethiopia—but it is far from consolidated. Only by expenditure of large additional sums on economic development—the field in which they have been least willing to spend and in which their own record is poorest—can they hope to maintain their grip for long. But even with such expenditure, the grip can hardly be regarded as assured.

NOTES

1. See Sergius Yakobson, "Russia and Africa," *Slavonic and East European Review* 17 (August 1939): and 19 (1939-40).
2. The best survey of Russian involvement with Africa in the 19th and early 20th centuries is Edward T. Wilson, *Russia and Black Africa Before World War II* (New York and London: Holmes and Meier, 1974). An often-cited earlier work, Czeslaw Jesman, *The Russians in Ethiopia—an Essay in Futility* (London: Chatto and Windus, 1958), is less complete. A late 20th-century author would have to be more hesitant about subtitling such a book "an essay in futility." What seemed like a closed chapter in the 1950s turned out to be a prelude to a great deal more history.
3. These activities have been treated in lively detail by Carlo Zaghi, *I russi in Etiopia*, 2 vols. (Naples: Guida Editori, 1972).
4. See Wilson, op. cit, pp. 54, 58.
5. Patricia Wright, *Conflict on the Nile—the Fashoda Incident of 1898* (London: Heinemann, 1972).
6. Milene Charles, *The Soviet Union and Africa* (Washington, D.C.: University Press of America, 1980), pp. 36-39.
7. It is hardly accidental that the Soviets and their surrogates appear not to have terminated support for the Eritrean insurgents until sometime in 1977, for they wished to keep open the option of expanding their influence in the Horn through exploitation of Somali irrendentism and Eritrean insurgency until they felt sure of gaining a solid grip on the centralized Ethiopian governmental structure. During the

first three years of the Ethiopian revolution, it was not clear that a centralized state would survive, though the Soviets opted for it decisively in December 1976 when they promised Mengistu major military assistance on condition that the U.S. military relationship be severed. It is possible that the Soviets reinsured themselves even after 1977 by continued ties to the Eritreans, with some support coming through East Europeans or the Italian Communists. Such links could remain to this day.

8. Paul B. Henze, "Russians in the Horn—Opportunism and the Long View," originally prepared for the Council on Foreign Relations in 1979 and shortly to be issued in expanded form by the European-American Institute for Security Research (P.O. Box 9844, Marine del Ray, CA 90291), deals with these questions at much greater length.

9. During 1961–70 Somalia received by far the largest foreign aid per capita of any country in the Horn, while Ethiopia received the least. Per capita averages for this decade are as follows: Ethiopia, $13.80; Kenya, $56.90; Somalia, $90.00; Sudan, $26.62. U.S. Arms Control and Disarmament Agency (ACDA), *World Military Expenditures and Arms Transfers,* annual issuances.

10. I. M. Lewis, *A Modern History of Somalia,* rev. ed. (New York and London: Longmans 1980), provides the most comprehensive interpretation of developments in the country since independence. Unfortunately, like most sympathetic treatments of modern Somali history, it reports on the break with the Russians at the end of 1977 with more insight and at greater length than the period of close friendship that preceded it.

11. These and most other military and economic aid statistics in this paper, unless otherwise noted, are derived from ACDA, op. cit., which has appeared regularly for more than a decade, usually summarizing data for ten years previous to the final date covered. Much of this data has been gathered and analyzed in Paul B. Henze, "Arming the Horn," presented to the VIIth International Conference on Ethiopian Studies, Lund, Sweden, April 26–29, 1982 and published as Working Paper #43, International Security Studies Program, Woodrow Wilson Center, Smithsonian Institution, Washington, D.C.

12. Exact figures on Soviet economic aid to Somalia are difficult to obtain. As of 1974, the USSR had offered approximately $90 million, but less than half of this sum appears to have been drawn down. During 1962–77 the United States supplied Somalia and Ethiopia with economic aid as follows (in millions of dollars):

	Loans and Grants	Peace Corps	Total Economic Aid
Somalia	73	5.4	78.4
Ethiopia	275.1	33.8	308.9

Given the fact that Ethiopia's population was at least eight times that of Somalia, per capita U.S. aid to Somalia was twice that to Ethiopia. U.S. economic aid to Somalia was probably equal to, and may even have exceeded, Soviet economic aid in value. See USAID, *U.S. Overseas Loans and Grants . . .* July 1, 1945¢September 30, 1981 (Washington, D.C.: USAID, 1982).

13. Good assessments of developments during this period include David Laitin, "The Political Economy of Military Rule in Somalia," *Journal of Modern African Studies* 14, no, 3 (1976); and Brian Crozier, "The Soviet Presence in Somalia," *Conflict Studies,* February 1975.

14. See Gabriel Warburg, *Islam, Nationalism and Communism in a Traditional Society—The Case of Sudan* (London: Cass, 1978), pp. 93-140.

15. Anwar Sadat maintained he gave Numeiry warning. See Warburg, op. cit., p. 135.

16. The best account of the period is Christopher Clapham, *Haile Selassie's Government* (New York: Praeger, 1969; London: Longmans, 1969).

17 The Russian approach to Haile Selassie is reminiscent in many respects of their approch to the shah of Iran until his fall.

18. For background on Eritrea, G. K. N. Trevaskis, *Eritrea, a Colony in Transition* (London: Oxford University Press, 1960), is indispensable. No study of the Eritrean rebellion that has appeared to date could remotely qualify as either objective or complete. The most extensive, Richard Sherman, *Eritrea—The Unfinished Revolution* (New York: Praeger, 1980), provides a great deal of data favorable to the Eritreans and ignores a good deal that is not. The most comprehensive and balanced study of the Eritrean problem that has yet appeared is Haggai Erlich, *The Struggle over Eritrea, 1962-1978—War and Revolution in the Horn of Africa* (Stanford, Calif.: Hoover International Studios, Hoover Institution Press, 1983).

19. The U.S. Military Aid and Assistance Group in Ethiopia refrained from direct involvement in Ethiopian operations against the Eritrean rebels, but U.S. military aid and counterinsurgency training of Ethiopian military personnel were important in improving Ethiopian performance. The Eritreans were well aware of these activities, but chose to avoid attacks on Kagnew and confrontation with Americans. Incidents that occurred were accidental.

20. Bereke Habte Selassie, *Conflict in the Horn of Africa* (New York and London: Monthly Review Press, 1980), provides both indirect and direct confirmation of Soviet and other Communist support. So do Fred Halliday and Maxine Molyneux, *The Ethiopian Revolution* (London: Verso; New York: Schocken Books, 1981).

21. For interesting data on student psychology, see David C. Korten, *Planned Change in a Traditional Society—Psychological Problems of Modernization in Ethiopia* (New York and London: Praeger, 1972), esp. pp. 239-71.

22. The Peace Corps became a special target of the left in many parts of the world about this time, a phenomenon that merits more comparative study. From its inception, the Peace Corps had evoked intense hostility from the left in Latin America. In Turkey, it fell victim even more rapidly than in Ethiopia to mounting leftist agitation. There was bitter irony in these developments, in light of the great lengths to which both Peace Corps leadership and rank and file had gone to demarcate Peace Corps undertakings from all other U.S. government operations.

23. Ethiopian Students Union of North America and Ethiopian Students Union of Europe.

24. Technically, Ethiopia remained a monarchy, with Crown Prince Asfa Wossen, incapacitated in London, declared king upon deposition of the emperor. The declaration was revoked in March 1975, when all royal titles were abolished.

25. So much so, in fact, that some of them provoke doubt by the very vehemence of their denials. This is especially true, for instance, of Halliday and Molyneux, op. cit., p. 214, who maintain that the United States tried to prevent the

Ethiopian revolution and go to great lengths to impugn American motives both before and after 1974 from a bewildering variety of contradictory angles. Marina Ottaway, *Soviet and American Influence in the Horn of Africa* (New York: Praeger, 1982), pp. 90, 91, 103, makes the same assertions more naively, pronouncing the Russians blameless of any involvement with the Ethiopian revolution until the end of 1976.

26. There had long been doubt about the crown prince's ability to succeed his father, and about his father's willingness to have him as successor, but during the early 1970s Haile Selassie had taken steps to underscore his commitment to his eldest son's succession, a position he reiterated to Asrata Kassa when he appointed him president of the Crown Council in August 1971. There was a widespread assumption among the Ethiopian elite, including younger government officials who were positive toward him, that on accession the crown prince would take immediate steps to share power with parliament as a committed constitutional monarch, and would permit political parties to function. He described these intentions to me at length in a private audience in August 1972.

27. This problem was compounded when U.S. Ambassador E. Ross Adair left his post in January 1974 for medical reasons. He was not replaced, and a weak embassy staff was hard put to maintain contact with Ethiopian officialdom, let alone influential private Ethiopians, during the confusing and fast-moving situation in the months that followed. There was an American ambassador in Ethiopia for only 16 of the next 54 months—between January 1974 and July 1978, when Frederick Chapin, appointed by President Carter and accepted by Mengistu, took up his post.

28. For one attempt at unraveling the still mysterious maneuverings in and among various elements in the armed forces that led to the establishment of the Derg (which means "committee" in Amharic), see Marina and David Ottaway, *Ethiopia—Empire in Revolution* (New York and London: Holmes and Meier, 1978), pp. 48-52.

29. I am currently involved in an attempt, in partnership with Haggai Erlich of Tel Aviv University, to chronicle in detail the year 1974 in Ethiopia, in order to establish what is known and can be explained, and what is not known and needs to be clarified in respect to this hectic and dramatic year.

30. I was told in 1982 by an Ethiopian now living in Europe, who was in continual contact with many leading figures in Addis Abada during 1974 (but was not in a governmental position) that the Hungarian embassy, and specifically the Hungarian cultural attaché, had served as an important point of contact with Derg elements during this time. The cultural attaché is said to have cultivated relationships with military and security officers who had been selected in the early 1970s for anti-hijacking and counterterrorist training, and came to form an activist clique whose members felt a strong link with each other. I have been unable to confirm this information from other sources, but note that Soviet use of satellite diplomatic and intelligence personnel for politically risky subversive operations in many parts of the world seems to have expanded from the late 1960s on. If the "antihijackers," as the group is said to have become known in 1974, actually fell under Communist influence and control, this was an ironic turn of events, for originally Ethiopian personnel were trained in various forms of countersubversion techniques by Israel and the United States.

31. A Gojjami Amhara, reputed to be a conservative nationalist at heart, he played a prominent role during the first three years of the revolution and was regarded as

second in power to Mengistu. He was liquidated in November 1977, charged with placing the interests of Ethiopia ahead of the interests of socialism.

32. For a more extensive review of this period, see Paul B. Henze, "Communism and Ethiopia," *Problems of Communism,* May–June 1981, pp. 55-74. Citations to this article include much of the published reporting and source material on this period.

33. COPWE, the Commission for Organizing the Party of the Workers of Ethiopia, was set up at the end of 1979 and held its first congress in June 1980. Though it performs some of the functions of a Communist-type party, it has not been allowed to develop an independent leadership structure—its leadership is identical with that of the Derg and government.

34. It was these efficient fighter aircraft, more than any other single factor, that enabled the Ethiopians to stem the Somali advance in the summer of 1977. The Soviet-supplied Somalia air force was quickly neutralized by the Ethiopians, whose American training as pilots was superior to that the Somalis had been given.

35. The reports were well-founded, and stemmed from advance briefings given by Derg members to meetings of Ethiopian diplomats in Europe and the Middle East on how to minimize the public relations consequences of the brutal and destructive offensive that was planned. Kissinger, as a result of such reporting, sent a strong personal warning to the Derg that is believed to have caused some modification of plans.

36. Revolutionary Ethiopia inherited a well-managed fiscal and financial structure from the imperial regime, and kept some of the same men who had managed it for the emperor in authority. The country's financial situation was also aided by high coffee prices during the mid-1970s.

37. In 1978 dollars, military aid received by Somalia during 1974–77, almost all of which came from the USSR or allied Communist states, is calculated at $398 million by ACDA, with a current ("then-year") dollar value of $340 million. See ACDA, *World Military Expenditures and Arms Transfers, 1970–1979,* publication no. 112 (Washington, D.C.: ACDA, 1982), p. 118.

38. The figure is from USAID, *U.S. Overseas Loans and Grants . . . Obligations and Loan Authorizations, July 1, 1945–September 30, 1981* (Washington, D.C.: USAID, 1982).

39. I have not gathered complete statistics on this subject, but it appears probable from available data that the United States actually supplied Somalia with more economic aid during 1960–77 than the Soviet Union did—$91.8 million, according to USAID, op. cit. With the enormous upsurge in refugee assistance after 1977, U.S. allocations rose dramatically, totaling $172.3 million during 1978–81 (exclusive of $40.4 million in military assistance, 1980–81). It is apparent that the United States has underwritten much of the cost of the refugees resulting from the Somali attack on Ethiopia. Seen in a broader context, the Soviet Union has poured in the arms, and the United States (and other Western countries) have paid for the consequences of the overarming: the refugees. The Soviets are not known to have contributed anything to refugee relief in either Somalia or Ethiopia.

40. Soviet Ethiopianist Maria Rait provided a summary of the current Soviet line in "Peaceful Borders on the Horn of Africa," presented to the VIIth International Conference on Ethiopian Studies, Lund, Sweden,

April 26–29, 1982. Ethiopians present at the conference did not find it convincing.

41. See for instance, Halliday and Molyneux, op. cit., p. 242.

42. Ibid., p. 266.

43. This rather scholastic distinction loomed large in Carter administration decisions on military aid to many countries. To most receiving countries, it appeared to be mere sophistry designed to camouflage American desire to withhold aid for various other reasons.

44. It can be argued that if the United States had withheld military aid in 1974 or 1975, instead of greatly increasing it and facilitating additional arms sales for cash, the Derg's already strong pro-Soviet declaratory stance might have been modified. Such an approach could also have had the result of forcing the Soviets to make binding commitments to the Derg much sooner on military aid—and perhaps even to furnish economic support. In retrospect, it is difficult to see how such an American approach could have been effective except as part of a more coherent effort to persuade the leaders of the Ethiopian revolution that orientation to the Soviet Union was not in their country's ultimate interest. This would have been a kind of sophisticated political initiative that the United States seemed incapable of undertaking during this period.

45. There are remarkable similarities between the miscalculation that led Iraq to attack Iran in 1980 and Somalia's attack on Ethiopia in 1977. In both instances attack caused countries that seemed to be disintegrating to rally. In both cases, armed forces that had been dependent upon American equipment, training, and concepts of military leadership performed better than those which the Soviets had trained. There are also interesting parallels—and substantial differences—between the Ethiopian and Iranian revolutions.

46. The assertions of many writers who have chosen to believe otherwise to the contrary (for example, Halliday and Molyneux, op. cit., who give a distorted account of these events on pp. 223–31)—no one in the Carter administration promised military support to Somalia for anything other than defense of its own territory.

47. If the Derg had not leaped to break the U.S. military relationship in April 1977, it might have been able to persuade the United States to provide military support when the Somalis attacked. Here it might also be argued, however, that if the Carter administration had had a larger view of U.S. strategic interests in the Horn/Southwest Asia/Indian Ocean region and less preoccupation with the morality of arms transfers, some degree of flexibility might have permitted supply of badly needed spare parts for F-5Es, for instance, which had a direct and clear relationship to defense of the country against aggression. Though no commitments to Somalia were made at this time or in the subsequent two years, there was nevertheless a small group of shortsighted advocates of support for the Somalis in the Carter administration. This group, surprisingly, included more men known as liberals than as conservatives. The principal result of its influence at this time was to discourage creative strategic thinking about Ethiopia.

48. For additional detail see Henze, "Communism and Ethiopia," loc. cit.

49. Though an ancient Muslim city with a distinct Semitic population and language of its own, Harar has a special emotional significance to Ethiopians, for it was the conquest of Harar by Emperor Menelik in January 1887 that completed the process of restoring the empire to what Ethiopians considered its ancient glory—the

Egyptians had occupied Harar and a large section of the adjacent coastal region in the previous decade. Ras Makonnen was governor of Harar when his son, the future Haile Selassie, was born in 1892. The site of Ethiopia's principal military academy, Harar has played a political role in modern imperial Ethiopia out of all proportion to the size of its population or its economic importance. Loss of it to the Somalis would have discredited Mengistu's regime as unable to protect true Ethiopian national interests. See "The Province of Harar" in Paul B. Henze, *Ethiopian Journeys* (London: Ernest Benn, 1977), pp. 187–212.

50. These figures are from ACDA, op. cit., p. 99. Figures are not yet available for Russian military aid deliveries to Ethiopia in 1980, 1981, and 1982, but some have continued each year.

51. The phrase is from Nimrod Novik, *On the Shores of Bab-el-Mandeb—Soviet Diplomacy and Regional Dynamics,* monograph no. 26 (Philadelphia: University of Pennsylvania, Foreign Policy Research Institute, 1979).

52. I have heard these complaints personally, both as a government official and as a private researcher, on many occasions since 1978. The Soviets have exploited these Ethiopian feelings—whether genuine or feigned, to encourage the conclusion that the United States is a country on which not a great deal of reliance can be placed over time. Nevertheless, the American visitor to Ethiopia at this time is invariably impressed with the vast amount of residual pro-American feeling in the country—much more so, unfortunately, than in Somalia, where the country's political and military misadventures, and the resulting refugee burden, have encouraged some degree of dour xenophobia.

53. See Henze, "Communism and Ethiopia."

54. Russians in Ethiopia are currently estimated to total between 1,200 and 1,500. This is a very small group compared with the size of the Russian advisory contingent in Egypt during the peak of the relationship with Nassar or in comparison to the Russian presence in Somalia until 1977. If Russians were present in Ethiopia at the same level as in Somalia, there would currently have to be over 30,000 of them in relation to the size of the population, or another 20,000 in relation to the size of the armed forces!

55. Through 1981, $40.4 million in U.S. military aid for Somalia had been authorized, but less than half of it had been delivered. For a current summary of Siad Barre's political status and some of Somalia's pressing problems, see my "How Stable is Siad Barre's Regime?" *Africa Report,* March–April 1982.

56. Assefa GMT, *Selected Poems—The Voice* (Addis Ababa: Chamber Printing House, 1980), p. 33.

SEVEN

The Soviet Union in Africa:
An Assessment
RAYMOND W. COPSON

INTRODUCTION

The Soviet Union has made significant gains in Africa since the early 1970s. Four African countries—Angola, Mozambique, Ethiopia, and the People's Republic of the Congo—are signatories to treaties of friendship and cooperation with the Soviet Union.[1] Soviet military advisers and Cuban troops are apparently well entrenched in Ethiopia, strategically located on the Red Sea opposite Saudi Arabia and along the approach to Suez. Cuban troops and Soviet advisers are also in Angola, a country in mineral-rich southern Africa that has considerable economic potential. A number of other countries have regimes that follow domestic and foreign policies that are broadly approved in Moscow. The dean of Soviet Africanists, Anatoly Gromyko, counts "over a dozen" "socialist-oriented"[2] countries on the continent.

Despite these gains in Africa, however, the Soviet Union has continued to suffer—as it had in earlier years—serious setbacks in its African policy. It has lost its position in Somalia, and seen its role in several other countries significantly reduced. Perhaps as a result of such setbacks, Soviet observers of Africa appear to have adopted a decidedly guarded view of the prospects for Soviet influence and Marxist socialism on the continent. This view is accompanied by a realistic assessment of Africa's grave economic, political, and social problems.

Soviet policy toward Africa at the present time is heavily concentrated on the Horn of Africa and the southern part of the continent. The strategic location of these areas, and the mineral wealth of southern Africa, are no doubt major factors attracting Soviet interest. Further Soviet gains in these areas in the short term are conceivable. A government favorable to the Soviet Union could come to power in Namibia at some point, although this is by no means certain. Coups might occur in the Horn, as elsewhere in Africa, that would bring pro-Soviet regimes into office.

The views expressed here are those of the author and do not reflect those of CRS or the Library of Congress.

Whether such gains would prove to be lasting, however, must be of concern to Soviet analysts. Soviet experience in Africa has demonstrated that friendly regimes can be overturned in countercoups. They can also undergo changes of heart that suddenly draw them to the West. Moreover, Soviet analysts, like their Western counterparts, must grapple with Africa's highly uncertain economic prospects in looking toward the future. Serious agricultural problems, burgeoning populations, and a host of other problems confront the majority of African countries with a future in which political instability and social turmoil loom as distinct possibilities.

Perhaps the Soviet Union can profit from instability and turmoil in Africa. But doing so would appear to require major economic, and possibly military, commitments that would compete with high-priority demands on Soviet resources elsewhere in the world. To date, Soviet capabilities for dealing with Africa have proved to be quite limited, and not always implemented with skill. Thus, the Soviet ability to achieve dominance in Africa or to exclude Western influence, even in the long term, is very much open to question.

CURRENT SOVIET ATTITUDES TOWARD AFRICA

Despite its gains, the Soviet Union today is by no means jubilant over the situation in Africa. Soviet officials and analysts are able to muster only guarded optimism when contemplating the prospects for Marxist socialism on the continent. President Brezhnev, speaking of the "newly free" nations to the 26th Congress of the Communist Party of the Soviet Union (CPSU) in 1981, said:

> These countries are very different. After liberation, some of them have been following the revolutionary-democratic path. In others, capitalist relations have taken root. Some of them are following a truly independent policy, while others are today taking their lead from imperialist policy. In a nutshell, the picture is a fairly motley one.[3]

Professor Gromyko is concerned about the fate of even the socialist-oriented states in Africa. Taking note of "economic disproportions, numerous social problems still unresolved, and scientific and technological backwardness" in Africa, he has written that "the position of the countries that are aiming to improve their people's welfare is not an easy one."[4]

Ideology no doubt compels the Soviets to continue to expect the eventual victory of Marxism in Africa, but they are making no predictions about when this victory will occur. Brezhnev issued no clarion call to revolution at the 26th Party Congress. But he made it clear that the Soviet Union would remain active in the Third World:

The CPSU will consistently continue the policy of promoting cooperation between the U.S.S.R. and the newly-free countries and consolidating the alliance of world socialism and the national liberation movement.[5]

Modest Soviet expectations for Africa are firmly rooted in hard experience. While there have been, on balance, a number of gains for socialist and Marxist forces on the continent, there have also been serious setbacks. Soviet influence in Sudan was virtually eliminated after a leftist coup against President Numeiry failed in 1971. In November 1977, Somalia, which had been the first African country to sign a treaty of friendship and cooperation with the Soviet Union, expelled all Soviet advisers and broke relations with Cuba. In August 1979, the regime in Equatorial Guinea, which had allowed the Soviet Union to use facilities in its territory as a jumping-off place for operations in Angola, was overthrown in a coup. The new government refused to renew a lease on a fishing depot used by Soviet trawlers apparently equipped with advanced electronic gear.[6]

Even the victory of Robert Mugabe, a self-declared Marxist, in the April 1980 elections in Zimbabwe was something of a setback for the Soviet Union. During the long guerrilla war in Zimbabwe, Soviet aid had gone primarily to Joshua Nkomo, Mugabe's non-Marxist rival. Soviet tacticians had evidently judged Nkomo to be the likely victor in any postwar leadership contest. Mugabe was understandably disappointed by his treatment at Soviet hands, and he waited six months after taking office before inviting the Soviets to open an embassy. U.S. and British embassies had been permitted from the beginning.

The history of Soviet setbacks in Africa extends back to the earliest days of Soviet involvement in independent Africa.[7] Soviet assistance to Prime Minister Lumumba in the Congo (Leopoldville), now Zaire, in 1960-61 helped to precipitate Lumumba's overthrow by pro-Western forces. Moreover, the Soviets were strongly criticized by many African leaders for unilateral interference in Africa and for sabotaging the U.N. peacekeeping operation in the Congo. Guinea, one of the first countries to receive Soviet assistance after independence, denied landing rights to Soviet planes during the Cuban missile crisis of 1962.[8] Governments that had been friendly to Moscow were overthrown in Ghana in 1966 and in Mali in 1968.

These experiences, together with other, lesser setbacks in bilateral Soviet relations with African states, have forced the Soviets to adjust to certain realities of the African situation. Two adjustments seem critical.

First is coming to a realistic estimate of Africa's political and economic problems. Soviet writers in the Khrushchev era were known for their optimistic assessments, from the Soviet perspective, of the prospects for economic and political development along socialist lines in Africa.[9] Experience tempered this enthusiasm. Soviet writings on Africa today are more likely to stress the obstacles to economic growth, political stability, and socialist development in Africa. Larded with condemnations of "international imperialism," "neocolonialism," and "provincial dependent capitalism" as the root causes of Africa's difficulties,[10] these writings also acknowledge hunger, disease, poverty, and adverse natural conditions as significant limiting factors on Africa's potential. The increase in petroleum prices during the 1970s is also recognized as a major economic problem, although (perhaps for diplomatic reasons) this increase is attributed to "transnational corporations" rather than to Middle Eastern and African oil producers.[11] Assessing such factors, one Soviet analyst reached the following conclusion:

> All this, in combination with the unfavorable forecasts for the trends in world capitalist production in the current decade, gives no grounds to hope for radical positive changes in the developing world.[12]

This vision of Africa must restrict Soviet expectations of what can be accomplished on the continent in the years ahead. Clearly there is a possibility of economic disintegration and political instability in Africa that would make it difficult for any outside power to exercise influence. A country that wishes to retain even marginal influence is going to have to respond to Africa's economic difficulties with large amounts of economic assistance. But the Soviet Union has not been a generous aid donor in the past, and its ability to become more generous is in question.

Second is appreciating the strength and appeal of the Western economies in Africa. As much as some Africans may denounce "economic imperialism" and "neocolonialism," the fact is that Western consumer goods, industrial and agricultural equipment, technology, and skills are widely recognized on the continent as superior to the Soviet equivalents. Western banks, Western corporations and businessmen, and Western technical personnel are widely dispersed around the continent. Countries that have undergone a reduction in the Western presence, such as Guinea and Angola, have suffered for it. Typically, they have sought at least a partial return of the Western presence. Angola, indeed, has welcomed a visit from David Rockefeller, retired chairman of Chase Manhattan Bank, for talks on increased U.S. private investment in the country.[13]

Soviet observers acknowledge the appeal of the Western economies in Africa, and accept that even the socialist-oriented governments must continue to operate in an economic environment strongly influenced by the West. According to Gromyko:

> Suffice it to say that the socialist orientation in Africa has come about and is developing with these countries still living within the framework of the world capitalist economy.[14]

This remark could, in addition, be interpreted to imply that a Western economic role in the socialist-oriented countries is necessary to the growth and development of those countries.

This is not to say that the Soviets are pleased by the continued strength of the Western economies in Africa. One writer has complained that Africa is "encountering fierce resistance on the part of the neocolonialists and their allies and their local henchmen."[15] But this and similar comments[16] only underlined the Soviet acknowledgment of the economic influence of the West in Africa.

Behind the vehemence of Soviet denunciations of "neocolonialists" in Africa lies a recognition of the limited Soviet ability to compete. Faced with serious economic problems at home, the Soviet Union has been able to contribute to Africa's economic development in only a modest way. Substantial efforts have been made in a few countries, but in 1954–79, the USSR provided only $1.2 billion in aid to sub-Saharan Africa.[17] The United States, which has historically been outpaced by some other Western donors in Africa, gave $5.7 billion over a comparable period,[18] while the Western nations and Japan together provided the same amount in 1979 alone.[19] The Soviets gave $1.7 billion in economic aid in 1979 worldwide,[20] so it is clear that they would be hard-pressed to compete with the West in aid to Africa. Reliable data on Soviet trade with Africa are not available,[21] but clearly the USSR is in no position to compete with the tens of billions that flow from the West to the African nations each year.

SOVIET STRATEGY IN AFRICA

An element of uncertainty must exist in any analysis of Soviet strategy. In the absence of an open policy discussion in the Soviet Union, or of an investigative press, the possibility of hidden plans and goals can never be dismissed. The analyst is left to examine official statements and authorized academic publications, both of which are usually couched in heavily propagandistic terms, and to draw inferences from Soviet actions.

This kind of analysis suggests that one goal of the Soviet Union on the continent is to weaken the West in a region where it is acknowledged to be quite strong. According to Brezhnev, "In a thousand ways, the imperialists are trying to bind themselves to these countries in order to deal more freely with their natural riches and to use their territory for strategic designs."[22] From this perception, it naturally follows for the Soviets that steps should be taken to counter the Western role in Africa, even if the Soviet Union and its friends on the continent are not yet in a position to terminate that role.

Soviet planners evidently hope that, with time, a large bloc of anti-Western, Marxist states with close ties to the USSR can be created. Angola,

Ethiopia, and Mozambique—states that are perceived as being on the "left flank" of socialist orientation in Africa[23]—are expected to lead in this movement. One Soviet analyst has written of their role:

> These states may come close to direct integration with the world socialist system, which in its turn will be a fresh factor in a further deepening of the crisis of present-day capitalism.[24]

Countering Chinese influence in Africa may still be a factor in Moscow's thinking, although China is only a marginal influence on the continent today. Anatoly Gromyko is still able to bluster against China for its "aspiration for hegemonism and anti-Sovietism,"[25] and for allegedly "aiding the neocolonialists" in Africa.[26] Soviet observers recognize, nonetheless, that the principal Chinese threat to their interests today is in Asia, not in Africa.[27] It may be, however, that one part of Africa, the Horn, is strategically significant to the Soviet Union, partly because of the rivalry with China in Asia. According to one analyst, the Horn has served as a way station and strong point on a key shipping route to Southeast Asia, where that rivalry is keenest.[28]

The Horn is probably more significant to the Soviets, however, because of its strategic location on the southern flank of the Middle East. Soviet interest in the Horn first became apparent in the mid-1960s, when Somalia was provided with the Soviet arms that made it a regional military power. In the 1970s, the region probably became more important to the Soviets because of their loss of influence in the Middle East. Thousands of Soviet advisers and military personnel were expelled from Egypt in 1976, and by the end of the decade, Egypt and Israel were implementing a peace settlement arranged entirely under American auspices. Losses at the center of the Middle East, however, seem to have increased Soviet interest in the flanks of the region. The Soviet intervention in Afghanistan, Soviet attempts to gain influence in Iran after the collapse of U.S. influence there, and the Soviet role in Ethiopia may thus form a pattern reflecting Soviet strategic concerns over the oil-rich region on its southern border.

Long-term Soviet plans for the Horn are not clear, and may not have crystallized even in Soviet minds. Soviet planners may envisage a linked system of socialist-oriented states in the region, perhaps including Somalia after a coup or a second realignment and—across the Red Sea—South Yemen. There may also be some hope that Sudan could eventually be included in such a system.

Bringing Ethiopia, long wary of encirclement by Islam, into a system of cooperation with Muslim nations would be a test for Soviet diplomacy and pressure tactics. But Ethiopia did enter into a cooperation agreement with Libya and South Yemen in August 1981,[29] suggesting that the idea may have some potential. A belt of friendly nations extending across the Horn and into Arabia would, it need hardly be pointed out, provide the Soviet Union with opportunities for extending its influence deeper into the Middle East. It could also offer significant military benefits in the event of a superpower confrontation in the Middle East or the Persian Gulf.

Southern Africa is the other region of Africa that is clearly of special interest to the Soviet Union. With Portugal's withdrawal from Angola and Mozambique, and the victories of Marxist, Soviet-supported revolutionary movements in those countries, Moscow scored two of its signal foreign policy successes of the 1970s. The prospect of a South African withdrawal from Namibia, a mineral-rich territory with a population of only 1 million, holds out the possibility of another gain in the region in the near future. Informed analysts, however, are not yet ready to predict the future behavior of an independent Namibian government headed by Sam Nujoma, the leader of the guerrilla opposition. Nujoma has received Soviet support (as well as support from African and other sources), but he is widely regarded as enigmatic and unpredictable. In any event, the Namibian peace process is being sponsored by five Western nations led by the United States, so that the final settlement may contain provisions that will limit Soviet opportunities. In 1983, it should be noted, a South African withdrawal from Namibia is far from certain.

Meanwhile, there is a palpable Soviet fascination with the future of South Africa itself, where in 1982 an alleged Soviet KBG major was expelled after what was reported to be his fourth mission to the country.[30] Soviet analysts are well aware of the mineral wealth and strategic location of this country. Moreover, because of what they see as "deepening class contradiction," a growing "African proletariat," and the inevitable failure of reform efforts directed by the "local big bourgeoisie,"[31] Soviet observers evidently believe that the country has revolutionary potential.

Just how strong this belief may be is difficult to assess. Soviet analysts also recognize the strength and effectiveness of the South African government. According to one Soviet writer:

> The Pretoria regime still possesses considerable economic and military potential and powerful repressive machinery. It is doing all it can to stem the tide of the revolutionary movement.[32]

But even if, as seems likely, the USSR is not expecting early revolutionary change in South Africa, it now has a foothold in the region from which it will undoubtedly seek to influence the direction of any such change, whether in the long or the short term. Soviet military advisers in Angola and possibly Mozambique, close Soviet ties to the governments of these countries, and Soviet aid to the African National Congress and the Mozambique-based

South African Communist Party have provided the Soviet Union with a position from which it can try to exploit developments in South Africa as they occur.

Elsewhere in Africa, it is difficult to discern clear military/strategic ambitions behind Soviet conduct. If such ambitions are present, they probably take the form of a desire for military access, to be used in the event of as yet undefined contingencies. Some observers, for example, believe that the Soviet Union may hope to use an 1,800-meter runway it is helping to build as an aid project in Mali.[33] This facility does not tie in with any immediate known Soviet objectives, but it would be useful in dispatching transport planes to a variety of African destinations.

In general, the Soviets seem concerned to maintain ties with a variety of regimes—ties that can have diplomatic, economic, and intelligence benefits—and to take advantage of opportunities for increased influence as they present themselves. Soviet broadcasts, for example, supported the new regime of Flight Lieutenant Rawlings, which took power in Ghana in a New Year's (1982) coup. Rawlings is popular among African youth, who see in him a zealous, pure-in-heart challenge to corrupt politicians. Backing Rawlings was good public relations for the Soviets, who probably had little expectation of long-lasting gain in a country as stricken with economic difficulties and political instability as Ghana.[34]

Meanwhile, the Soviets are careful to keep on the good side of the very different government in Nigeria. Nigeria's civilian regime is at the apex of a boisterous political system, in which charges of corruption often fill the air, and it oversees an active capitalist economy. Nigeria, in short, is far from a socialist orientation. But Nigeria is also Africa's most populous nation, its economy is the largest on the continent, and its army—130,000 men—is second in size only to Ethiopia's on the African continent. This is not a country from which the Soviet Union can afford to be excluded if it is to play a major role in African affairs. Thus, Soviet publications are full of praise for Nigeria as, in the words of one writer, a country that "pursues both a realistic foreign and a rational domestic policy."[35] Nigeria is singled out for its efforts to restrict the activities of "transnational corporations";[36] academic exchanges are carried on;[37] and substantial economic assistance is sent to Nigeria.

SOVIET TACTICS IN AFRICA

But ambitions alone cannot assure a successful foreign policy. The fact that the Soviet Union has ambitions in the Horn, in southern Africa, and elsewhere by no means guarantees that these ambitions will be realized. Estimating the prospects for Soviet success requires an assessment of the

Soviet Union's tactics on the African continent and of its capabilities for successfully implementing those tactics in the future.

With tactics as with strategy, an element of uncertainty must hang over the discussion. To some degree, Soviet tactics in Africa remain hidden. The outside observer may never learn what is said in private meetings when the leaders of "socialist oriented" states visit Moscow. Are strong-arm techniques employed? Are threats made? How often? Nor is it easy to discover how Soviet advisers in Africa carry out their activities on a day-to-day basis.

Questions linger over the possibility of Soviet involvement in a number of specific events in Africa. Were the Soviets, through their Cuban allies, involved in the 1978 uprising in Zaire's Shaba Province, or did the Carter administration badly misread this crisis by implicating Cuba? Did the Soviet Union have foreknowledge of the 1977 Angolan coup attempt launched by a faction thought by some to be more pro-Soviet than President Neto? Was any encouragement provided to Rawlings, who visited Libya prior to his second takeover in Ghana? These are fascinating questions, but the answers may never be known.

In Liberia, there has been some suspicion of the Soviet Union. The new government in Liberia, which seized power in April 1980, flirted briefly with Libya and the Soviet Union, but in May 1981, for unexplained reasons, it ordered a reduction in the size of the Soviet embassy staff. In June, Liberian authorities seized a cargo of electronic equipment being off-loaded from a Soviet ship directly into a Soviet embassy car.[38] But again, the details of Soviet covert activity, if any, remain shrouded.

ECONOMIC ASSISTANCE

Soviet economic assistance to African countries is an important instrument of policy, even if it is a limited instrument. While only a few countries are likely to receive Soviet aid in a given year, more than 25 countries have benefited from Soviet assistance since their independence.

The impact of Soviet assistance may be magnified by the way it is channeled into large-scale infrastructure projects. The U.S. development assistance program is focused on directly aiding the poorest of the poor in Africa, and it goes primarily to the rural areas.[39] The future may judge that this approach has made the greater contribution to African development, but the Soviet approach, some argue, enhances the usefulness of aid for political and propaganda purposes. Much Soviet aid supports industrial projects,[40] such as a major pipeline and the Ajaokuta steel project in Nigeria. Some 6,000 Soviet personnel are expected to come to Ajaokuta,[41] located in a country that does not receive U.S. economic assistance because of its oil wealth. In

Mozambique, Soviet personnel are reported to be engaged in the development of coal mining and in oil exploration,[42] and the Soviets have supported railway and road construction in Angola.[43] Insofar as agriculture is supported, the Soviets concentrate on assisting large-scale farming and on providing farm machinery.

Economic assistance as an instrument of Soviet policy is largely constrained by the limits, noted above, on the Soviet economy. The Soviet Union, given its other priorities at home and in the defense field, is simply not in a position to provide aid to Africa on a vast scale.

Another difficulty for the USSR in the field of economic aid is that the Soviet economic experience may be of only limited relevance in Africa. Food and agriculture are critical problems on a continent where per-capita food production is falling at a rate of 1.4 percent annually.[44] But the Soviet Union, facing a food crisis of its own, can hardly become a major supplier of food aid in Africa. Its background in collective agriculture and state farms restricts its ability to contribute to raising agricultural output in Africa, where rapid production increases by individual small farmers are widely seen as the only road to early food sufficiency.

When Soviet aid for infrastructure projects brings in large numbers of Soviet technicians, the opportunities for friction with Africans increase. Reports suggest that Soviet personnel show a tendency toward clannishness in Africa, forming tightly knit communities that disdain social interaction with Africans. Soviets are also reputed to be condescending and impatient in dealing with their African counterparts. In August 1979, Nigeria expelled a number of Soviet air force instructors, and offensive behavior may have contributed to the decision to do so.[45] Certainly the expulsion raises questions about the possibility of significant frictions when large numbers of Soviets arrive at Ajaokuta.

The Soviet Union, moreover, has acquired a reputation for sharp dealing and attempts to exploit its economic relationships with African countries. According to one report, Angola "provides the rent and utilities for the Soviets' housing, pays $600 a month for every Cuban school teacher, allows the Soviet Union to keep 75 percent of the fish caught off the Angolan coast, and repays its debts for weapons with most of its income from oil and coffee."[46] Reports that Ethiopian coffee sent to Eastern Europe in repayment of debts has been resold on world markets in competition with exchange-earning Ethiopian export coffee are not likely to have been well received in Addis Ababa. The Soviet negotiations with Nigeria over the Ajaokuta project were extremely prolonged, lasting from 1967 until 1976.[47] This may have indicated Nigerian wariness over the terms of the deal—and perhaps over possible Soviet political intentions toward Nigeria.

Nor are African recipients satisfied with the quantity and quality of Soviet aid. President Sékou Touré of Guinea, once the foremost Soviet ally on the African continent, has complained openly about the Soviet failure to develop his country's bauxite industry. Colonel Mengistu, the Ethiopian head of state, actively seeks increased Western assistance and is making some effort to rebuild his country's tourist industry—suggesting dissatisfaction with the volume of Soviet assistance flowing into his country. Angola and Mozambique also encourage aid from a variety of sources, and apparently do not regard Soviet aid alone as adequate. Soviet economic assistance in Africa, in short, is a foreign policy instrument of decided limits.

SECURITY ASSISTANCE

The Soviet Union far outstrips the United States as an arms supplier to the African continent, and its role has been expanding in recent years (see Table 1). Soviet security aid, however, has been geographically concentrated. In terms of dollar value in 1975–79 (the most recent period for which unclassified data are available), 44 percent of Soviet assistance went to Ethiopia.[48] Angola, with 15 percent for the same period, has been the second-ranking recipient, and lesser amounts of military aid have been spread to at least 17 other countries.

Soviet military advisers have assumed increasing importance in Africa in recent years. They are thought to have directed the Ethiopia offensive against the Somali invasion of 1977–78, and are probably playing a role in Ethiopia offensives against Eritrean guerrillas. A few have been killed or captured in southern Angola. It is estimated that there are 4,000 Soviet military advisers on the African continent at present, heavily concentrated in these two countries and in Mozambique.[49] Approximately 11,000 military personnel from these countries and from several others have received training in the Soviet Union.[50]

Cuban troops in Africa also serve as an instrument of Soviet policy. Cuba no doubt has its own leadership ambitions among the Third World nations. In pursuing these ambitions, it is more than a surrogate for the Soviet Union. But without Soviet financial and logistical support, the presence of these troops in Africa would be impossible. While providing such support, the Soviets are using the Cuban troops for their own purposes.

The Cuban forces were particularly useful to the Soviet Union in 1975–78, when they played a crucial role in consolidating the power of the Marxist MPLA Party in Angola and in beating back the Somalis in the Ogaden. Their attraction for the Soviet Union probably lies in their ability to engage in combat in Africa without arousing the sort of alarm that Soviet forces would create. The Cubans, in African eyes, can appear to represent a

TABLE 1
Weapons Delivered by Major Suppliers to Sub-Saharan Africa[a]

Weapons Category	United States	USSR	Major Western European[b]
1973–76			
Tanks and self-propelled guns	10	460	60
Artillery	20	940	230
APCs and armored cars	30	850	240
Major surface combatants	0	1	2
Minor surface combatants	0	16	37
Submarines	0	0	0
Supersonic combat aircraft	0	120	50
Subsonic combat aircraft	0	50	10
Other aircraft	10	10	200
Helicopters	10	30	80
Guided missile boats	0	2	0
Surface-to-air missiles (SAMS)	0	600	190
1977–80			
Tanks and self-propelled guns	20	1,060	20
Artillery	200	2,150	170
APCs and armored cars	10	1,520	520
Major surface combatants	0	4	9
Minor surface combatants	0	44	30
Submarines	0	0	0
Supersonic combat aircraft	20	210	20
Subsonic combat aircraft	0	90	10
Other aircraft	10	60	80
Helicopters	0	100	110
Guided missile boats	0	2	1
Surface-to-air missiles (SAMS)	0	1,360	10

[a]U.S. data are for fiscal years, and cover the period from July 1, 1972, through September 30, 1980. Foreign data are for calendar years.

[b]"Major Western European" includes France, the United Kingdom, West Germany, and Italy totals as an aggregate figure.

Source: Reprinted in part from U.S. Congress, House Committee on Foreign Affairs, Subcommittee on International Security and Scientific Affairs, *Changing Perspectives on U.S. Arms Transfer Policy* (Washington, D.C.: U.S. Government Printing Office, 1981), p. 21.

minor power, far away, that is of little threat to African independence. Moreover, the Cuban troops—culturally influenced by long ties between their island and the African continent—are more accepting of Africans than Soviet troops could ever be.

Today an estimated 23,000 Cuban troops remain in Angola, as well as 12,000–17,000 in Ethiopia and small contingents in a few other countries. For the present, they appear rather inactive. In Angola Cuban casualties have occurred in clashes with UNITA guerrillas, but the Cubans have avoided engaging South African forces during their incursions. Cuban troops in Ethiopia, as far as is known, are not taking part in the fighting in Eritrea, but are positioned to resist a new Somali attack (which is not regarded as likely). The reasons for this apparent inactivity are not known. It may be that the Cuban government has grown wary of the domestic impact that deaths in foreign wars can have; that, in Angola, Cuban troops are reluctant to engage South African forces for military reasons; and that in Ethiopia, Cuba is reluctant to fight Marxist Eritrean groups it once supported. Some combination of these and other factors may be at work.

On rare occasions, the Soviets have undertaken overt naval movements in order to bolster their African allies and intimidate opponents. Soviet naval vessels appeared off Angola in 1976,[51] and South Africa charged that a Soviet naval task force was moving along its coast after the South African incursion into Angola in August and September 1981. In February 1981, Soviet ships were sent to ports in Mozambique following a South African raid against opposition movements based in that country. The Soviet ambassador to Mozambique said that the vessels had come under the 1977 Soviet-Mozambique treaty of friendship and cooperation, and warned, "if anyone attacks us or our friends, we will give a suitable response."[52]

Security assistance can be a powerful instrument of foreign policy on a continent where so many regimes are threatened by internal and external enemies. The Soviets made their greatest gains in Nigeria when they provided weapons during the 1967–70 civil war. Somalia's attack on Ethiopia, carried out with Soviet-supplied arms, initiated Ethiopia's dependence on the USSR. Arms aid, however, is also a limited instrument.

Too prominent a role as a supplier of weapons on the African continent can be damaging to a superpower's reputation. The Soviet role as an arms provider to Idi Amin's Uganda, which continued even as evidence of Amin's bizarre behavior in domestic and foreign policy accumulated, damaged the Soviet Union in African opinion. The same is true of Soviet aid to Equatorial Guinea's repressive Macias Nguema, overthrown in 1979.

Most African governments regard requests by other governments for assistance from outside powers as a legitimate exercise of sovereignty, and do not openly object when even large-scale arms shipments or Cuban troops arrive by request. But all are highly sensitive on the issue of maintaining Africa's independence, and many are worried that the Soviet role in supplying arms could one day threaten that independence. General Olusegun Obasanjo, then the Nigerian head of state, warned the Soviets in

1978 that they should not "overstay their welcome," and added, "Africa is not about to throw off one colonial yoke for another."[53] Too many reactions of this sort could lead to a reduction of Soviet influence on the continent.

Africans are not always pleased with the Soviet arms that are delivered, and this can lead to frictions. Nigeria was reportedly dissatisfied with both the quality and the rate of delivery of Soviet weapons during the civil war.[54] Moveover, in the arms field, as in economic aid, the Soviets are known for their parsimony. Zambia, with a deeply troubled economy but facing repeated raids from Rhodesian armed forces, signed an arms deal with the Soviets in 1979 that cost it $100 million.[55] Ethiopia's coffee crop appears to be heavily mortgaged to pay for Soviet military aid.

PROPAGANDA

The Soviet Union carries out a major propaganda campaign in Africa. Radio Moscow beams 273 hours of broadcasting in 10 languages to Africa each week, compared with 219 hours for the BBC and 135 hours for the Voice of America.[56] In addition, the Soviets circulate numerous press reports aimed at the continent, and sponsor the publication of journalistic and academic articles with the African audience in mind.[57]

Soviet propaganda directed toward Africa often stresses ideological themes that have a sympathetic audience there. A favorite claim is that "transnational corporations," driven by the quest for scarce raw materials and "superprofits," are ruthlessly exploiting Africa and its people.[58] Meanwhile, it is argued, the United States, in the search for strategic facilities, is accelerating the arms race in Africa and sowing the seeds of international discord. Such ideas, which attribute Africa's problems to non-African forces, inevitably have a certain appeal.

Misinformation is frequently provided in Soviet propaganda. In 1982, for example, Soviet sources alleged that the United States was cooperating with South Africa in order to produce chemical and biological weapons for use against South Africa's black population.[59] They also charged that the United States had conspired with Britain to overthrow the new Ghana government;[60] plotted to overthrow President Kaunda of Zambia;[61] and attempted the ouster of Zimbabwe's Prime Minister Mugabe.[62] The United States is repeatedly portrayed as engaged in intensive military cooperation with South Africa and as aiding Jonas Savimbi's UNITA opposition in Angola. U.S. "military penetration" of an impoverished Somalia is another frequent complaint.[63]

The effect of this propaganda in Africa is difficult to assess, but appears limited. The few listener surveys that exist, as well as unscientific observation, indicates that African audiences are far more likely to listen to the BBC and the Voice of America (or Radio France in the Francophone nations) than to Radio Moscow. The clear bias and heavy-handedness of Moscow's broadcasts apparently deter listeners, who seek objectivity elsewhere. Nor does Soviet propaganda in the print media seem to have a significant African audience. Nonetheless, it is striking that the charges made against the United States in Soviet propaganda sometimes recur when the United States is criticized in the African media or on African campuses. This could be entirely coincidental, but it may also be that the Soviet propaganda effort does have some influence.

Soviet tactics in Africa have their mundane side as well. A steady stream of visitors between Africa and the Soviet Union is apparently intended to cement relationships. "Uzbek people's representatives,"[64] Lithuanian officials, and a host of other Soviet delegates have made the journey to Africa, while officials of African labor unions, political parties, and governments travel to the USSR. Medical care is available in the Soviet Union for the leaders of friendly countries. These things are also done by the Western nations and, at least as far as medical care is concerned, it seems likely that the Western version is better appreciated in Africa.

THE FUTURE

Speculation on the future of the Soviet Union in Africa centers on two issues: whether the Soviets will be able to retain the gains they have already made, and whether they can achieve additional gains. From time to time, reports in the press suggest that the Soviets are losing influence in Angola, Mozambique, and Ethiopia—the countries where their effort has been concentrated in recent years—or are on the verge of being expelled. A break or a major reduction in Soviet relations with any of these countries would be a major setback for the USSR.

In none of these countries has Soviet involvement been an unequivocal success. To Angolan, Ethiopian, and Mozambican observers, the contribution of the Soviet Union to solving national problems must still be open to question. The military contribution is certainly of value, but clearly has its limits. South African forces are able to move into southern Angola at will, meeting no counterattacks from Cuban troops. Perhaps these troops would join battle if South Africa penetrated into central Angola or threatened major towns, but South Africa encounters only local resistance as it ranges over southern Angola.

Meanwhile, UNITA guerrillas can mount attacks over a wide part of Angola. They have apparently kept the Benguela railway, once an important link to the Atlantic for Zaire, virtually closed. Mozambique was unable, despite the Soviet security assistance it has received, to prevent the January 1981 South African raid, and it faces a small but possibly growing resistance movement, which it alleges is backed by South Africa. Nor, despite an offensive in the first months of 1982, has Ethiopia been able to defeat the Eritrean guerrilla movement.

All three countries face serious economic problems. These problems are by no means entirely the fault of the Soviet Union, which cannot be blamed for drought in Ethiopia or for declining world commodity prices. But the Soviet Union's inability to respond fully to the economic needs of Angola, Ethiopia, and Mozambique means that all three remain interested in increased Western aid. Angola's avid interest in attracting private Western capital is particularly evident. The West remains culturally attractive in Angola, Ethiopia, and Mozambique. A revival of a bourgeois life-style has been reported in the Ethiopian capital,[65] where Western shortwave newscasts and newsmagazines are popular.

The Soviet Union seems to be wary of possible breakaways, particularly on the part of Angola and Ethiopia. Should the Western peace initiative in Namibia succeed and the UNITA rebellion somehow end, Angola's need for Cuban troops would probably cease. A withdrawal of these troops, in turn, would open the way for a dramatic improvement in relations with Washington and a possible influx of U.S. investment. This prospect probably explains Soviet Premier Nikolai Tikhonov's warning that the Namibia initiative is a "broad plot of international imperialism" intended to "intimidate" Angola and return it to the Western "sphere of influence,"[66] Tikhonov gave this warning to an Angola delegation visiting Moscow in January 1982. In Ethiopia, meanwhile, the Soviet Union continues to press Colonel Mengistu for the establishment of a civilian Marxist party. Such a party would become the base for a permanent Marxist-socialist government, removing affairs of state from the hands of a single, rather unpredictable individual.

Will any of the three most closely allied states break away from the Soviet Union? Much counterevidence could be cited to suggest that they are solidifying, rather than reducing, their relations with the USSR. The Angolan delegation that visited Moscow in January 1982 pledged to strengthen relations with the USSR and entered into a new ten-year cooperation agreement. Mozambique's March 1981 expulsion of U.S. embassy personnel as alleged "spies" abruptly ended progress that had been made in improving relations with the United States. Mengistu's August 1981 decision to enter into a treaty linking his country's foreign and defense policies with those of Libya and the People's Democratic Republic of Yemen cut off speculation at the time on an Ethiopian turn to the West. In any event, as long as the Angolan, Mozambican, and Ethiopian regimes are threatened by internal and external enemies, they are likely to remain dependent on Soviet security assistance.

Would the Soviets leave these countries if asked? They have, in the past, packed up and departed from Egypt, Sudan, Somalia, and other countries.

But if the Soviet intervention in Afghanistan marks a new era of intensified Soviet strategic concern over the Middle East, the USSR might well be highly reluctant to leave Ethiopia. A variety of covert and overt techniques might be used to assure that an Ethiopian regime favorable to Moscow's staying came into office. Angola and Mozambique are farther from the Middle East, and perhaps less important to the realization of the Soviet Union's major immediate foreign policy goals. Perhaps these countries would be easier to leave. But southern Africa is strategically and economically important to the West and therefore, inevitably, of keen interest to the Soviet Union. Thus, here too the Soviets could well resist a forced departure.

The strategic significance of the Soviet presence in Angola, Ethiopia, and Mozambique for neighboring states is inevitably a source of concern. The Soviet-advised offensive in Ethiopia's Ogaden halted at the Somalia border in 1978. But Somalia is understandably worried that a Soviet-armed Ethiopia will look its way if the rebellion in Eritrea is brought to an end. Kenya and Sudan maintain cordial relations with Ethiopia at present, and Colonel Mengistu appears convinced that peace with these pro-Western neighbors is an essential condition for defeating the Eritrean insurgents and for deterring Somalia from any new attacks. But Sudanese and Kenyan leaders, one suspects, must have occasional pangs of doubt about the prospects for long-term friendship with a Marxist Ethiopia.

South Africa, of course, is highly sensitive on the issue of Soviet involvement in southern Africa. Clearly, Soviet-supplied opposition forces based in Angola and Mozambique are in no position to engage in regular war with South African forces, and could not do so for many years to come. But guerrillas infiltrating from those countries can cause damage that would encourage black opposition within South Africa, lead to dissension among white political forces on the best means of countering the threat, and perhaps precipitate white emigration. Such developments could eventually result in major political change in South Africa, although in directions that can hardly be predicted today.

Whether such developments occur, however, is a highly contingent matter. They would depend, among other factors, on whether political reform in South Africa moves forward or stagnates; on whether there is a Cuban withdrawal from Angola, leading to a U.S–Angolan rapprochement; on whether there is a settlement in Namibia; and on the nature of any new Namibian regime. These interacting contingencies could work themselves out in ways that would reduce Soviet influence in the region. Certainly an expansion of Soviet influence is by no means a forgone conclusion. Similarly, in the Horn, an expansion of Soviet influence to other countries will be affected by the ability of those countries to resolve their economic problems, to cope with religious and ethnic conflicts, and a host of other factors. Permanent Soviet gains in other countries in the Horn are not inevitable.

Elsewhere in Africa, the Soviets can reasonably expect occasional coups that will bring friendly governments to power. Socialism is a political philosophy that enjoys wide appeal in Africa, and new (often young) military leaders quite often proclaim their allegiance to socialist development. This gives the Soviet Union, which proclaims itself as the champion of socialism in the world, a ready entrée. Elected governments also may at times warm to the Soviet Union, particularly as a way of increasing the military and economic assistance they receive. For the Soviet Union to consolidate gains such as these, however, would require major commitments of resources. Even then, as the Soviets have learned, recipient governments may be overthrown or grow dissatisfied with Soviet assistance, and look to the West for aid.

To summarize, consolidating gains requires the use of tactics that are flawed and, at least as applied by the Soviets to date, of limited effect. Improvements in these tactics are likely to require substantial changes in Soviet attitudes, and perhaps even in the Soviet system. If the Soviet Union is to give greater economic aid in Africa, it will have to become more generous, and possibly wealthier. If its way of life is to be made more appealing to Africans, it will have to become a more open and more tolerant society. If Soviet broadcasts to Africa are to attract a wider audience, they will have to be made more objective. Finally, if force is to be used against recalcitrant African governments—and the Soviet Union has learned that these governments can be recalcitrant—costly diversions of military resources to sites at great distances from the Soviet Union itself would have to be considered. Whether such diversions could be considered at a time when the USSR is facing a range of other military problems is far from certain. The long-term expansion of Soviet domination and control over a large part of the African continent, in short, would require policy changes in commitments of resources that are difficult to imagine under present circumstances.

NOTES

1. The Soviet-Angolan treaty, signed on October 8, 1976, appears in Colin Legum, ed., *African Contemporary Record, 1976-1977* (London and New York: Africana Publishers, 1977), pp. C151-C53. The Mozambique treaty, of March 1977, is in ibid., *1977-1978,* pp. C17-C19; and the treaty with Ethiopia, of November 20,

1978, is in ibid., *1978–1979*, pp. C84–C86. The treaty with Congo was signed on May 13, 1981, and ratified on March 23, 1982. For text, see Foreign Broadcast Information Service (FBIS), *Daily Report Soviet Union*: (*Soviet Union*), May 9, 1981, pp J1–J3. FBIS relayed the text from *Pravda*.

2. Anatoly Gromyko, "Socialist Orientation in Africa," *International Affairs* (Moscow), September 1979, p. 96. Gromyko, who was probably including Libya and Algeria in his count, is director of the Institute of Africa, USSR Academy of Sciences.

3. *Report of the Central Committee of the CPSU to the XXVI Congress of the Communist Party of the Soviet Union and the Immediate Tasks of the Party in Home and Foreign Policy*, delivered by Leonid I. Brezhnev, February 23, 1981 (Washington, D.C.: Information Department, USSR Embassy, 1981).

4. Anatoly Gromyko, "The Imperialist Threat to Africa," *International Affairs*, July 1981. pp. 47–48.

5. *Report of the Central Committee*, p. 14.

6. *Washington Post*, December 19, 1979, p. A28.

7. David E. Albright, "Moscow's Africa Policy in the 1970s," in David E. Albright, *Communism in Africa* (Bloomington: Indiana University Press, 1980), pp 38–40.

8. Robert Legvold, *Soviet Policy in West Africa* (Cambridge, Mass.: Harvard University Press, 1970), p. 157.

9. This was particularly true in the early years of African independence. See ibid., pp 60–98, 209–13.

10. See G. Roschin, "Africa Battling for Economic Liberation," *International Affairs*, March 1981, pp. 107–17; Y. Tarabrin, "Problems of Africa in the 1980s," *International Affairs*, June 1981, pp. 47–57.

11. Gromyko, "The Imperialist Threat to Africa," p. 47.

12. A. Dinkevich, Commenting in "Round Table, the Strategy of Economic Development in the Young States," *Asia and Africa Today* (Moscow), January–February 1982, p. 19.

13. *Washington Post*, March 3, 1982, p. A1.

14. Gromyko, "The Imperialist Threat to Africa," p. 48.

15. Tarabrin, op. cit., p. 54.

16. Gromyko has quoted Lenin on the alleged tendency of "imperialism" to put up "an increasingly furious resistance the closer death approaches." "Socialist Orientation in Africa," p. 99.

17. U.S. Central Intelligence Agency (CIA), National Foreign Assessments Center, *Communist Aid Activities in Non-Communist Less Developed Countries, 1979 and 1956–1979* (Washington, D.C.: CIA, 1980), p. 18.

18. Calculated on the basis of data appearing in U.S. Agency for International Development (USAID), *U.S. Overseas Loans and Grants and Assistance from International Organizations, July 1, 1945–September 30, 1980* (Washington, D.C.: USAID, 1981). Data are for fiscal years 1953–79.

19. Organization for Economic Cooperation and Development (OECD), *Geographical Distribution of Financial Flows to Developing Countries, 1976–1979* (Paris: OECD, 1980), p. 2.

20. CIA, op. cit., p. 18.

21. Roschin (op. cit., p. 116) places Soviet trade with Africa at 1.3 billion rubles in 1978. Setting a figure for this amount in dollars is problematic because the ruble is not a convertible currency and because much of the trade probably took the form of commodity exchanges. The value set on commodities is open to question.

22. *Report of the Central Committee,* p. 12.

23. Georgy Kim, "Deepening Socio-Class Differentiation," *Asia and Africa Today,* January–February 1982, p. 5.

24. Ibid. Kim is a corresponding member of the USSR Academy of Sciences.

25. Anatoly Gromyko, "Soviet Foreign Policy and Africa," *Asia and Africa Today,* January–February 1982, p. 48.

26. Ibid.

27. Asia remains the main objective of Peking's expansionist plans. Nikolai Karinin, and Boris Pavlov, "On the Road of Expansion," *Asia and Africa Today,* September–October 1981, p. 48.

28. Gary D. Payton, "The Somali Coup of 1969: The Case for Soviet Complicity," *Journal of Modern African Studies,* September 1980, pp. 495–98.

29. The published terms of this treaty call for economic, political, and security cooperation. FBIS, *Daily Report: Middle East and Africa (MEA),* September 2, 1981, pp. R1–R3.

30. According to South African Prime Minister Botha, the officer was exchanged for eight high-ranking Western agents and a South African soldier captured in Angola. *Washington Post,* May 12, 1982, p. A19.

31. A. Makarov, "South Africa—Mainstay of Racism and Apartheid," *International Affairs,* January–February 1981, pp. 61, 62, 64.

32. Ibid., p. 67.

33. Christoph Gudel, "Mali—Potential and Problems," *Swiss Review of World Affairs,* September 1981, p. 9.

34. Rawlings, for his part, seemed more interested in building a strong relationship with Libya, rather than the Soviet Union. By 1983, as Ghana's economic woes deepened, Rawlings' main foreign policy concern was increased aid from the Western nations and their financial institutions.

35. Tarabrin, op. cit., p. 49.

36. Roschin, op cit., p. 112.

37. See, for example, transcripts of speeches given at the Second Soviet-Nigerian Round-Table Scientific Conference, *Asia and Africa Today,* November–December 1981, pp. 44–45.

38. FBIS, *MEA,* June 25, 1981, p. T1. FBIS cited a Liberian report.

39. Under the Reagan administration, aid under the Economic Support Fund has increased substantially. This aid, as distinct from development aid, need not go directly to the poorest of the poor. Much of it is used to provide balance of payments support in Sudan and a few other countries. Neither development assistance or Economic Support Fund aid is being used to support large-scale infrastructure projects comparable to those funded by the Soviet Union.

40. For a Soviet summary, see Ivan Kapranov, "Cooperation Between the U.S.S.R. and the Developing Countries, *Asia and Africa Today,* January–February 1982, pp. 31–34.

41. FBIS, *MEA,* June 5, 1981, p. T1. FBIS cited a Lagos, Domestic Service broadcast.

42. FBIS, Soviet Union, April 7, 1982, p. J4.

43. Ibid., February 9, 1982, p. J4.

44. USAID, *Congressional Presentation, FY 1983* (Washington, D.C.: USAID, 1982), p. 16.

45. *New York Times,* August 22, 1979, p.3.

46. Report by David Lamb of the *Los Angles Times,* in *Washington Post,* June 5, 1980, p. A29.

47. Oye Ogunbadejo, "Ideology and Pragmatism: The Soviet Role in Nigeria," *Orbis* 21 (Winter 1978): 821–22.

48. U.S. Arms Control and Disarmament Agency (ACDA), *World Military Expenditures and Arms Transfers, 1970–1979* (Washington, D.C.: USACDA, 1982), p. 127.

49. CIA, op. cit., p. 15.

50. Estimate is for 1954–79. Ibid., p. 16.

51. Daniel S. Papp, "The Soviet Union and Southern Africa," in Robert A. Donaldson, ed., *The Soviet Union in the Third World, Successes and Failures* (Boulder, Colo.: Westview Press, 1981), p. 74.

52. *Africa Research Bulletin* (London), February 1981, p. 5957.

53. Ibid., June 1978, p. 4893.

54. Ogunbadejo, op. cit., pp. 813–19.

55. *Africa Research Bulletin,* December 1980, p. 5911.

56. Data are for 1981. U.S. International Communications Agency, *Voice of America Handbook* (Washington, D.C.: USICA, 1982).

57. Many are found in the bimonthly publication *Asia and Africa Today.*

58. Roschin, op. cit.

59. FBIS, monitoring Radio Moscow broadcasts, *Soviet Union,* March 19, 1982, p. J2; March 25, 1982, p. J2.

60. FBIS, relaying TASS reports, *Soviet Union,* February 1, 1982, p. J2; March 22, 1982, p. J3.

61. Anatoli Khaznov, "The White House and the 'Black Continent;'" *Asia and Africa Today,* January–February 1982, p. 8.

62. FBIS, relaying a TASS report, *Soviet Union,* March 12, 1982, p. J1.

63. FBIS, relaying Soviet commentaries, *Soviet Union,* March 12, 1982, pp. J1–J2; March 22, 1982, pp. J4–J6.

64. FBIS, relaying a Tashkent report, *Soviet Union,* April 7, 1982, p. J3.

65. David Ottaway, "Coptic Church, Home Restaurants Thrive in Marxist Ethiopia," *Washington Post,* December 12, 1980, p. A49.

66. *Washington Post,* January 22, 1982, p. A25.

EIGHT

Vanguard Parties in the Third World
DAVID E. ALBRIGHT

Recent years have witnessed increased attention by Moscow to vanguard parties in the Third World as instruments of Soviet foreign policy. This has stemmed to some degree from lessons that the leaders of the USSR have distilled from their dealings with Third World countries since the mid-1950s. At the same time, it has reflected a broadening during the 1970s of the Soviet concept of a vanguard party.

To assess the precise import of the heightened Soviet interest in vanguard parties, therefore, it is essential to understand both the lessons that Moscow has learned and the new Soviet notion of a vanguard party. Each of these considerations strongly colors current Soviet perspectives on the exploitation of vanguard parties to further the USSR's ends in the Third World.

LESSONS LEARNED

Soviet experiences in the Third World since the mid-1950s have caused Moscow to arrive at several key judgments. First, Soviet leaders now believe that in the foreseeable future the chance of "genuine" revolutionary breakthroughs—that is the emergence of Soviet-style Communist regimes that would associate themselves closely with the USSR and thereby afford vehicles for the projection of Soviet influence—are poor throughout at least the great bulk of the Third World. This assessment runs counter to that which prevailed during the late 1950s and early 1960s. It was a series of major Soviet setbacks during the earlier period that triggered the reversal in Moscow's view.

The views in this chapter are those of the author and do not necessarily reflect the views of the U.S. Air Force or the U.S. government.

As the British, French, and Belgian territories of sub-Saharan Africa moved toward independence in the last half of the 1950s and "anti-imperialist" ferment spread to Latin America with the Cuban revolution of 1959, Moscow became convinced that the demise of colonialism finally loomed on the near horizon. Along with this new evaluation went an upsurge of Soviet revolutionary optimism regarding the Third World in general.

Leninist doctrine conditioned Soviet leaders to see the breakup of the colonial system as the harbinger of a revolutionary tidal wave that would sweep over the Third World and leave Communist regimes in its wake, and Soviet commentary about the Third World took on a tone that betrayed Moscow's belief that such a course of events would ensue. A retrospective critique in the mid-1960s by a prominent Soviet writer affords a highly revealing insight into the temper of the times. Speaking specifically about Africa, he observed:

> The effective achievements of the national liberation movement on the continent, the establishment, in a few years, of dozens of new national states tended to create the erroneous impression that the struggle was almost at an end, that the way to liberation was easy and the forces of imperialism were played out.[1]

For nearly a decade, Soviet leaders clung tenaciously to this revolutionary optimism, despite the sharp adversities that they encountered. In fact, what preoccupied them was figuring out how the revolutionary process might develop and how the USSR might hasten the process along. Initially, they seemed inclined to assume that the process would proceed fairly rapidly on its own steam. However, efforts in the late 1950s by some Third World rulers, such as Gamal Abdel Nasser of the United Arab Republic, to repress local Communists soon threw that assumption into question.

Moscow then decided that it was both desirable and possible to speed up the revolutionary process by encouraging greater militancy on the part of radical elements of the Third World within a framework of cooperation with the currently dominant "national bourgeois" forces. This calculation underlay the calls in 1959–60 for the establishment of "independent national democracies" in the Third World. In Soviet eyes, the struggle to achieve such a goal would have several distinct characteristics. Local left-wing elements would continue to participate in—or, in certain instances, seek to promote—broad national-front alliances composed of all "anti-imperialist" forces. While temporarily accepting the primary role of the "national bourgeoisie" within these alliances, left-wing forces would attempt to build up their strength and eventually take control of the alliances by championing the "progressive" economic and social measures that the masses presumably wanted.

Depending upon circumstances, the alliance would take one of two forms. Where a Communist party already existed or where the dominant non-Communist party contained few leftist elements, the alliance would involve separate parties in classical Leninist tradition (thereby necessitating the formation of a Communist party in the latter case). But where the main non-Communist party was an umbrella organization and included visible left-wing forces, the party itself might serve as the alliance, and the struggle for hegemony might take place within its ranks.[2]

At about the same time that this evolution in Soviet thinking was going on, the USSR suffered a severe reversal of fortunes in the Congo (Leopoldville) (now Zaire), which had gained independence from Belgium in June 1960. After the emergence of the new state, the USSR had developed close ties with Premier Patrice Lumumba, but it quickly found him ousted at the behest of President Joseph Kasavubu, who was suspicious of Soviet blandishments. More galling, the U.N. General Assembly, with major backing from Third World countries, recognized a Kasavubu delegation, and spurned a Lumumba delegation, as the legal representatives of the Congo (Leopoldville) in late November 1960.

This setback, and especially the divisions among Third World states that contributed to it, seems to have persuaded Moscow that the revolutionary tide was not running with equal force in all places in the Third World, and such a judgment induced the USSR to focus its attention on those countries where "progressive" representatives of the "national bourgeoisie" appeared to be in charge. These included the United Arab Republic, Ghana, Guinea, Mali, Cuba, Indonesia, and eventually Algeria and Burma.[3]

Quite soon after the completion of this two-step reappraisal of the situation in the Third World, however, a split began to emerge among Soviet observers as to the validity of aspects of the new approach. While one group upheld it in all particulars, a second group evinced misgivings about elements of it.[4] The latter, highly conscious of the weakness of left-wing forces in many "progressive" states, questioned the ability of these forces to carry out a struggle for hegemony with the "national bourgeois" rulers there; furthermore, they worried about the growing tendency of at least portions of the local left-wing forces to side with China in the intensifying Sino-Soviet dispute. Perhaps most important, these observers doubted the willingness of extant "progressive" leaders to tolerate activities that threatened to undermine their regimes. As Soviet commentators were plainly aware, Ahmed Sékou Touré of Guinea had reacted sharply in late 1961 to a local effort to push his government in a more radical direction than he wished to go; this affair cast a pall over Moscow's relations with Conakry.

Moreover, the adherents of the second school of thought discerned an alternative way of furthering the revolutionary process. They noted that

Cuba had undergone a rapid transition to socialism through Fidel Castro's conversion to "scientific socialism," and they pointed out that "progressive" countries such as the United Arab Republic, Algeria, Ghana, Mali, and Burma were undergoing domestic radicalization under the auspices of rulers who had at least verbally embraced "scientific socialism." Therefore, they argued, the USSR might accept the commitment of these "revolutionary democrats" as geniune and seek to guide them toward a "true understanding" of "scientific socialism." The transition to socialism would thus result from the transformation of extant rulers into traditional Marxist-Leninists, rather than from their replacement by others of such a persuasion.

In late 1963, Nikita Khrushchev, against some high-level opposition, formally endorsed the Third World "revolutionary democrats' "[5] and this outlook, which subsequently remained the operative one for the USSR until early 1966. Over the intervening months, however, the formidable requirements of inducing socialism even in the states under "revolutionary democratic" leadership hit home to Soviet analysts.[6] Hence, they increasingly suggested that the revolutionary process in the Third World would probably be more protracted than originally anticipated.[7]

More critical, events in these countries highlighted the possibility that the "revolutionary democracts" might not be up to bringing about a transition to socialism. Ahmed Ben Bella's fall in Algeria in 1965 showed that they might not even have the requisite skills to fend off internal challenges, and the ousters of Kwame Nkrumah of Ghana in February 1966 and President Sukarno of Indonesia in March 1966 demonstrated that their realms could well pass into the hands of "reactionary" rulers.

The debacle in Ghana prompted the Soviet leadership to launch a full-scale review of Soviet Third World assumptions. Out of this came some basic shifts in perspective. Not only did the existing "revolutionary democrats" have such grave faults and they would in all likelihood never carry out transitions to "true" socialism in their countries,[8] but prospects for "real" revolutionary breakthroughs in the Third World in the discernible future were bleak. A commentary on Africa observed that "as the African revolution gains in depth, the internal weaknesses and objective difficulties in the liberation movement on the continent become increasingly evident."[9] The fundamental problem, as Soviet analysts saw things, lay in the prevailing conservatism of Third World societies.[10]

To be sure, Moscow subsequently recognized the appearance during the 1970s of a new breed of "revolutionary democrats" in Third World countries such as South Yemen, Angola, Mozambique, and Ethiopia.[11] Nevertheless, the reserve it displayed about revolutionary prospects in the Third World in the late 1960s has persisted to the present. Soviet commentators, for example, have continued to stress the impediments to "geniune" revolution there, paying special heed to the low level of class and political consciousness of the masses. Indeed, they have underscored the "instability in the revolutionary process" in even the most advanced "revolutionary democratic" states, and they have carefully called attention to "the possibility of aberration and reversals" in these as well as other countries.[12]

The second conclusion that Soviet leaders have reached about the Third World concerns the present rulers of the states there. Moscow today sees the vast majority of these rulers as having little in the way of a shared outlook with the USSR. Furthermore, it feels that they tend to try to use ties with the Soviet Union to advance their own particular interests. Such a perception represents a major departure from the view to which Soviet leaders subscribed in previous periods, and reflects disappointments that Moscow has suffered as a consequence of what it now regards as excessive sanguineness.

During the late 1950s and early 1960s, when neutralism and nonalignment were acquiring considerable vogue in non-Western areas, Soviet commentators repeatedly spoke of common purposes that bound the developing countries and the USSR together. They cited two in particular: the developing states and the Soviet Union alike desired to prevent war, and they also wished to follow their own economic paths, free of interference from Western imperialism and colonialism.[13]

Events connected with the Congo (Leopoldville) imbroglio of 1960–61, however, revealed the shakiness of such a premise. Many Third World countries failed to rally behind the USSR and other champions of Patrice Lumumba that endeavored to restore him to power after his deposal. According to Moscow, "had the Afro-Asian states displayed the same unity and resolve they displayed together with the socialist countries at the time, for instance, of the 1956 Suez crisis, the imperialists' criminal designs in the Congo would have stood no chance of success.[14]

The behavior of most Third World countries in the context of mounting Sino-Soviet discord in the 1960s merely confirmed the gulf between them and the USSR. Despite the latter's frequent attempts to pressure them into backing Moscow against Peking, they insisted on staying out of the quarrel.

Nonetheless, the mounting attention paid by Third World states to global economic issues, their push for the creation of a new international economic order, and their general "anti-imperialist" rhetoric in the 1970s seemed to Moscow to offer new grounds for encouragement regarding shared perspectives. Soviet leaders, for example, took pains to depict the USSR as a "natural ally" of the nonaligned. In the words of Leonid Brezhnev, the real division in the world lay "not between 'big' and 'small,' 'rich' and 'poor,' but between socialism and imperialism".[15]

What finally induced the USSR to shed its illusions on this score was Third World responses to the Soviet invasion of Afghanistan in December 1979. In January 1980, the overwhelming majority of Third World states endorsed the U.N. General Assembly resolution calling for the removal of all foreign troops from Afghanistan. Of those that did not, most either abstained or failed to vote. Only Angola, Mozambique, Ethiopia, Grenada, South Yemen, and Afghanistan supported the USSR.[16] Moreover, the U.N. ambassador of one of the Third World's most important member states, Nigeria, pointedly observed: "I think that after Havana [the sixth nonaligned summit meeting, in September 1979], the nonaligned movement is undergoing tremendous strain. But in the end certain things become clear. There are no natural allies."[17]

A Soviet analyst recently capsulized the revised Soviet viewpoint in the following manner:

> One apparently has to bear in mind that in their approach to all international questions the developing countries are guided first and foremost by their own national interests, as they understand them. Indira Gandhi said that India does not adhere to a pro-Soviet or anti-American stand. India only adheres to a pro-India stand.[18]

In light of all the preceding considerations, Soviet leaders have decided that they need some means of ensuring a Soviet presence in Third World states and a Soviet voice in Third World affairs. Since the early 1960s, Moscow has revived the claims of global power status that Nikita Khrushchev made in the 1950s for the USSR. Yet, as Brezhnev and his associates know full well from the problems that Khrushchev encountered in seeking to validate his claims, global power status must be not only self-asserted but also self-achieved and self-sustained; it does not flow from the consent of the international community. And upholding claims to such a status requires a country to demonstrate global reach. That is, it must have a continuing presence and exert influence throughout the world.[19]

The USSR does, of course, possess certain assets of an economic and military nature that are exploitable in this regard. But these tend to be limited in scope or of dubious utility for guaranteeing a local Soviet presence and a Soviet say in local affairs over the long haul. Not surprisingly, then, Moscow has looked with increasing favor on political means to further its purposes in the Third World. In this context, ties with vanguard parties have had special appeal.

CONCEPT OF A VANGUARD PARTY

The extent of the appeal of such ties has related directly to the expanded Soviet definition of a vanguard party. Prior to the late 1970s, the

Soviet notion of a vanguard party followed conventional Leninist lines. Such a party, in Soviet eyes, had to be an organization of tested cadres, not a mass body open to all, and it must operate according to the principle of democratic centralism, with its lower levels closely subordinated to its upper ones. At the same time, Moscow held that a vanguard party must have deep organizational roots among the masses, so as to be able to mobilize them behind its programs. In the wake of the Ghanian coup of 1966, Soviet analysts severely criticized the ruling parties in what Moscow had earlier dubbed "revolutionary democracies" for failing to "work hard enough to achieve organizational fusion with the rank and file." Instead, they reassmbled "clubs for revolutionary intellectuals who love to talk and argue, to air their views on theoretical problems, organizational structure, points of procedure and other obvious aspects of revolutionary organizations."[20] With the growing fragmentation of the international Communist movement in the early 1960s, Moscow also made explicit what it had hitherto left implicit. A vanguard party had to accept not just "scientific socialism" but the Soviet version thereof. Thus, self-classification as a Marxist-Leninist entity would not qualify a body as a vanguard party unless it met Soviet standards as well.

During the late 1970s, however, the USSR modified its concept in significant ways. To begin with, it now bestowed Marxist-Leninist legitimacy upon at least certain parties that had originally formed in opposition to pro-Soviet Communist parties. The Communist Party of India-Marxist (CPI-M) afforded the classic illustration.[21]

This party had come into being in 1964 as a result of an apparently irreconcilable split in the Indian Communist movement triggered by Nikita Khrushchev's revision of the fundamentals of Marxism-Leninism in the USSR, and the CPI-M had pursued a domestic programmatic line during the 1960s and 1970s that was sharply at variance with the line of the Moscow-backed Communist Party of India (CPI). While the CPI had opted for a combination of the parliamentary path and cooperation with the government of Indira Gandhi, the CPI-M had adopted a political strategy of peasant mobilization, focusing upon India's eastern flank, and unremitting opposition to the Gandhi government.

Its approach had yielded substantial dividends in the electoral upheavals of 1977-78 in India. The CPI-M had garnered 4.30 percent of the vote and 22 Lok Sabha seats in the 1977 national elections; in elections held three months later for legislative assemblies in two territories and ten of India's states, it had won 205 of 2,455 seats. By obtaining 174 of 294 seats in West Bengal, it had captured control of that state's government, and at the end of the year a leftist front led by the CPI-M had swept to power in Tripura. The CPI, in contrast, had seen its share of the national vote drop from 4.73 percent in 1971 to 2.82 percent in 1977, and its number of seats in the Lok Sabha fall from 23 to 7. Worse yet, it had been virtually wiped out in the elections for legislative assemblies.

In the wake of these developments, the CPI, with Moscow's unmistakable blessing and perhaps even at Moscow's instigation, moved to restore links with the CPI-M and to forge a "left and democratic" front including it. After much pulling and tugging, the two parties finally reached a quid pro quo in the autumn of 1979—to the unconcealed delight of the USSR. Thus, in the January 1980 national and state elections the two parties divided up constituencies, campaigned together, and extended each other a degree of logistical support.

This unity strategy produced some impressive fruits. The two parties won a total of 47 seats in the Lok Sabha (35 for the CPI-M and 12 for the CPI). In the voting for the Kerala state legislature later in January, the "left and democratic" front led by the CPI-M there garnered 93 seats in a legislature of 140.

But the big winner was the CPI-M. In the parliamentary elections, it polled 12 million votes nationwide, as compared with 83.5 million for Mrs. Gandhi's victorious Congress-I and 37.2 million and 18.5 million, respectively, for Janata and Lok Dal, the two main non-Communist opponents of Congress-I. The CPI, in contrast, captured just 500,000 votes (some 80,000 fewer than it had received in 1977).

Far from being oblivious to these realities, Moscow in the 1980s has continued to encourage unity of the two Indian Communist parties and has pushed as well for rapprochement between the Communist Party of the Soviet Union (CPSU) and the CPI-M. In July 1980, for example, a CPSU team headed by Boris Ponomarev, director of the International Department, welcomed Jyoti Basu, a member of the CPI-M Politburo, to the USSR and had "wide-ranging" discussions with him. Leonid Brezhnev also spoke briefly with several members of the CPI-M Politburo at official functions during his visit to New Delhi in December 1980, although no formal meeting took place between the CPSU general secretary's delegation and the CPI-M.

Even more striking than Soviet acceptance of the Marxist-Leninist credentials of parties such as the CPI-M was Moscow's recognition of a wholly new category of vanguard bodies. For shorthand, it referred to these as Third World "vanguard parties" or "vanguard revolutionary parties," but it made clear that they were "revolutionary democratic parties of a new type." That is, it carefully distinguished such entities from Communist parties.

Beginning with the Labor Party of the People's Republic of the Congo in 1969, a number of ruling parties in the Third World had proclaimed a commitment to Marxism-Leninism and an intention to transform themselves into "vanguard" parties. Throughout much of the

1970s, however, Soviet observers had either ignored these developments or had passed over them lightly. A typical commentary had more or less equated the outlook of the ruling elements of countries like the Peoples's Republic of the Congo with that of the leaders of such avowedly non-Marxist-Leninist states as Tanzania, Egypt, Algeria, and Guinea. Specifically, it had classified all of these countries as merely "socialist-oriented states"—that is, all had "proclaimed, at one time or another, their adherence to socialist ideas" and had "refused to take the capitalist road of development."[22]

About the spring of 1978, signs appeared that the Soviet perspective was undergoing change. For example, one of the major Soviet journals dealing with world politics carried an article that remarked that "the development of social relations . . . has shown the vitality and great political advantages of a one-party system, provided it reflects the anti-imperialist and anti-colonial mood of the people and makes progressive changes in the interests of the working masses." "This," the piece said in elaboration, "has been convincingly illustrated by such vanguard parties as the MPLA Party of Labour of Angola, resting on a broad-based national liberation movement, and the FRELIMO of Mozambique based on the movement so named." Then it went on to contend that "vanguard parties are created, as a rule, in what have become socialist-oriented countries," and it stressed that "their role . . . is difficult to exaggerate."[23]

What set a reappraisal in motion remains somewhat foggy. Perhaps it was nothing more than the recent proliferation of self-styled Marxist-Leninist "vanguard" parties in the Third World. Such parties had emerged in Benin and Somalia in 1976 and in Angola and Mozambique in 1977. Or other circumstances may have entered into the calculations. For instance, all of the "vanguard" parties that had come into being prior to 1977 had done so under the auspices of radical military leaders, but 1977 had witnessed the birth of some under civilian aegis.

In any event, a new Soviet attitude had become manifest by early 1979. Soviet media now devoted long disquisitions to the "vanguard" parties of the Third World.[24] These analyses initially identified six specific parties as belonging to the group: the Popular Movement for the Liberation of Angola Labor Party (MPLA-PT), the Mozambique Liberation Front (FRELIMO), the Congolese Labor Party (PCT), the Benin People's Revolutionary Party (PRPB), the (South) Yemen Socialist Party (YSP), and the People's Democratic Party of Afghanistan (PDPA). Over time, the Commission for Organizing the Party of the Workers of Ethiopia (COPWE) has been added to the list, although this body's organization is conceded to be in its infancy. One final point is worth noting here. While Soviet sources have not yet explicitly labeled the New Jewel Movement of Grenada and the Sandinist National Liberation Front of Nicaragua "vanguard" parties, they have come quite close to doing so.[25]

Such parties, in Soviet eyes, have a number of distinct characteristics. They constitute "revolutionary democratic" alliances of workers, peasants, artisans, the state petit bourgeoisie, the radical intelligentsia, and employees. Although they are still in the beginning stages of formation, they strive to strengthen their "organizational and ideological unity" and to reinforce their "influence on the working masses." They are also in the process of "conversion to Marxist-Leninist teaching about the path of the revolutionary transformation of society." Last but not least, they are "broadening and deepening" cooperation "with the world Communist movement, and in the first instance with the ruling parties of the countries of the socialist commonwealth."[26]

Neither of these broad innovations in Soviet thinking about vanguard parties in the Third World, it should be emphasized, took place in the abstract. Both represented Soviet responses to developments in the real world. In this sense, they reflected evolving Soviet views of the opportunities that the Third World offered the USSR.

EXPLOITATION OF VANGUARD PARTIES

In paying increased heed to Third World vanguard parties as a means of advancing the USSR's interests in the Third World, Moscow has not yet reverted to the wholesale and virtually total reliance on them that typified its policy in the late 1940s and early 1950s. Rather, it has differentiated the political situations in individual countries and has tailored its approach to each country to try to maximize the USSR's position there. Thus, both the extent to which and the way in which vanguard parties now figure in Soviet policy toward the Third World vary from context to context.

One can, however, discern some patterns in this regard. These deserve exploration in detail.

At the outset, it is important to bear in mind that no vanguard parties have formed yet in a substantial number of states in the Third World. This includes most of the countries of sub-Saharan Africa and the smaller countries of the Persian Gulf region. Nor has the USSR taken any concrete steps to foster the creation of such parties in these states, even though Soviet analysts have spoken of the need for the establishment of "vanguard" parties there to ensure "progressive development."[27]

Where vanguard parties do exist, their role in Soviet policy is the least complicated in countries that have only Communist parties with a staunchly pro-Chinese orientation. Moscow has long simply ignored these parties. This has been the case regardless of the nature of the USSR's relations with the governments of the states concerned. The countries that fall into this category lie exclusively in Asia, with Malaysia, Thailand, and Burma being the key representatives.

The situation is far more complex with respect to states in which (a) there exists either a single pro-Soviet Communist party or two or more Communist parties, at least one of which displays a pro-Soviet orientation, but (b) no Communist party has much clout. The degree to which any of these parties enters into Soviet policy depends upon the importance that Moscow attaches to the specific countries in which they operate.

Soviet leaders appear to see a number of the states in this group as of relatively minor consequence in the overall Third World picture. These countries, for example, are outside the southern rimlands of the USSR, which have constituted the prime focus of Soviet concern in the Third World since the mid-1960s.[28] They are also fairly small entities in terms of both size and population, and they enjoy little influence beyond their own borders. The African states of Senegal and Lesotho and such Latin American and Caribbean states as Bolivia, Chile, Colombia, Costa Rica, the Dominican Republic, Ecuador, Haiti, Panama, Paraguay, Suriname, and Uruguay provide good illustrations.

In keeping with its generally low level of interest in these countries, Moscow has not really tried to employ the indigenous Communist parties there as instrumentalities for affecting local conditions favorably from its standpoint. This has been true no matter how warm or cool the USSR's relations with the governments of the states involved.

The remainder of the countries in the group clearly qualify as significant in the eyes of Soviet leaders on at least one of several grounds. A good many make up part of the southern rimlands of the USSR. Some are large countries of considerable regional importance. Others occupy territory of particular strategic significance. Some are especially well endowed with natural resources. Egypt, Israel, Brazil, Sudan, Tunisia, and Saudi Arabia offer first-rate examples.

Although plainly cognizant of the weaknesses of the pro-Soviet Communist parties in these states, Moscow has nevertheless sought to capitalize, to the degree possible, on their presences there to further the USSR's purposes. The exact way in which it has done so, however, has varied.

In countries with whose governments the USSR has been on poor terms, Soviet leaders have not entirely eschewed attempts to foster alternatives to these governments with the aid of local Communist parties. Soviet media commentaries on Sudan in the 1980s, for instance, have strongly suggested Moscow's endorsement of the efforts of the Sudan Communist Party and other opposition forces to topple Jaafar al-Numeiry, a firm backer of the Camp David peace process and of former Egyptian President Anwar al-Sadat.[29]

But by and large, Moscow has endeavored to use the Communist parties in these states to alter official attitudes toward the USSR and/or to induce the local governments to adopt policies beneficial to it. During the last years of Sadat's rule in Egypt, for example, Soviet officials in Cairo maintained clandestine contacts with the outlawed Egyptian Communist Party and other opposition elements, but these contacts appear to have been aimed essentially at fomenting sufficient internal unrest to render it difficult for Sadat to sustain his rapprochement with Israel and his hostility to the USSR.[30] Motives of a comparable sort seem to have underlain the amount of publicity that Moscow has given to the anti-Zionist, pro-Arab-nationalist stance of the Communist Party of Israel (RAKAH). This party, it should be noted, draws the great bulk of its membership and electoral support from Israel's Arab minority.

In countries with which the USSR has fairly decent-to-close official relations, Soviet leaders have adopted quite a different tack. They have encouraged local Communist parties to behave in a manner that bolsters these relations—or at minimum does not affect them adversely. Iran furnishes an excellent illustration. Moscow has counseled the Tudeh Party to endorse the government of Ayatollah Ruhollah Khomeini and to seek to fan its anti-Westernism, and the party has gone along with this advice, even though it has encountered some difficulties as a result of such a policy.[31] One could cite evidence of a similar kind in the cases of Algeria, Jordan, Morocco, Nigeria, Nepal, and even Argentina.

Not surprisingly, the USSR shows a much greater inclination to assign Third World vanguard parties a role in its foreign policy in countries where these entities possess substantial influence than in those where they do not. Indeed, demonstrable influence plainly matters more to Moscow in this general connection than even the niceties of ideological viewpoint.

In all cases where a non-ruling Communist party of any kind enjoys some local political clout, Soviet leaders in recent years have extended it their firm support. However, the calculations entailed in rendering such support have differed from context to context.

In a few states, the USSR, through its championing of influential Communist parties, has lent its weight to efforts to displace existing governments by violent means, for the local parties have been carrying on armed struggles against these governments—usually within the framework of broad political fronts embracing non-Communists as well as varied kinds of Communists. El Salvador, Guatemala, and South Africa provide the leading examples. Such decisions have required Moscow to give up any thought of productive ties with the current governments there, but it has lost little in the process, because its relations with them have ranged from bad to nonexistent anyway. Moreover, the prospects for success of the efforts to bring down the governments have been at least fair over the medium run.

Elsewhere, Soviet backing of Communist parties of local consequence has been designed to enhance the USSR's capacities for dealing effectively with the governments of the countries concerned, but the precise goal has not been the same in all instances. One can distinguish three settings that have resulted in diverse preoccupations.

Where governments have maintained a distant or at best correct attitude toward the USSR, Moscow has appeared to see links with important local Communist parties as means of improving the climate of official relations. That is, it has viewed these parties as useful advocates of an expansion of ties with the USSR and articulators of foreign-policy positions generally compatible with Soviet ones. The Soviet approach to the new United Socialist Party of Mexico has reflected such a perspective. In contacts with the party, Soviet officials have played down its Eurocommunist orientation.

Where governments have in the past looked upon the USSR with great favor but have recently cooled toward it, Moscow has tended to regard links with significant local Communist parties as insurance against a further deterioration of the relationships. Such ties guarantee the USSR forceful domestic voices for continued relations of some intensity, and they constitute reminders to local governments that the USSR has the ability to cause them trouble internally if it is alienated.

India furnishes perhaps the prime illustration of circumstances in which a consideration of this kind has been operative. After the defeat of Indira Gandhi in the elections of 1977, Soviet-Indian relations took a turn for the worse, and even though Mrs. Gandhi returned to power in 1980, she has not displayed her old warmth toward the USSR. In part, her new reticence probably stems from ire at the vehemence with which Soviet commentators criticized her in the late 1970s for the emergency rule that had precipitated her downfall in 1977; in part, it is clearly a reaction to the Soviet invasion of Afghanistan.[32] At any rate, Moscow seems to have concluded that support of a leftist front involving both the CPI and CPI-M would help give it leverage to restrain Mrs. Gandhi from moving farther away from close alliance with the USSR. Comparable developments in Iraq since the late 1970s appear to have led Soviet rulers to adopt a similar tactic there, centered on the Iraqi Communist Party. But this party has proved to be a relatively ineffectual instrument for stopping the decline of official Soviet-Iraqi amity.[33]

Where governments at present maintain cordial relations with the USSR, Moscow seems to have viewed strong links with Communist parties influential in local milieus as a hedge against the sort of evolution that has occurred in India and Iraq. Not only do such ties help to deepen Soviet involvement in internal political life in these states, but they also force local governments to keep in mind the Soviet capacity for mischief making. Motivations of this nature appear to have accounted for Soviet behavior in places like Syria, Guyana, and Peru.

Finally, the ruling "vanguard" parties of "revolutionary democratic" countries have been the object of intense Soviet courtship in world affairs. Because they control governments, the USSR has solicited their support on a wide range of international issues. By the same token, it has joined with them on a variety of causes that they have promoted in the world community.

CONCLUSION AND PROSPECTS

As the preceding analysis has tried to suggest; the increased use that the USSR has made of vanguard parties in conducting its foreign policy in recent years and the new elements of diversity that it has introduced into its approach to them represent attempts to come to grips with the Third World's contemporary reality. Yet that reality is by no means fixed. Moscow's experiences with "bourgeois-nationalist" rulers throughout much of the Third World may for the moment justify a high degree of wariness toward them, but fresh opportunities associated with them could open up and significantly alter its attitude toward them. Such a development, in turn could reduce its attention to vanguard parties.

Already one can detect a tentative drift in this direction. For example, increasingly since 1979 Soviet analysts have perceived a major "contradiction" between those Third World states that have embarked on the capitalist path and Western "imperialism." A growing number of these states are following or want to follow a "national capitalist" road, while Western "imperialism" seeks to channel them along the road of "dependent capitalism."[34] Such an analysis implies that this "contradiction" offers an opportunity for the USSR to exploit. Similarly, Soviet commentators have recently displayed a fascination with the resurgence of Islam in the Muslim world. They have indicated that Islamic movements with a political tinge may take one of two forms, progressive or reactionary. The first is "anti-imperialist, antimonopolist, and antifeudal," while the second, is "anti-Communist and antisocialist."[35] Implicit here is the proposition that movements of the first sort present openings upon which the USSR might capitalize.

In addition, Moscow's stretching of its concept of a vanguard party to encompass unorthodox entities has greatly complicated the task of advancing its ends through exploitation of vanguard parties. As long as it dealt essentially with pro-Soviet Communist parties, it could exercise a reasonable amount of control over events. Now, however, it has lost much of that advantage. To pursue its goals, it must engage in persuasion to get many key parties to behave in the manner it wishes, and there is no certainty that such undertakings will prove successful. Under these circumstances, the USSR could suffer some setbacks to its interests.

In light of these considerations, it is crucial to recognize that the role that vanguard parties play today in Moscow's foreign policy may not stay the same in ensuing years. If Soviet leaders see new opportunities emerging that require exploitation by other means and/or if they encounter severe problems in trying to induce diverse vanguard parties to act in ways the USSR desires, they could significantly modify the role that they assign to vanguard parties.

NOTES

1. K. Brutents, "African Revolution: Gains and Problems," *International Affairs*, No. 1 (January 1967), p. 21. When this article appeared, Brutents had long been a major Soviet commentator on Third World affairs. Later, in the mid-1970s, he joined the International Department of the Central Committee of the Communist Party of the Soviet Union (CPSU) as a deputy director.

2. For more extended discussion of the theory and practice of "national democracy" from the Soviet standpoint as well as for sources, see David E. Albright, *The Dilemmas of Courtship: The Soviet Union, China, and Ghana* (Bloomington: Indiana University Press, forthcoming), Chaps. II and IV. The seminal analysis of "national democracy" is Richard Lowenthal's "On 'National Democracy': I. Its function in Communist Policy," *Survey*, No. 47 (April 1963), pp. 119-134.

3. See Albright, *The Dilemmas of Courtship: The Soviet Union, China, and Ghana*, Chap. II; Robert Legvold, *Soviet Policy in West Africa* (Cambridge, Mass.: Harvard University Press, 1979), Chaps. 3 and 4; Lowenthal, loc. cit.

4. See Albright, *The Dilemmas of Courtship: The Soviet Union, China, and Ghana*, Chap. IV; Legvold, op. cit., Chap. 5. For a seminal treatment of the debate, see Uri Ra'anan, "Moscow and the 'Third World,' " *Problems of Communism*, vol. 14, No. 1 (January-February 1965), pp. 21-31. The nature of the second group's critique, it should be underscored, was never explicit in the open literature. That critique must be inferred from the character of the group's positive proposals and the contextual setting.

5. See what purported to be an interview with the editors of two Algerian newspapers, a Ghanaian one, and a Burmese one in December 1963, as reported in *Pravda* and *Izvestiia*, December 22, 1963. For a more detailed analysis of the opposition, see Albright, *The Dilemmas of Courtship: The Soviet Union, China, and Ghana*, Chap. VI; Legvold, op. cit., pp. 194-201; Ra'anan, loc. cit.

6. For illustrative purposes, see Victor Maevskii's report on a trip around Africa under the auspices of the World Peace Council, in *Pravda*, March 31, 1965; Adakemiia Nauk SSSR, Institut Afriki, *Nezavisimye strany Afriki: ekonomicheskie i sotsial'nye problemy* (Moscow: Izdatel'stvo "Nauka," 1965); A. Vladin, "Professional Education in Ghana," *New Times*, no. 27 (July 7, 1965), pp. 16-17; L. Aleksandrovskaia, *Gana* (Moscow: "Mysl," 1965).

7. See, for example, K. Ivanov, "National-Liberation Movement and Non-Capitalist Path of Development," *International Affairs*, no. 5 (May 1965), pp.

59-60; K.N. Brutents, "Several Peculiarities of the National-Liberation Movement," *Voprosy filosofii*, no. 6 (June 1965), p. 36; Fedor Burlatskii's article in *Pravda*, August 15, 1965; "The National-Liberation Movement and Social Progress," *Kommunist*, no. 13 (September 1956), pp. 20-24; R. Ul'ianovskii, "Several Questions of Noncapitalist Development of the Liberated Countries," ibid., no. 1 (January 1966), pp. 113-115; and K. Ivanov, "The National-Liberation Movement and Non-Capitalist Path of Development," *International Affairs*, no. 2 (February 1966), pp. 20-21.

8. For a particularly biting capsulization of the thinking on this issue, see the remarks of Lufti El Kohli, an Egyptian Communist, at a seminar held in October 1966 on "Africa's national and social revolution." The seminar was sponsored jointly by the Soviet-dominated *Problems of Peace and Socialism* and *At-Talia*, a monthly Egyptian journal that El Kohli edited. El Kohli's observations may be found in the North American edition of *Problems of Peace and Socialism* (entitled *The World Marxist Review*), no. 1 (January 1967), pp. 18-19. That his comments accurately mirrored Moscow's feelings about "revolutionary democrats" was confirmed by Soviet reactions to the events prior to and after the fall of Modibo Keita's regime in Mali in November 1968. See Legvold, op. cit., pp. 290-302.

9. Brutents, "African Revolution: Gains and Problems," p. 21.

10. See Yuri Bochkaryov, "The Outlook in Africa," *New Times*, no. 17 (April 27, 1966); N. Gavrilov, "Africa: Classes, Parties and Politics," *International Affairs*, no. 7 (July 1966); the report of the October 1966 seminar in Cairo on "Africa's national and social revolution," in *The World Marxist Review*, no. 1 (January 1967), especially the contributions of Alexander Sobolev, the Soviet deputy editor of *Problems of Peace and Socialism*, and Ali Yata, the head of the Moroccan Communist Party; G. Kim and A. Kaufman, "Non-Capitalist Development: Achievements and Difficulties," *International Affairs*, no. 12 (December 1967); R. Ul'ianovskii, "Scientific Socialism and the Liberated Countries," *Kommunist*, no. 4 (March 1968); K. Brutents, "On Revolutionary Democracy," *Mirovaia ekonomika i mezhdunarodnye otnosheniia*, no. 3 (March 1968).

11. See, for instance, K. Brutents in *Pravda*, February 10, 1978; Y. Tarabrin, "The National Liberation Movement: Problems and Prospects," *International Affairs*, no. 2 (February 1978); Radio Moscow in English to Africa, April 21, 1978, in Foreign Broadcast Information Service, *Daily Report: Soviet Union* (hereafter FBIS-SOV), May 4, 1978, pp. H/1-2; V. Kudryavtsev, "Africa Fights for Its Future," *International Affairs*, no. 5 (May 1978); C.P. Nemanov, "Parties of the Vanguard Type in the African Countries of Socialist Orientation," *Narody Azii i Afriki*, no. 2, (1979); K.N. Brutents, *Osvobodivshiesia strany v 70-e gody* (Moscow: Izdatel'stvo politicheskoi literatury, 1979); Yu. N. Gavrilov, "Problems of the Formation of Vanguard Parties in the Countries of Socialist Orientation," *Narody Azii i Afriki*, no. 6 (1980); Vl. Li, "Social Revolution in the Afro-Asian Countries and Scientific Socialism," *Aziia i Afrika segodnia*, no. 3 (March 1981); G. Kim, "The National Liberation Movement Today," *International Affairs*, no. 4 (April 1981); Institut Afriki Akademiia Nauk SSSR, *Ieologiia revoliutsionnykh demokratov Afriki* (Moscow: Izdatel'stvo "Nauka," 1981).

12. See, for example, O. Orestov, "Independent Africa in the Making," *International Affairs*, no. 11 (November 1975); V. Solodovnikov and N. Gavrilov,

"Africa: Tendencies of Non-Capitalist Development," ibid., no. 3 (March 1976); Tarabrin, loc. cit.; Viktor Sidenko commentary, Radio Moscow in English to Africa, May 9, 1978, in *FBIS-SOV*, May 11, 1978, pp. H/4-5; *Pravda*, August 26, 1978; A. Iskenderov, "Unity of the World Revolutionary Process—A Factor of Stronger Peace," *International Affairs*, no. 12 (December 1978); G. Kim, "The Successes of the National Liberation Movement and World Politics," ibid., no. 2 (February 1979); Brutents, *Osvobodivshiesia strany v 70-e gody*; Gavrilov, "Problems of the Formation of Vanguard Parties in the Countries of Socialist Orientation"; Kim, "The National Liberation Movement Today." The quotations in the text are drawn from the last item, p. 35.

13. For illustrative purposes, see A. Guber, "The Crises of the Colonial System," *International Affairs*, no. 12 (December 1957); "The 21st Congress of the CPSU and the Tasks of Orientalists," *Problemy Vostokovedeniia*, no. 1 (1959); "Foreign Policy Problems at the CPSU Congress," *New Times*, no. 5 (January 1959); V. Nikhamin, "New International Role of Eastern Countries," *International Affairs*, no. 5 (May 1960); N. Inozemtsev, "The Development of World Socialism and the New States in International Relations," *Kommunist*, no. 9 (June 1961).

14. Soviet government statement of December 7, 1960, on the situation in the Congo, *New Times*, no. 51 (December 1960), p. 39.

15. Message to the 1973 Algiers summit of the nonaligned movement. For the text, see *FBIS-SOV*, September 5, 1973. On the changing character of the nonaligned movement and the Soviet response, see William M. LeoGrande, "Evolution of the Nonaligned Movement," *Problems of Communism*, vol 29, no. 1 (January-February 1980), pp. 35-52.

16. *The New York Times*, January 15, 1980.

17. *The Washington Post*, January 11, 1980.

18. Y. Alimov, "The Newly-Free Countries in World Politics," *International Affairs*, no. 9 (September 1981), p. 23.

19. For elaboration, see Vernon V. Aspaturian, "Soviet Global Power and the Correlation of Forces," *Problems of Communism*, vol. 29, no. 3 (May-June 1980), pp. 1-18.

20. The specific quotations come from the remarks of Lufti El Kohli at the seminar on Africa's national and social revolution in October 1966, loc. cit., pp. 18-19. But the report on the proceedings of the seminar makes plain that he was stating a view with which the Soviet participants concurred. See "Africa: National and Social Revolution," *World Marxist Review*, no. 1 (January 1967). Moreover, commentaries in Soviet media hewed to a similar position. See, for instance, N. Gavrilov, "Africa: Classes, Parties and Politics"; T. Kolesnichenko in *Pravda*, November 2, 1966.

21. The following discussion draws heavily upon the work of Bhabani Sen Gupta. See especially his "Indian Communism and the Peasantry," *Problems of Communism*, vol. 21, no. 1 (January-February 1972), pp. 1-17; "India's Rival Communist Models," ibid., vol 22, no. 1 (January-February 1973), pp. 1-15; "Indian Politics and the Communist Party (Marxist), ibid., vol. 27, no. 5 (September-October 1978), pp. 1-19; *The CPI-M: Promises, Prospects, Problems* (New Delhi, Young Asia Publications, 1979); "Communism and India: A New Context," *Problems of Communism*, vol. 30, no. 4 (July-August 1981), pp. 33-45.

22. Orestov, loc. cit., p. 75.

23. Kudryavstev, loc. cit., p. 32.

24. Among the first were A. Shin, "Vanguard of the Yemen Revolution," *Aziia i Afrika segodnia*, no. 1 (January 1979), and Nemanov, loc. cit. For a representative sampling of subsequent items, see Gavrilov, "Problems of the Formation of Vanguard Parties in the Countries of Socialist Orientation"; Ye. Primakov, "The Law of Uneven Development and the Historical Fate of Liberated Countries," *Mirovaia ekonomika i mezhdunarodnye otnosheniia*, no. 12 (December 1980); O.I. Grishchina, "The Benin People's Revolutionary Party in the Vanguard of Social-Economic Transformations," *Narody Azii i Afriki*, no. 2 (1981); Li, loc. cit.; Ye. Primakov, "Countries of a Socialist Orientation: Difficult but Feasible Transition to Socialism," *Mirovaia ekonomika i mezhdunarodnye otnosheniia*, no. 7 (July 1981).

25. In the fall of 1980, the Soviet-line *World Marxist Review* described Grenada and Nicaragua as the sole countries aside from Cuba to have "taken the road of building a new society in Latin America." See "The Latin American Proletariat and Its Allies in the Anti-Imperialist Struggle," *World Marxist Review* (London), August 1980, p. 48. Over ensuing months, Soviet media have reported statements by leaders of the New Jewel Movement and the Sandinist National Liberation Front which have referred to the parties as "vanguards." See, for example, the text of the speech delivered by the Nicaraguan Daniel Ortega at a dinner in the Kremlin in honor of his visiting delegation on May 4, 1982, in *Pravda*, May 5, 1982.

26. The specific quotations come from Nemanov, loc. cit.

27. See, for instance, N. Gavrilov, "The New Africa Emerging," *International Affairs*, no. 7 (July 1980) pp. 36-37.

28. The southern rimlands encompass all those states forming an arc around the USSR's southern borders—from South Asia around to North Africa. For more extended treatment of Soviet preoccupation with the southern rimlands in recent years, see Richard Lowenthal, "Soviet 'Counterimperialism,' " *Problems of Communism*, vol. 25, no. 6 (November-December 1983), pp. 52-63; David E. Albright, "Moscow's African Policy of the 1970s", in David E. Albright (ed.), *Communism in Africa* (Bloomington: Indiana University Press, 1980), pp. 35-66.

29. See particularly the radio broadcasts published in *FBIS-SOV*.

30. For relevant discussion, see Richard F. Starr (ed.), *Yearbook on International Communist Affairs 1982* (Stanford, Cal,: Hoover Institution Press, 1982), pp. 15-16.

31. For analysis, see Shahram Chubin, "Leftist Forces in Iran," *Problems of Communism*, vol. 29, no. 4 (July-August 1980), pp. 1-25; Starr, *Yearbook on International Communist Affairs 1982*, pp. 18-22; *Christian Science Monitor*, February 24, 1983.

32. For more detailed treatment of events in India since the mid-1970s, see Sen Gupta, "Communism and India: A New Context."

33. On the current status of the Iraqi Communist Party, see Starr, *Yearbook on International Communist Affairs 1982*, pp. 24-25.

34. See, for instance, Brutents, *Osvobodivshiesia strany v 70-e gody*, especially pp. 31-50; Kim, "The National Liberation Movement Today," pp. 32-33. Kim, incidentally, employs the terminology of "Westernisation from above" and "mass 'democratic' capitalism 'from below' " to describe the two categories.

35. See, for example, A. Vasilyev, "Islam in the Present-Day World," *International Affairs* no. 11 (November 1981); S. Aliev, "Islam and Politics," *Aziia i Afrika segodnia*, no. 12 (December 1981).

NINE

Aid and Trade: Soviet Attitudes toward African Client Economies
HERBERT BLOCK

IDEAS, AID, AND TRADE IN GREAT POWER RIVALRY

Centuries of colonizing effort made a handful of nations masters of vast territories on all continents. In a few decades their empires were broken up, the only exception—as yet—the Soviet empire. Since 1943, 94 new states have come into being—that is, 60 percent of all states recognized as sovereign (of which there are 168 counting the Republic of China). Africa had only four formally independent states before 1943 (Ethiopia, Egypt, Liberia, South Africa); since then 47 have been added. Of these, all but four (Libya, Morocco, Tunisia, Algeria) are sub-Saharan. Two more candidates for statehood, Namibia and Western Sahara, are waiting in the wings for their cue.

Of the new sub-Saharan states—one fourth of all the nations of the world—some are viable and fairly solid. The majority have had hardly any experience in self-government, their populations are unprepared for life under modern conditions, and their boundaries are as accidental and fragile as those the European nation-states inherited from their dynastic predecessors. At odds with each other and often internally disunited, the new states either draw the great powers of today into their quarrels or great and greater powers, directly or through proxies, interfere uninvited, to bar or eject hostile forces, foreign or local. As throughout history, great power conflicts enable small and smallest countries to play the big ones off against each other, provided they have the right mix of impudence, luck, and perspicacity.

In regard to the economies, the postcolonial rivalries take place in three rings. There is, first, the business sphere of ordinary commercial and financial deals meant to reap the advantages trade usually bestows on all partners, though their political side effects cannot be overlooked. Second is the domain of political transactions pure and simple, strengthening local regimes with outside resources, in the interest of the donor and to the detriment of some other foreign power. Finally, high up an ideological spectacle is going on between social and economic philosophies. The Soviet superpower performs in all three rings. Reversing the order, we will comment first on ideological aspects.

Marxism in the Wrong Habitat

Ideology operates also in three regions. In the highest, the intellectual sphere, it teaches its devotees how to understand life or at least provides arguments for the all-important intradoctrinal squabbles. Marxism-Leninism is well suited for sophisticated and contentious scholasticism. Ideology serves political leaders a ready-made world view on a silver—or, rather, a paper—platter, and thus spares them precious time for action. Marxism-Leninism complements its philosophy with strategic advice. For the people ideology is an opium. The firebrands Marx and Lenin were neither original nor clear in their views of a desirable society; they were pungent in their excoriation of "capitalism" and "imperialism" and above all, of everybody not in tune with them. If the two men had been contemporaries, they would have quarreled bitterly; so would have, decades later, two other headstrong men, Stalin and Mao. Lenin was free to interpret Marx at will because the dead man couldn't object and Mao could extol Stalin after 1953 to spite the dead despot's successors without fear that the teacher might turn against the disciple.

Marx, under the influence of Hegel, understood history as law-governed progress from lower to higher stages of social development. The sequence leads from primitive communalities to feudalism, capitalism and its higher form called imperialism, and socialism-communism. Each phase is separated from the next by cataclysmic events until, with the advent of socialism, society becomes nonantagonistic. The doctrine, with its later Soviet interpretations, poses several ideological problems in its application to sub-Saharan Africa.

Marxism does not explain how history, moving by necessity, achieves progress without a benevolent Providence. Sub-Saharans, differing in their beliefs but, on the whole, deeply religious, are not easily reconciled to an anti-religious Marxist ideology. But such sentiments need not prevent their governments from turning to the USSR for political and military reasons. Moreover, among their leaders are unpredictable characters embodying an unstable mixture of fervor and cunning; witness Benin's President Kérékou who in a matter of years veered from opportunistic moderation to "scientific socialism" and then, unexpectedly, to a Libyan-inspired Islamism. The prevailing ideological confusion, after 1980, with sudden conversions to this or that creed, is reminiscent of the twists and turns during the Reformation and Counter-Reformation. Atheism is a handicap in Africa.

Marxism, teaching that the predestined ascent of societies comes to pass in the strict order of their economic development, cannot explain why the most advanced nations its creator had in mind, England and France, have persistently rejected Communism. It was Russia, backward compared with them—though not an underdeveloped country in the present meaning of the term—that fell into the hands of the Bolsheviks. When Lenin's expectation that the West would join his revolution came to naught, he resorted to an imperialism theory developed by Rudolf Hilferding and Rosa Luxemburg. The colonial powers, it proposed, had postponed the day of reckoning for a while by exploiting, in the interest of their capitalists but also of their workers, their possessions overseas. The "Storm over the East," to quote the title of an impressive early Soviet motion picture (Lenin called East what we now call South; even today Soviet experts on the Third World are called "orientalists"), was to dislodge the capitalist overlords in the dependencies and then, their colonial lucre gone, in the West.

The imperialist issue has been ideally suited to stirring the imagination of underdeveloped nations and has toughened their demands against the advanced West. Yet, the underlying arguments have not been borne out by the facts of history. The decolonization of recent decades has not diminished the prosperity of the divested nations more than marginally. It has not converted any of them to Communism; the only developed countries joining the Soviet bloc, Czechoslovakia and East Germany, were conquered by force of arms. Finally, only a handful of the newly sovereign nations have taken the "socialist path." Mainland China does not fit the scheme either. It had never been colonized, and its rulers have called their socialist brethren in Moscow the true imperialists.

Nor was decolonization achieved solely on the wings of Marxist-Leninist thought, which means that in sub-Saharan Africa, as part of the decolonized world, the Soviet ideology faces other philosophies. Both the demands for independence and the concepts underlying the new governmental and legal institutions have drawn on liberalist ideas of self-determination and human rights, on nationalist emotions, on syndicalist notions, and on other Western creations. Socialism is only one of the contending ideologies. In fact, disregarding a recent wave of religious fundamentalism and, faute de mieux, a romantic glorification of traditional tribal communal life, the whole decolonization movement has lived on occidental thought—a condition that some Third World intellectuals brand as "cultural imperialism."

Even though the historical progress of the world economies as envisaged by Marxism is truncated by the failure of the advanced West to turn Communist (before as well as after the loss of the colonies), Sovietism insists on a ceremonial pecking order within the socialist camp. The uncontested head of the hierarchy is the USSR as the historically first socialist country. Other members of the Council of Mutual Economic Aid (CMEA) are trailing, but they, at least, are "states of real socialism." Further down, ranked in an order reflecting their usefulness and obedience, are less-developed followers. Until the late 1960s they were called "countries attempting a non-capitalist course"; since then they have been countries "with a socialist orientation."

Each bears an additional label with its current rank, which is now and then updated according to ideological fashion and political circumstances. Examples are the May Day slogans of 1982: "Salute the people of Ethiopia, who have chosen the path of socialist transformation" (slogan no. 67), and "the peoples of Angola, Mozambique, and other African countries that"—slightly less exalted—"have chosen the path of socialist development" (slogan no. 68). Still further down were "Africa's peoples struggling against imperialism and racism" (slogan no. 71). The Somalis are now a nonpeople. It is unlikely that the Africans are happy with this official pyramid, reminiscent of the ranking of colonies in the empires of yesteryear.

Whenever a doctrine establishes a hierarchy, believers among the disadvantaged orders, fervent but impatient, wonder whether they could not leapfrog to a higher rank. Marx himself, a refugee from a less-developed Germany, asked the question on behalf of his former compatriots, and in 1850 expressed at least the hope that the forthcoming revolution of the French proletariat (there was none) would accelerate the advent of German socialism. Around 1882, when Russia was plagued by assassinations (terrorism is not a specialty of our time), Marx expected Russia to become "the vanguard of revolutionary action in Europe"; vanguards, however, may skirmish successfully but do not win the war. At the same time, Russian revolutionaries asked Marx whether Russia, blessed with quasi-Communist peasant collectives, might not bypass capitalism and enter socialism directly. Marx was embarrassed, and weasel-worded. Now, a century later, Africans raise a similar question. They do not aspire to the elevated rank of the USSR, but they would like to speed up their historical development and perhaps, with the help of their tribal communities, bypass the obnoxious capitalism with Soviet aid.

The Kremlin's attitude toward such a notion is a clear-*nyet*. Soviets have as little use for rudiments of a primitive stage of African life as Marx had for Russian peasant communes. The Soviet vanguard of history does not tolerate local attempts, touching though they may be, to salvage an outdated remnant of their own past. African leaders, whether out of conviction or convenience, could not avoid declaring on various occasions that "there cannot be an African or European socialism . . . there is only Scientific Socialism"[1]— that is the Soviet variety of that vague contraption.

How to Let African Clients Flirt
with Capitalism Without Losing Them

Deciding against a major role for tribal communities does not answer the question whether a sub-Saharan state, by choosing the socialist path, might bypass capitalism altogether or whether it would have to undergo the capitalist experience, though for only a brief period. Should its leadership eradicate the beginnings of "capitalism" in favor of Soviet institutions and policies, or allow them to unfold so that the country traverses its preordained capitalist phase as quickly as possible? Since Marxism is highly history-minded, since Sovietism uses Russian history as a pattern, and since any proposition can be proved or disproved with one of the many (ambiguous) Lenin quotations, the discussion is carried on in terms of NEP (New Economic Policy) or no NEP.

In 1921, when Lenin's ruinous measures had become unbearable, he embarked on the "New Economic Policy." He restored the market economy and a stable currency, permitting small businesses to operate in industry, agriculture, and trade: the government retained the "commanding heights"—that is, in addition to general policy direction, ownership of the large plants. Russia still had a reservoir of entrepreneurs, and they brought about seven years as fat as possible under Bolshevik rule. But in 1928, Stalin ended the "strategic retreat" and established his command economy with full nationalization and planning. Yet we may indulge in counterfactual history by assuming that Bukharin, a radical turned moderate, had ousted Stalin instead of becoming his victim. The result would have been a strengthened NEP, and in the end the USSR might have become a mixed economy. If in an African country, Soviet and local Communists would permit a comparable strategic retreat, they might, for all practical purposes, "NEP" the socialism in the bud.

Soviet references to the NEP experience in the context of African policy are not an accident. The Soviet economy is in considerable trouble exactly because it has preserved the Stalinist system; among the possible remedies would be a modernized version of NEP. While it would please economists with a bent for market procedures, the reigning doctrinaires would have no use for it, and prefer not to regard it as an option for the USSR. But the subject has been broached in general and for underdeveloped countries in an almost precapitalist phase, and "orientalists" have produced a series of papers on pros and cons of a NEP in the Third World.[2]

Soviet client regimes hold power in countries that have receded precipitously from a very modest level of prosperity under an inefficient colonial administration (Angola, Mozambique) or have belonged to the poorest of the poor since time immemorial (Ethiopia). And their problem is not only poverty but also ignorance, corruption, and inexpert leadership.

The Soviets, as Lenin's own people in history's avant-garde, do not mince words when discussing Africa. In 1981, Viktor Sheynis of the Moscow Institute of World Economy and International Relations tried to explain why African states reversed their connection with the USSR and left the socialist path:

> Prerequisites for such countercoups and degenerations are contained in the fact that a number of negative social phenomena like corruption, nepotism, economic and administrative inefficiency, the stagnation or slow rise in the living standard, the passiveness of the masses, nondemocratic government, and the like are rooted in the existing socioeconomic and sociocultural structure of many developing countries.[3]

He continued by complaining about the "political leadership in certain states and the absence of a broad proletarian class basis." In truth, African Sovietism is dictatorship not of the proletariat, but without one.

Clients of this type, useful for the USSR's global strategy, could cost Moscow a pretty penny and, since their orientation is reversible, money and effort may ultimately be wasted. With this possibility in mind, advocates of an African NEP have argued that it would create the best of two worlds. The country, while remaining a Soviet satellite, would profit from the activities of its own "capitalists" and from Western aid, both private and public, including the entrepreneurship and technology of foreign-owned companies. In the end, thanks to these class enemies, the economy would be ripe to plunge into socialism, with both native and foreign capitalists the losers.

What of the threat that a local Bukharin or, worse still, an openly antisocialist leader would turn the Soviet-oriented economy toward an occidental path? On condition that the government remains faithful to its Sovietist inclinations, it would have to defend the "commanding heights"—which in underdeveloped countries are not particularly impressive. It would have to refrain from debasing the national patrimony to "bureaucratic capital (that is, a distinctive variety of monopoly capital the economic predominance of which is based mainly not on enterprise in the sphere of material production or circulation but on the direct use of the political power of a narrow group of persons in mercenary interests)."[4] The "state capitalism" of a government stumbling on the socialist path would be in danger of becoming the tool either of international corporations or of the "grande bourgeoisie," a somewhat grandiloquent expression for native businessmen cooperating with foreigners, and therefore also called "dependent capitalists."[5] Finally, it would be necessary to watch the "native capitalists," defined as petit-bourgeois local entrepreneurs, who, however, as part of the "national bourgeoisie," might be rather submissive.

The Soviets would have to control the local administration as much as possible. This is difficult in a faraway country that cannot be invaded as easily as the adjoining Warsaw Pact countries or Afghanistan. The next best thing is the presence of Cuban troops, a local Communist party sufficiently under Moscow's influence to offer alternative leaders, and government chiefs in need of Soviet protection (emperors of the declining Roman Empire relied on, or were the glorified prisoners of, bodyguards recruited from the Huns or Teutons; African satraps depend on secret police from East Germany or of similar provenance). Needless to say, the system can never be foolproof. In each case the USSR has to ponder, first, whether the strategic advantages obtained or expected match the outlays and possible entanglements, and, second, whether the African associates are reliable or, if necessary, expendable. In the case of Ethiopia versus Somalia, Moscow decided in favor of the stronger nation; in Egypt and Mali, it was the Africans who made the decision.

All of this is déjà vu in history. During the Thirty Years War the Swiss Confederation maintained a prudent, heavily armed neutrality, but what is now the canton of Grisons, with its important Alpine passes, tried to play Hapsburg and Bourbon off against each other. When Protestant clergymen (the mullahs of their time) and their Catholic counterparts were not just killing each other, the international power game was not without temporary success. In 1637, when Paris was behind in payments to Grisons, a French army had to capitulate to the mountain people and its illustrious commander, the duke of Rohan, became virtually a prisoner in Chur, now the canton's capital. Richelieu was sick at heart. "This disaster," he wrote to one of his friends, "is only due to lack of money. For each écu paid in time [to Grisons] we will now need ten and even they will not repair the loss. For a long time I have preached to our treasury; if they do not believe me now, one has to give up all hope."[6] Richelieu's predicament may console lesser statesmen of today. France was perfectly capable of paying Grisons, not by reducing the court's expenditures but by economizing elsewhere or by levying higher taxes on the poor.

A great power must make up its mind where it wants to spend its resources (and the resources of satellites previously subdued or suborned). Strategic advantages, their acquisition, and their retention, cost money and blood. The inclusion of Cuba in the Soviet bloc shows that the USSR has been willing to spend heavily on an overseas associate, undoubtedly far more than it anticipated in the early 1960s. But the Kremlin has judged a strategic position close to the American mainland to be worth the cost. This consideration leads to the second issue: the use and flow of resources accompanying political intervention and penetration in sub-Saharan Africa.

AID

Soviet Aspirations Backed by a Costly Power Structure

When the Kremlin contemplates the cost-benefit ratio of aid to sub-Saharan Africa, it does not limit its scrutiny to what is usually called "aid"—that is, the grants and concessional credits provided for the economic development of backward client states and, in cases aside from troops from the Soviet camp in combat, for military modernization. Moscow also estimates the resource outlay of military (and intelligence) operations conducted by the USSR itself or by proxies expecting compensation and support in one form or another. Nor can the Kremlin farm out economic and military assignments to the Warsaw Pact members without a quid pro quo. These are no longer the days of Stalin, when satellites were simply given orders. But the main expense for the USSR arises insofar as African ventures exacerbate superpower rivalry and call for larger Soviet security efforts.

Incorporation of Cuba into the Soviet empire brought forth not only hefty annual subsidies for the Castro regime but, in the course and as a consequence of two major American-Soviet crises, increased Soviet security outlays. The USSR's Cuban undertaking was economically costly, but up to the early 1980s quite profitable in terms of power politics; likewise the succor for Vietnam. The outcome is not always positive. Khrushchev reportedly complained in 1957 that China was "milking us dry;"[7] this must have been a typical Khrushchev exaggeration, buy even more economic and military help—the Chinese called the USSR niggardly—would not have prevented the Sino-Soviet rift. Egypt is another example of a Soviet political as well as economic loss. In the Horn of Africa, the Kremlin experienced the typical dilemma of two "friends" at loggerheads; it opted, reasonably enough, for the one with population and national product at that time ten times as large as those of the other.

The USSR penetration of Africa was facilitated by American handicaps at the time of the Vietnam venture and the Watergate crisis; they must have figured on the Kremlin's balance sheet of reasons for and against activities in Africa. But such calculations are known to be speculative and hazardous, if not in the short, then in the long, run, and the Soviet armament efforts of the 1970s were inevitably meant to back the prospective expansion into Africa. On the American side, the Soviet forays into Angola, Ethiopia, and other places have been reasons for preparedness measures; thus, a new arms race has begun at a time of economic slowdown in the Soviet bloc and, coincidentally, in the Western world.

But East and West are different in that the defense burden, measured by the share of the national product devoted to defense, is twice as high in the USSR as in the United States and three to four times as high as in NATO

Europe. It would, of course, make no sense to impute, say, one or two percentage points of the Soviet defense share of 14–15 percent to the USSR's African extravaganzas—and yet some of the Soviet defense burden is related to them. Whatever this imponderable increment, it is far heavier than the generally modest Soviet bloc grants and credits for African aid. Obviously, the superpower rivalry is an open-ended affair with political and economic efforts in the offing.

To what extent do the Soviet allies help their protagonist carry the burden of sub-Saharan ventures? The Warsaw Pact members in Eastern Europe give economic and military aid, send technicians to Africa, and train Africans at their educational institutions. Cuba has troops in Africa.

Eastern Europe's economic aid in 1975–79 to Soviet clients in Africa was estimated in current dollars as follows: Angola, close to $100 million; Mozambique, $15 million; Ethiopia, some $70 million; Somalia, $5 million; Congo, $12 million; Guinea, $85 million; and small amounts to others.[8] Using the purchasing power of the dollar in 1980, the value of the commitments might be 20 percent higher. But these amounts refer to aid extended; aid actually delivered is always lower (of Eastern Europe's economic aid to all non-Communist developing countries in 1975–79, only 43 percent of the amounts extended were actually drawn: $1.73 billion of $4.02 billion).[9] Between 1975 and 1979, Czechoslovakia and Poland transferred arms to Angola valued at $30 million, to Mozambique valued at $5 million, and to Ethiopia valued at $40 million at current prices;[10] there were undoubtedly military deliveries from East Germany and other East European countries.

All of this is sizable from the point of view of the recipients, but negligible from that of the donors. The outlay is minute in comparison with either Eastern Europe's national security expenditures—influenced, in turn, by an international tension intensified by the USSR's Africa policy—or with Soviet subsidies for shaky East European economies. If we accept Thad Alton's calculations,[11] Eastern Europe's military expenditures in 1979 amounted to 5.1 percent of its combined national product. Whatever the exact figure, the burden was heavier than in NATO Europe (3.6 percent) with its greater prosperity. In fact, Poland and Romania—with populations of 57.3 million out of Eastern Europe's 108.8 million—are practically bankrupt. And while up to 1956, the USSR exploited Eastern Europe, the shoe is now on the other foot.

A 1980 study by Jan Vaňous and Michael Marrese[12] arrives at the conclusion that, in 1980 dollars, the USSR subsidized its six East European associates to the tune of $7 billion in 1978, $11.6 billion in 1979, and $21.7 billion in 1980. In the early 1980s, Poland must have cost the Soviets a substantial amount in goods and hard currency. The subsidies just mentioned include opportunity costs—that is, the resources the Soviet

Union forwent by selling oil and other goods not to the West but at concessional prices to Eastern Europe. Whether the USSR would actually have realized these gains in deals on the world market is another question. If it were true that at the same time the Soviets are fleecing their satellites in sales of military goods and services, the net subsidies would be somewhat lower.

Uncertainty also surrounds Soviet subsidies for Cuba. With an allowance for concessional prices in trade of primary products (low for Soviet oil, high for Cuban sugar), Cuba appears to cost the USSR between $3 and $3.5 billion annually. Inevitably, the USSR has had to back the Cuban military efforts in Africa with goods and services; moreover, Castro's proxy role must have given him political clout vis-à-vis the Kremlin and a degree of freedom to pursue his own goals.

Modest Soviet Resources for African Aid Projects

Compared with the resources the USSR, pursuing its great-power aspirations, has been putting into its military establishments and into satellites requiring succor, its economic aid to Third World countries is paltry; its military aid, answering strategic necessities, is somewhat larger. Moscow, of course, does not reveal aid statistics, so we have to rely on Western calculations. The CIA prepares them annually, and published them through 1979.[13] Since then, the information has remained classified. The OECD has come out with its own data on economic aid flows,[14] and the U.S. Arms Control and Disarmament Agency (ACDA) continues to publish estimates of arms transfers.[15] All these compilations are in current dollars, which means that a sum totaling several years with significant inflation would be higher if expressed in purchasing power of the dollar of later years.

Concepts complicate matters still further. As mentioned above, it is important to differentiate between aid extended or committed and aid drawn or delivered. In 1977–80, the advanced West's Development Assistance Committee (DAC) actually disbursed 80.5 percent of the aid committed; the USSR, according to the CIA, in 1976–79 disbursed 32 percent (between 1954 and 1979, 45 percent). We do not know the ratio of Soviet aid promised and delivered to sub-Saharan clients. Furthermore, all CIA information on "non-Communist LDCs" excludes Soviet associates such as Cuba and Vietnam, but includes the African states currently tied to Moscow. Needless to say, all figures are estimates, and in some cases guesstimates.

Military aid, subsidized or fully paid, is as old as history and is supplied on purely political grounds. International help after catastrophes, natural or man-made, is also time-honored; during and after the two world wars, American relief was worldwide. A novel undertaking, however, was President Truman's Point Four program; it started the systematic flow of economic aid from developed to underdeveloped countries. It is a common practice to misrepresent political stratagems as philanthropic; hypocrisy, said La Rochefoucauld, is homage that vice pays to virtue. In the case of American economic aid, we could observe the reverse. While political motives were by no means absent, they were stressed to mask generosity; Machiavellian justification was homage that virtue paid to vice, so that it did not look naive.

A few years later, the program took on a universal scope: between 1954 and 1979, DAC provided gross official bilateral capital flows of $215.9 billion in current dollars, of which the United States contributed $94.4 billion. This statistic starts in 1954, and not earlier, because at that time the USSR entered the aid scene with a bang. To the West's unnecessary dismay, it launched "an aggressive program of economic diplomacy."[16] The program allowed the Third World to play East and West off against each other and then, as time passed and the Soviet deliveries remained modest, it provoked spokesmen for underdeveloped countries occasionally to criticize Soviet niggardliness. By now the Third World takes aid programs for granted; largess has become a human right.

In 1954–79 the USSR supplied economic aid valued at $8.23 billion in current dollars. Even Mainland China, itself an underdeveloped country with a GNP estimated at one-tenth of the Soviet Union's, gave economic aid of $2.825 billion during the same period—one third as much as the USSR. In 1979—and, of course, in the dollar's purchasing power of that year—gross bilateral official capital flows were, according to the CIA,[17] $7.012 billion from the United States, $23.351 billion from DAC as a whole, $3.050 billion from OPEC (which started this type of aid in 1974), $180 million from Mainland China, $575 million from the USSR, and $265 million from Eastern Europe. There was an additional $12 billion of Western-supplied multilateral aid.[18]

Turning to sub-Saharan Africa and, first, to the important arms transfers, ACDA reports that in 1975–79, Soviet shipments amounted to $2.88 billion in current dollars, an annual average of $576 million. How much of this amount was cash, how much credit, and how much grants is not known. Three-quarters of this amount ($2.17 billion) went to Ethiopia, Angola, and Mozambique, $21 million to a Somalia later abandoned, and the rest to sundry governments leaning at least for a time toward Moscow (Mali, $110 million; Congo, $50 million; Madagascar, $30 million; Benin, $20 million). Arms that the Cubans wielded probably were not all included in these figures, but the estimates are very tentative.

Economic aid committed to sub-Saharan states with Soviet ties, varying in degree and time, is precariously estimated as follows.

The Somali Republic, which came into being in 1960 and sided with the USSR from 1969 to 1977, in 1975 received Soviet economic aid promises totaling $62 million in current dollars; it is not known to what extent they were honored. Eastern Europe did not extend economic aid. Since it reversed the alliance, CMEA countries have steered clear of the Somali Republic. The DAC made bilateral commitments increasing from $29.9 million in current dollars in 1977 to $234.4 million in 1980, with the U.S. contributing bilateral aid rising from $0.8 to $74.7 billion.[19] Expressed in 1980 dollars and with a supplement designed to come closer to purchasing power equivalents than conversion at official exchange rates achieves, the Somali GNP was $666 million in 1969 and $856 million in 1980; in terms of per capita product, it declined from $300 to $244.[20]

Ethiopia was given practically no economic aid until 1977 and 1978, when Eastern Europe extended $23 and $45 million in current dollars; in 1979, the USSR, which until then had refrained from economic aid, committed $95 million. OECD estimates CMEA's 1979 commitments at $99.4 million; those for 1980 (no breakdown by donors), at $37.8 million. The latter amount represents 0.4 percent of the Ethiopian GNP ($9.2 billion in 1980 dollars), or $1.16 for each of the country's 31.8 million inhabitants. Size and development of the Ethiopian GNP can only be guessed. Our figures show a slight decline of the real GNP per capita from $298 in 1974, when the Ethiopian revolution took place (total GNP in that year was $8.4 billion), to $283 in 1980; in reality it may have decreased more. DAC aid rose from $51.2 million in 1977 to $79.9 million in 1980 (the U.S. contribution increased from $6.9 million to $13.4 million); multilateral aid was $131.1 million in 1977, declined somewhat, then rose again to $147.3 million in 1980 (all aid data in current dollars).

Angola received Soviet economic aid promises of $20 million, $6 million, and $1 million in 1976, 1977, and 1978, and East European promises of $10 million in 1976 and of $76 million in 1978. OECD estimates total CMEA commitments at $0.1 million for 1979 and at zero for 1980. DAC aid increased from $7.4 million in 1977 to $57.7 million in 1980 (with the American bilateral contribution rising from $0.2 million to $5.3 million); multilateral aid declined from $42.2 million to $28.5 million between 1977 and 1980. Angola is one of the retrodeveloping countries. In 1974, the troubled year before it gained independence, the GNP in 1980 dollars was an estimated $7.725 billion; in 1980 it was $5.889 billion. The per-capita GNP declined from $1,283 to $890.

Mozambique was extended Soviet economic aid only in 1976 and 1977, in the amounts of $3 million and $5 million, respectively; East European aid in 1977 and 1978 was $12 million and $2 million, respectively. OECD estimated CMEA aid in 1979 at $0.4 million, and in 1980 at $2.8 million. DAC commitments in 1977 were $108 million; in 1980, $123.9

million, including U.S. contributions of $5.2 million and $14.8 million. In 1979 and 1980, OPEC gave bilateral aid of $11.4 million and $10.3 million. Multilateral aid rose from $29.2 million in 1977 to $50 million in 1980. Mozambique's GNP in 1980 dollars declined from $7.9 billion in 1974, the year before independence, to $7.71 billion in 1980 (per capita, from $960 to $561).

The People's Republic of the Congo received practically no economic aid from the USSR and Eastern Europe, if we use the CIA's data. OECD lists CMEA commitments of $31.0 million in 1977 and $0.4 million in 1978; afterward, nothing. DAC bilateral commitments were $30.9 million in 1977 and $64.0 million in 1980, of which the United States contributed $0.8 million and $0.9 million. In 1978 and 1980, OPEC bilaterally committed $3.6 million and $21.1 million, respectively. Multilateral aid commitments increased from $16.1 million in 1977 to $60.2 million in 1980. The Congo's GNP is estimated at $1.137 billion (in 1980 dollars) in 1970, and at $1.47 billion in 1980; in that period the per-capita GNP moved from $961 to $951.

Benin has received no Soviet or East European aid worth mentioning. DAC aid rose in 1977–80 from $12.7 million to $57.8 million (U.S. share, from $0.8 million to $7.9 million). In 1978, OPEC promised $8.2 million. Multilateral aid fell from $63.1 million to $45.6 million. GNP in 1960, when Benin became independent, was $1.25 billion; in 1980, $2.17 billion (both figures in 1980 dollars). Since the population increased by 70 percent in that period, GNP per capita rose only from $608 to $622.

Guinea in 1974 received USSR aid commitments of $2 million; Eastern Europe commitments, of $80 million (allegedly promised). Since then, there have been no increases. DAC commitments rose from $7.1 million in 1977 to $12.4 million in 1980, with no U.S. contributions. In 1977 and 1979, OPEC added $6.2 million and $6.9 million bilaterally. In 1960, when Sékou Touré turned Guinea toward the Communist world, its GNP (in 1980 dollars) was $1.65 billion; in 1980, it was $2.35 billion ($538 and $430 per capita, respectively).

Madagascar, according to the CIA, received Soviet economic aid of $6 million in 1978; apparently it has received nothing since. OECD lists CMEA aid between 1977 and 1980 as $14 million, $28 million, $0.4 million, and zero. DAC in 1977 provided $52.3 million, and in 1980, $95.7 million (the United States in 1977 gave $0.8 million; in 1979, $2.1 million; in 1980, nothing). OPEC's bilateral contributions, as promised, were $8.3 million in 1977, rose to $34.2 million in 1979, and declined to $9.4 million in 1980. Multilateral aid increased from $45.1 million to $132.6 million. Between Malagasy independence in 1960 and 1980, total GNP grew from $4.2 billion to $6.05 billion; per capita GNP fell from $767 to $707.

The data thus assembled, fragile though they are attest to three hard facts:

1. The poor condition of these nations' economies, which are not only backward but moving backward in terms, if not of total, then of per-capita, GNP, only the population increasing
2. The meager resources these nations receive from CMEA, and the Soviets in particular, with drawings of course remaining behind commitments
3. The far larger transfers from the West in bilateral and multilateral funds, both of which are supported by the United States.

For the Soviets all of this is not a question of capability but of willingness. They feel that throughout their history they have pulled themselves up by their bootstraps; they disparage outside help received in the process. At any rate, the Politburo is not a philanthropic committee; it follows the dictates of power policy (which do not exclude an occasional act of generosity). Thus, they are willing to underaid in resources and overaid in ideology, all the while welcoming "capitalist" aid for their clients while they hope the latter will not be tempted to orient themselves toward the West.

How useful is the ideological help—the Soviet example implemented with Soviet advice—for sub-Saharan countries? Insofar as the Soviet system conforms to Oskar Lange's famous definition "a war economy *sui generis*" —fashioned, in fact, after the ineffective German war economy of World War I—it may serve in regions under actual war conditions, and sub-Saharan Africa still has its share of armed hostilities. But allocation of men and matériel according to emergency priorities, regulation of the production processes, and rationing in distribution are wasteful and invite corruption; they are not a model for economic development, once a degree of quiet is restored. Nor is Stalin's system of comprehensive planning advisable for African countries. It has worked badly in the USSR even after more than half a century of practical experience; it would create a mess in sub-Saharan countries without the prerequisite statistics and a seasoned administration.[21]

Stalin's policy of strengthening arms and arms-supporting industries by throttling personal consumption is not applicable in areas where living conditions are at rock bottom and the industrial preconditions—which Stalin inherited from the tsars—are completely absent. The ruling party in Mozambique, FRELIMO (Frente de Liberacão de Mozambique) declared at its Third Congress in February 1977: "Only by building up heavy industry will our country be able to insure control of the production processes, free itself from dependence and increase its economic capacity decisively."[22] For Africans this is a castle in Russia. Except in some light and labor-intensive industries, industrial investment is rational only where it serves to export low-cost raw materials (oil in Angola, bauxite in Guinea). Such activity, however, does not free a country "from dependence"; it integrates it into the world economy—a profitable undertaking, but not for FRELIMO.

Africa, with crude birth rates of almost 5 percent among the Soviet clientele and a population growth of about 2.5 percent per year, requires agricultural development; in this respect the USSR offers the worst model imaginable, for the country, with an almost stagnant population (outside its Muslim areas) is not able to feed itself in a modern fashion. Its mechanized state and collective farms require irrationally heavy investments far beyond African means, and at the same time Soviet farm equipment is rusting in the fields—as has been the case where African collectives received tractors and related implements of Soviet bloc manufacture. Poland, with a combination of food shortages and inefficient industries, is an example of what happens even to a highly educated population forced to introduce the Soviet system.

Regimes politically and ideologically close to Moscow do not imitate Soviet patterns only because the USSR urges them on. Their leaders are either fanatic in their beliefs—which need not be shared by their peoples—or sycophants. In their desire to please their overlords, they sometimes out-Kremlin the Kremlin. In such cases Moscow has to brake their enthusiasm, fearful that they may have to be bailed out. Stalin told Bulgaria's Dimitrov to go slow on farm collectivization; Cuba received warnings during the Guevara experiments; and Angola was advised "not to expel Portuguese businessmen and specialists."[23] All this is a question of degree, and the results cannot always be foreseen. For Angola, retrodeveloping and pinched by lower world market prices for oil, ties to the West have been vital. Its leader, President José dos Santos, is a flexible man; we have even witnessed Portugal's President António Eanes invited to Luanda only seven (lean) years after Angola's break with Lisbon. Dos Santos, after mentioning the country's socialist path, drank a toast to "friendship and cooperation" between the two peoples and "to the health of his Excellency the President of the Portuguese Republic."

Much will depend not only on Angola's leadership but also on the international situation. Up to now, as the preceding survey by country shows, the West has been willing to help Soviet clients in sub-Saharan Africa, in the hope that they may reverse their association. If East-West tension should further increase, and sub-Saharan Africa's geopolitical position grow in importance in the light of Latin American developments, the West might, as a minimum, reduce its aid and trade cooperation with Soviet clients (at least in bilateral dealings; multilateral agencies have achieved quite a degree of independence—a political problem in itself). In such an eventuality the USSR would have to step up its economic and military aid to African clients. The Kremlin will not shy away from expenditures, provided it expects the strategic advantages to match the cost. The second largest economy in the world, with apparently the largest military budget in the world, can afford the resource outlay—smallish compared with its other preparedness expense—as much as France could have sent some écus to Grisons if Richelieu had prevailed over the royal treasury. The issue is not the economy but politics, both foreign and domestic.

TRADE

Smallish with Soviet Export Surplus: Guns For Coffee

The transfers of military and civilian goods described in the preceding section are—or should be—reflected in the trade statistics of donors and recipients, except that commercial statistics are unreliable in backward countries and, often, in advanced countries. Arms flows in particular are frequently disguised or remain unrecorded in public. If, for instance, in 1981 the USSR shipped goods valued at 136.2 million rubles to Ethiopia while importing merchandise valued at 20.1 million rubles, there can be no doubt that the exports were made up chiefly of military supplies and, to a lesser degree (judging precariously by the 1980 economic aid commitments), of civilian goods on concessional terms or otherwise. Military aid apart, trade of the USSR and its CMEA partners with Soviet clients in Africa has been as inconsiderable as their economic aid. After their conversion to the Soviet-oriented path, African governments proclaimed their intention to greatly increase their commercial dealings with CMEA. Ethiopia even obtained observer status in that organization, but there is not much to observe, and other countries that were not admitted (for instance, Mozambique) have not missed much. CMEA already has several ailing members, and is not eager to become a nursing home for the chronically ill.

The client states, in turn, have become quite pragmatic, and have continued their economic relations with "capitalist" nations, including their former colonial overlords and even South Africa. In the context of their total exports and (civilian) imports, the role of the USSR and other CMEA countries is small. This, it is hardly necessary to add, makes them more vulnerable to possible control measures by "capitalist" trading partners while, on the other hand, it would facilitate a break with the Soviet camp along the lines of Somalia's reversal of alliances.

Viewed from Moscow—and this is the concern of the present paper—trade with the African clients is insignificant. As long as there is a worldwide sellers' market for weapons, even the Soviet arms could probably be sold to other shoppers on more advantageous terms. Nor is the USSR particularly interested in export goods from Africa. Angola, for instance, offers three main export commodities: petroleum, diamonds, and coffee. The USSR exports both oil and diamonds; faute de mieux, it imports

Angolan and Ethiopian coffee—a consumer good Moscow assigns a very low priority. Grain cannot be bought in sub-Saharan Africa; it is a deficit commodity both in Africa and in the Soviet Union. If Guinea had remained closer to the USSR, it would have been a major exception: the USSR, purchasing Guinean bauxite, in 1981 imported merchandise valued at 63.1 million rubles while exporting only 20.9 million rubles worth of goods to that country. The Soviet clients, having little to offer that interests Moscow, have import surpluses with the USSR, a situation that does not please the Soviets who are interested only in trade partners supplying high-priority goods or paying in hard currency.

This, then, is the record, as expressed in Soviet trade statistics: The values are in current rubles; they do not, of course, reflect domestic Soviet prices, but world market prices, rising throughout recent years, minus the depreciation of the dollar in terms of the official ruble-dollar rate. Merchandise movements are sanitized to protect Soviet strategic interests—for instance, in regard to arms shipments.

Soviet exports to Ethiopia amounted to only 2.6 million rubles in 1974, the year the emperor was ousted; they climbed to 136.2 million in 1981, obviously as the result of such deliveries as the Soviet government saw fit to acknowledge. Imports rose from 3.6 million to 20.1 million rubles, a coffee break for the Soviet consumer.

Trade with Angola began with exports of 14.4 million rubles; they increased to 107 million in 1981. Imports are given as 2.2 million rubles in 1976 and 8.1 million in 1981; they filled a few more Soviet coffee cups.

Mozambique became the USSR's trading partner in 1976. Soviet exports did not reach 4 million rubles, but rose to 35.7 million in 1981. Imports are given for 1978 as 0.8 million rubles; in 1981 they were as low as 1.3 million.

Benin's trade was minuscule in the mid-1970s as well as in 1981, when the USSR exported goods worth 1.6 million rubles and imported goods worth 0.4 million.

Congo received Soviet exports worth 2 million rubles in 1976, and 6.9 million in 1981; Soviet imports in 1976 were worth 2 million rubles, and in 1981, 5.5 million rubles.

Madagascar's trade was insignificant except for slight increases in Soviet imports in 1976 and 1977.

For Somalia, Soviet exports reached a maximum of 22.2 million rubles in 1975, while imports amounted to only 4.3 million rubles. Trade was discontinued in 1978.

Adding East European trade to the Soviet record would change the picture only marginally. It is a picture of Soviet bloc export surpluses, reflecting military and economic aid with insufficient offsets through African merchandise, all on a miniature scale. As a share of the USSR's total exports, trade with Ethiopia, Angola, Mozambique, Benin, and the Congo amounted to less than 0.4 percent; imports were only 0.2 percent of the Soviet total.

Nor is there room for much expansion in real terms. In theory, the economies are complementary: Africa could supply the USSR with tropical products in exchange for Soviet manufactured goods, particularly machinery, vehicles, and, of course, arms. In practice, the Africans prefer Western articles, and the USSR has no resources to spare for luxuries such as coffee or tropical fruit. Only in the hypothetical case that political conditions were to isolate African clients from the world outside the Soviet bloc would trade increase of necessity, but the assumption may never become reality. If, on the other hand, sub-Saharan clients were separated from commerce with the Soviet bloc, they could continue their dealings with Western countries. This they could do by severing or at least deemphasizing their relations with the Kremlin, without necessarily abandoning some sort of socialism, Marxist or otherwise. Politics has, and will continue to have, a clear-cut priority in the Soviet connection with African states.

NOTES

1. From the Report of the First Congress of the MPLA (Movimento Popular para a Liberacao de Angola), quoted in Nicos Zafiris, "The People's Republic of Angola: Soviet-Type Economy in the Making," in Peter Wiles, ed., *The New Communist Third World* (New York: St. Martin's Press, 1982).

2. Books aside, much of the Soviet discussion has taken place in scholarly journals such as *Narody Azii i Afriki* (Peoples of Asia and Africa), issued by the Oriental Studies Institute and the African Institute, and *Aziya i Afrika segodnya* (Asia and Africa today), published by the Oriental Studies Institute. See Elizabeth K. Valkenier, "The USSR, the Third World, and the Global Economy," *Problems of Communism*, July–August 1979, pp. 17-33. Foreign Broadcast Information Service (FBIS), *Soviet Guidelines for Third World Regimes: Political Control, Economic Pluralism*, Analysis Report, FB 81-10010, March 12, 1981, provides both useful comments and bibliographical references.

3. Quoted from FBIS Trends: *USSR-Ghana*, March 31, 1982, p. 10.

4. From Yurity N. Rozaliyev, "State Capitalism and the Developing Economy," *Narody Azii i Afriki* (1980), no. 1. Rozaliyev, of the Institute of General History, is one of those "orientalists" who believe that African states should make use of the "capitalists."

5. See FBIS, *Soviet Guidelines for Third World Regimes*, on Karen Brutents and his book *Osvobodivshiyesya strany v 70-ye gody* (The liberated countries in the 1970s) (Moscow: Izdatel'stvo politicheskoi literatury, 1979). Brutents, a Soviet government official whose general outlook is similar to that of Rozaliyev, made the distinction between "native" and "dependent" capitalists.

6. Quoted in Carl J. Burckhardt, *Richelieu*, III (Munich: Georg D.W. Callwey, 1966), pp. 265-66.

7. Quoted in Joseph S. Berliner, *Soviet Economic Aid* (New York: Frederick A. Praeger, 1958), p. 147.

8. National Foreign Assessment Center, *Communist Aid Activities in Non-Communist Less Developed Countries, 1979 and 1954–79*, ER 80-10318U (Washington D.C.: CIA, 1980). Previous issues of the same publication were also used for the present paper.

9. Ibid, Table A-S.

10. U.S. Arms Control and Disarmament Agency (ACDA), *World Military Expenditures and Arms Transfers 1970–1979* (Washington, D.C.: ACDA, 1982), Table III.

11. Thad P. Alton and his associates published their latest estimates in Research Project on National Income in East Central Europe, Occasional Paper no. 65 (New York: L.W. International Financial Research, Inc.).

12. From "Implicit Subsidies in Soviet Trade with Eastern Europe," Discussion Paper no. 80-32 (Vancouver: Department of Economics, University of British Columbia, 1980). Dr. Vaňous supplied the writer with slightly revised figures for 1979 and 1980.

13. See Wiles, op. cit., p. 13.

14. Organization for Economic Co-Operation and Development (OECD), *Geographical Distribution of Financial Flows to Developing Countries, 1977/1980* (Paris: OECD, 1981).

15. ACDA, op. cit.

16. U.S. Congress, Joint Economic Committee, *Dimensions of Soviet Economic Power* (Washington, D.C.: U.S. Government Printing Office, 1962), p. 416.

17. CIA, *Handbook of Economic Statistics 1981*, NF HES 81-001 (Washington, D.C.: CIA, 1981), Table 73. The report cited in note 8 has slightly different estimates for the USSR ($500 million), East Europe ($255 million), and Mainland China ($160 million); all these figures should be viewed as indicating general magnitudes.

18. OECD, op. cit, p. 231.

19. All DAC data from OECD, op. cit.

20. See Herbert Block, *The Planetary Product* (Washington, D.C.: U.S. Department of State, annual).

21. Western experts are as able as those of the USSR to gum up their own activities. The following quotation from the report by the executive director of the U.N. World Food Council—WFC/1982/4/pt. I (February 22, 1982)—describes how advice squads of international agencies descend on a helpless country, discombobulating its already overtaxed government: "For example, Upper Volta can hardly cope with the number of assistance projects that it is receiving. For 1981 there were 340 external assistance missions, and the government was not always able to keep up with the management and coordination requirements, with resulting confusion at all levels and a loss of resources and efficiency. Many of these missions give an impression of less than full effectiveness."

22. Wiles, op. cit., p. 129.

23. Valkenier, loc. cit.

INDEX

246

Libya and Soviet Union, 133-149; constraints on, 145-146; economic achievements, 143-144; economic objectives, 141; interest in location, 137-139; international terrorism, 136-137, 140-141; military aid, 136; objectives, 137-141; political achievements, 144; strategic achievements, 142-143; strategic objectives, 137-139; success, 141-144

Machel, Samora, 9
Machiavellli, Niccolo, 46
Madagascar, 3; Soviet economic aid to, 238; Soviet trade with, 242
Mali, 44, 62, 73
Marxism, 13, 15, 17-19, 26, 30, 38, 85, 214-217; Third World, 227-229; in wrong habitat, 227-229
Mediterranean area, 2
Mengistu (Colonel), 13, 44, 160-173, 197, 202, 203
Menon, Krishna, 48
"merchants of death," 32
"military intelligentsia," 35
military option, 32-37
Ministry of Foreign Affairs, 43
"mirror-imaging," 18
Moroccan Communist Party, 22
Morocco, 2, 5, 17, 30
Mosaddeq, Mohammed, 113, 118
Moscow Institute of World Economy and ternational Relations, 231
Mozambique, 3, 9, 13, 19, 33, 43, 44, 45, 74, 76; economic problems, 202; Mozambique Liberation Front (FRELIMO), 45, 61, 65, 216, 239; relations with U. S., 202; Soviet economic aid to, 237-238; Soviet trade with, 242
Mozambique Liberation Front (FRELIMO), 45, 61, 65, 216, 239
MPLA, 13, 45, 61, 69, 73, 197-198, 216; Russian support of, 64-66
Mugabe, Robert, 15, 76, 189
Mukhabarat, 38
Muslims in Soviet Union, 21-23

Namibia (South-West Africa), 14, 42, 43, 45; Soviet strategy in, 193
Nasser, Gamal Abdel, 2, 3, 24, 30, 33, 134, 209
Nehru, Pundit Matilal, 2; and Soviet diplomacy in India, 47-48; Third World, 47-48

Neto (Nito) Augustinho, 44, 64, 68
New Economic Policy (NEP), 230-231
New Jewel Movement of Grenada, 216
Nguema, 14
Nicaragua, 3, 14, 30; Sandinist National Liberation Front of, 216
Nigeria, 63
Nixon Doctrine, 57
Nkomo, Joshua, 15, 189
Nkrumah, Kwame, 2, 13, 59-61, 211
nonaligned countries, 2, 4; "fronts," 8-9; movement of, 8-11; strain of, 213
Non-Proliferation Treaty, 104
North Korea, 3
al-Numeiry, Jaafar, 71-72

Odinga, Oginga, 62-53
Ogaden campaign, 13, 67-68
Oman, 17
OPEC, 10, 32, 162, 236
Organization of African Trade Union Unity, 62
Organization of African Unity (OAU), 140, 144, 147

pacifist movement, 8-9
Pakistan: Chinese influence in, 84; communist party in, 54; Indo–Pakistan conflict, 52-54; Simla Agreement, 55; Soviet aid to, 100-101; Tashkent, 55
parallelism, 86
Partisans of Peace, 8, 9
People's Democratic Party of Afghanistan (PDPA), 216
People's Democratic Republic of Yemen (PDRY), 17, 22, 136, 202
PLO, 3
Popular Movement for the Liberation of Angola Labor Pary (MPLA-PT), 216
populism, 19
power rivalry, Third World, 241-243
"progressive," 2, 3, 6, 85, 209, 210-211, 217

al-Qaddafi, Mu'amar, 16, 22, 35, 69, 72, 74; American relations of, 136; *Green Book*, 135, 145; *jamahiriya*, 135; Organization of African Unity, (OAU), 140, 144, 147; politics of, 135; "positive neutralism" of, 135; post-Qaddafi era, 146-147; relationship with Soviet Union, 133-149; seizure of power by, 134-135; Soviet objectives, 137-141

248

ABOUT THE EDITOR

WALTER LAQUEUR is chairman of the International Research Council at the Center for Strategic and International Studies of Georgetown University. He is also editor of *The Washington Quarterly*, and editor of the Washington Papers series published by the Center. He has been director of the Institute of Contemporary History in London and editor of the *Journal of Contemporary History* as well as of *Survey*. He is university professor in government at Georgetown University and has taught in the past at the University of Chicago, Brandeis, Harvard, and elsewhere. He is author of numerous books on contemporary history and current affairs that have appeared in many languages—including *Communism and Nationalism in the Middle East* and *The Soviet Union and the Middle East,* which have long been the standard works in the field.

LIST OF CONTRIBUTORS

AMBASSADOR ARIEH EILAN, now retired, acquired his knowledge of third world problems when representing Israel in the General Assembly's Colonial Committee of the United Nations and later when serving as Israel's consul general in Bombay, ambassador to Kenya, and ambassador to Burma. As head of the East European desk in Israel's Ministry of Foreign Affairs and later ambassador to Finland, Mr. Eilan had the opportunity of following Soviet affairs. He now contributes to American publications.

ROBERT H. DONALDSON, provost of Herbert H. Lehman College, The City University of New York, is author of *Soviet Policy toward India: Ideology and Strategy* (Cambridge: Harvard University Press, 1974), coauthor (with Joseph Nogee) of *Soviet Foreign Policy since World War II* (New York: Pergamon Press, 1981), and editor of *The Soviet Union in the Third World: Successes and Failures* (Boulder, Colorado: Westview Press, 1981).

MURIEL ATKIN, Assistant professor of history at George Washington University,is the author of *Russia and Iran, 1780-1828* (Minneapolis: University of Minnesota Press, 1980) and several articles on Russian and Soviet relations with Iran.

ELLEN LAIPSON is an analyst in Middle East and North African Affairs at the Congressional Research Service, Library of Congress.

PAUL B. HENZE served in the U.S. Embassy in Addis Ababa in the late 1960s and early 1970s. From 1977 through 1980 he served in the National Security Council where his responsibilities included the Horn of Africa. He wrote "Getting a Grip on the Horn" while a Wilson Fellow at the Smithsonian Institution. He is now a resident consultant at the RAND Corporation.

RAYMOND W. COPSON is a specialist in African affairs with the Congressional Research Service of the Library of Congress. He holds a PhD in political science from Johns Hopkins University and has lectured in international relations at the University of Ibaden (Nigeria) and the University of Nairobi (Kenya).

DAVID E. ALBRIGHT is currently professor of national security affairs at the Air War College in Montgomery, Alabama. He served previously as senior text editor of the journal *Problems of Communism* and research associate at the Council on Foreign Relations in New York. His many publications on the Soviet Union and the Third World include *Communism in Africa* (Indiana University Press, 1980) and the *The USSR and Sub-Saharan Africa in the 1980's* (forthcoming).

DR. HERBERT BLOCK has been the leading expert on Soviet bloc economic and ideological issues. He has been an officer and later consultant to the U.S. State Department for close to forty years, preparing, among other reports, an annual survey of the planetary product. From 1962 to 1973 he lectured at the School for Advanced International Studies (SAIS) of Johns Hopkins University on comparative planning and Communist ideology. Dr. Block has written papers for the Center for Strategic and International Studies (CSIS) and the Brookings Institution. He cooperated with Walter Laqueur on *A Continent Astray* (Oxford University Press, 1979) and with Edward Luttwak on *The Grand Strategy of the Soviet Union* (forthcoming).